The CROSSINGS

A Memoir of Lives Well Lived

Susan Bussard

SUSAN BUSSARD

The Crossings: A Memoir of Lives Well Lived
© 2021 by Susan Beth Bussard

Passage from *To the Friend Who Did Not Save My Life* by Hervé Guibert quoted in "Death Sentences" by Julian Lucas in the *New Yorker*, Sept. 21, 2020, p. 65.

ISBN: 978-1-94429-884-5

Cover and Interior Design by Scot McDonald

LCCN: 2021904602

Printed in the United States of America
1 2 3 4 5 6 7 8 9 10 Printing/Year 24 23 22 21 20

In loving memory of my mother's family:
Marvin, Ruth, Sue, Edgar—and for Ingrid

CONTENTS

INTRODUCTION

FROM GENERATION TO GENERATION

The central figures of this memoir—grandmother Ruth Collier Gilliam Dillon (1890–1958), mother Sue Dillon Bussard (1913–1960), and friend from Sweden Ingrid Eva Linnea Jaensson (1914–2012)—blessed the lives of everyone they met. Strong women all, they loved, married, raised children, achieved higher-education degrees, and excelled in careers at a time when women were not supposed to have careers. They became lifelong friends and faced overwhelming health and financial challenges that infused their lives with joys and sorrows. Their friendship reached across an ocean and two continents. Their very natures and personalities embodied the good of humanity. Ruth, Sue, and Ingrid left indelible marks on their friends and descendants. The distinctive voice of each one rings in my head and blesses my heart. I have been shaped by the charismatic goodness embodied in each of them: selfless love, compassion, generosity, faith in God, determination to succeed, courage, confidence, a strong sense of individuality, an independent spirit, patience, love of adventure, and, above all, kindness. Because of how these three women live inside me, I am the woman I have become. May this memoir, four years in production from 150 letters, two diaries, and the re-membering of a century of experiences, speak into the lives of all who read it.

THE DILLONS

The story begins in the early 1800s with William Dillon, who was born in Bedford, Virginia, in 1805 and died in Kentucky in 1843. Milton Dillon, son of William, was also born and died in Kentucky. His son, William Jasper Dillon, was born December 17, 1858, in Burnside, Kentucky. Erman Laura Turner (she always went by Laura) was born October 6, 1864, in Adair, Kentucky, located in Hancock County, east of the town of Owensboro on the south side of the Ohio River. The town of Adair no longer exists. When Laura was a child, the family moved south to Burnside, Kentucky. The Civil War ended in 1865. In 1883, William Jasper Dillon, age twenty-four, began "keeping company" with Erman Laura Turner, age nineteen. When Laura found herself to be with child, it was incumbent upon William to marry her and establish a home for his family in Burnside, Kentucky.

The timeline from here is intuited, as precise documentation is missing. However, it seems plausible that the following took place. In Burnside, Kentucky, Laura Turner Dillon gave birth to three children: daughter Cora in 1883, daughter Bessie in 1887, and son Marvin Davis in 1890. Bessie remembered the family's traveling by covered wagon from Burnside, Kentucky, to Celina, Texas, in 1892 when she was five. It would have been an arduous journey of at least several weeks if not several months. The Dillon family caravanned with the Turner family. Laura's sister Josephine Turner had married James Ingram Dillon, an uncle of William Jasper Dillon, so these families were closely connected.

James Ingram had fought on the Union side of the Civil War and was with Sherman in Atlanta and on the following march through the South. He lost a leg in the Battle of Bentonville, North Carolina, which was the last battle of that march. Even though the Turners were from Kentucky, which remained part of the Union, we do not know on which side of the Civil War conflict the Turner family aligned themselves; perhaps it was both, which was common at the time. Whatever the circumstances, it is worth noting that Laura Turner was born in 1864, before the end of the Civil War. She grew up near the border between Kentucky and Tennessee hearing stories of the war, and it is likely that members of her own family fought and died on both sides. Therefore, it is plausible that she named her firstborn son Marvin Davis Dillon, giving a nod to Jefferson Davis, president of the Confederacy.

After the wagon caravan journey from Kentucky to northeast Texas, the families settled in Celina, in what is now Collin County. A fourth child, daughter Lera, was born in 1893. The family continued to grow with the births of sons Olan in 1895, Clifford in 1897, Milton in 1899, and Bernie in 1903. The family of nine children was complete with the birth of daughter Frieda in 1906. Mother Laura was forty-two. Family lore relates that William Jasper Dillon was something of a slacker and a ne'er-do-well, so it was Laura who supported the family by running a boardinghouse in Celina. However, the family did not live in poverty, as all the children survived to adulthood. William Jasper Dillon must have engaged in some enterprising employment that contributed to the support of his large family.

When the story picks up in 1910, the oldest son, Marvin, now twenty, is employed as a traveling salesman of agricultural equipment in northeast Texas for John Deere Plow Co. An ambitious entrepreneur, he learned on the job the principles of business management and salesmanship. When the relationship between Marvin and Ruth began that same year, the six younger Dillon children still lived at home. Other than knowing that Lera played piano quite well, other details about the talents or personalities of these children are lacking.

THE GILLIAMS

The Nuclear Family

Ruth Collier Gilliam Dillon: March 3, 1890–July 25, 1960, age 69

Marvin Davis Dillon: February 11, 1890–November 14, 1943, age 53

Married: September 21, 1912

Two children:

Erman Sue Dillon Bussard: July 26, 1913–May 23, 1960, age 46

Edgar Marvin Dillon: January 21, 1915–November 30, 1967, age 52

The Gilliams were from Dallas, but like the Dillons, they had also migrated to Texas after the Civil War. The Gilliams' town of origin was Farmville, Virginia.

Ruth's grandparents, Moses Everard Gilliam and Catherine Temple Jennings, married on December 16, 1842, in Farmville, Virginia. They were the parents of Oscar Augustus Gilliam, my great-grandfather, born May 10, 1846, in Halifax, Virginia. His siblings were Sue Gilliam, Wyndham Macon Gilliam, John Jennings Gilliam, and Adie Gilliam. O. A. Gilliam married Susan Collier Thornton, born August 15, 1848, in Charlotte, Virginia, on December 16, 1868. He was twenty-two and she was twenty. A total of seven children followed: an unnamed baby girl, born December 10, 1870, and died December 25, 1870; Eula Tuggle Gilliam, born March 31, 1874; John Wyndham Gilliam, born November 7, 1877; Kate Augustine Gilliam, born July 27, 1880; Robert Walton Gilliam, born September 14, 1883, and died in 1889; James Betterton Gilliam, born January 13, 1888; and my grandmother Ruth Collier Gilliam, born March 3, 1890. Their mother, Susan Collier Thornton Gilliam, died on March 24, 1906. Her obituary reads:

> PIONEERS CALLED: Death Has Heavy Harvest Among Aged
> Dallas Citizens
>   Dallas: March 24, 1906—(Special)—Mrs. O. A. Gilliam,
> aged 58 years, and for twenty-eight years a resident
> of Dallas died at her home at Gilliam street and Ewing
> avenue, today from apoplexy. Mrs. Gilliam (Nee Susan
> Collier Thornton) was born in Virginia August 15, 1848.
> She is survived by a husband and five children, all who
> reside in Dallas.

My great-grandfather, O. A. Gilliam, met and married his bride in Charlotte, Virginia, after the Civil War. At age fifteen, O. A. volunteered to serve in the Confederate army in Virginia. Because he was too young to be a soldier, he became a groom for General Robert E. Lee's horse, Traveller. He was wounded at the Battle of Sailor's Creek, the last battle before Lee's surrender at Appomattox, Virginia, on April 9, 1865.

O. A. might have been a witness to the surrender. The full story of that encounter is given later in this volume. So how did O. A. and Susan meet? It would have been at a town or church social function after the Civil War. Their families, the Gilliams and the Thorntons, lived in the same town or on nearby farms. O. A. had been shot in the face at the Battle of Sailor's Creek, which rendered it difficult for him to eat and impossible for him to smile. However, it must have been a sweet chemistry between them that led to the marriage. Of course, just following the Civil War, when so many young men had died, it stands to reason that courtships would have been short. After all, life was short.

O. A. and Susan grieved the death of their first child, only fifteen days old, on Christmas Day 1870. At this time, the couple resided in Trigg County, Kentucky. The next child wasn't born until 1874. During that interval, O. A. and Susan migrated by covered wagon from Kentucky to Dallas, Texas. They started their family again in Dallas and made a life for themselves. O. A. bought land on the outskirts of Dallas and leased it to tenant farmers. The family prospered, the children were educated, and his youngest daughter, Ruth, even went to North Texas State Normal College, located in Denton, Texas, graduating with a teacher's certificate in 1909.

MARVIN AND RUTH

Draw back, look down, and picture northeast Texas in 1910—Dallas at the hub of the several contiguous counties, postage-stamp communities.

Marvin Dillon and Ruth Gilliam, both age twenty, engaged in an intense friendship that blossomed into romance from the summer of 1910 until their wedding day, September 21, 1912. If we pan out and assume an aerial posture to peer down on the landscape, we notice the intricate web of railroad tracks and two-lane unpaved roads that crisscross the landscape, connecting small farming communities, intersecting with the city of Dallas at the hub of it all. When a traveler disembarked from a train at the local station, he would have been met by friends or family in a horse-drawn buggy or a horseless carriage—if the roads were dry.

The young lovers were never very far apart by today's measure.

Usually not more than fifty miles lay between them. However, as the letters reveal, meeting for a weekend rendezvous was never easy. Marvin courted Ruth by letters—lovingly written often daily while he crisscrossed the contiguous counties of northeast Texas selling agricultural and farm equipment, evidently with some success. He knew the territory. But the emotional center of his life was always Ruth.

While Marvin traveled throughout northeast Texas, Ruth, armed with a teacher's certificate from North Texas State Normal College, took a position teaching reading and English literature in Jean, Texas, located in Young County, positioned at the intersection of Highway 114 and FMR 1769. She lived in a boardinghouse owned by a local doctor and his wife. At the same time Marvin slept in hotels or boardinghouses in each town where he stopped to market his wares. The chatty letters they exchanged recount personal details of their daily activities and, of course, words of affection for each other and a shared desire to be together. Both Marvin and Ruth registered concern for the health of one another, as well as that of family members and friends. Scarlet fever and meningitis were highly contagious, life-threatening diseases that often resulted in the closure of local schools when an outbreak was detected. The letters make no reference to politics or current events of the day. The Civil War had ended forty-five years earlier, and William Howard Taft was president of the United States. Ruth and Marvin's world centered on themselves, their families, and friends, as revealed in the sentiments of the young lovers' letters.

Marvin continued to market agricultural equipment in northeast Texas after he and Ruth were married on September 21, 1912. My mother, Erman Sue Dillon, was born in Dallas on July 26, 1913, and her brother, Edgar Marvin Dillon, followed on January 21, 1915. In the years between 1913 and 1920, Marvin learned the business of materials handling. In 1920, Marvin and two partners founded Dillon Scale Company in Dallas, Texas. The business survived the Great Depression of the 1930s and prospered during World War II. Marvin died suddenly of a heart attack on November 11, 1943.

By the end of World War II, the postage-stamp existence of northeast Texas country people had been transformed by depression and war.

From across the Atlantic Ocean, along with thousands of émigrés to America from Europe, Ingrid Eva Linnea Jaensson arrived in New York from Sweden on the MS *Gripsholm* in September 1948. She had come to the US to pursue her dream to study American nursing practices and hospital administration. She stopped in Dallas for a weekend to visit a cousin who was working at Dillon Scale. Whether you want to call it fate or an act of the Holy Spirit, Ingrid's arrival in the US and her subsequent entry into the life of my family through her cousin changed everything.

The first part of the story that follows is constructed from letters exchanged between Marvin and Ruth beginning in mid-1910 through the summer of 1912. The letters contain references to the Texas towns of Jean, Celina, Tioga, Gunter, Prosper, and Newark: all located in counties contiguous to Dallas County. All these towns still exist. The second part of the story unfolds in the relationships documented in diaries and surviving letters written between members of my family— Ruth, Sue, Edgar, Jimmy (my father), and me (Susibeth)—and Ingrid from 1950 to 2012.

Moses E. Gilliam and Catherine T. Jennings circa 1842. Parents of Oscar Augustus Gilliam

*Oscar Augustus Gilliam in Confederate uniform,
age 19, circa 1865*

Dillon family circa 1894. Clockwise from left: *Marvin, age 4;
father William Jasper, age 25; Cora, age 11; mother Erman Laura,
age 25; Bessie, age 7; Lera, age 1*

PART ONE

The Love Story of Ruth and Marvin

THE FRIENDSHIP AND COURTSHIP: 1910–1911

*M*y grandmother, Ruth Collier Gilliam Dillon, born on March 3, 1890, the youngest of seven children and undoubtedly her father's favorite, was intelligent and ambitious. A cultured woman, Ruth was well-read, wrote poetry, played the piano, painted watercolors, produced needlepoint, crocheted baby clothes, taught Sunday school, and enjoyed an active social life. She pursued higher education at North Texas State Normal College, now the University of North Texas, in Denton. She graduated with a teaching degree in 1909. Historians have labeled the years between 1890 and 1900 the Gilded Age. The years between 1901 and 1910, before World War I, are called the Edwardian Age. Both the Dillon and Gilliam families thrived as part of a still small but growing American middle class. Ruth would have attended socials in the summer and embraced the fashion of the day—corsets, long dresses, wide-brim picture hats trimmed with sashes and feathers. Ruth's childhood ended the day her mother, Susan Collier Thornton Gilliam, died when Ruth was sixteen. Between March 1906 and spring 1910, Ruth earned a college degree and met Marvin Davis Dillon, the man who would become her husband.

Marvin Dillon, a traveling salesman for John Deere Plow Company, marketed tractors, plows, tillers, and all manner of agricultural tools to farmers in northeast Texas. His family lived in Celina, Texas, in Collin County, just north of Dallas. He frequently traveled by train, horse and buggy, and occasionally by automobile, still a novelty mode of transportation in the early twentieth century. Since Marvin and Ruth were both Baptists, they probably met at a church social, likely hosted by Cliff Temple Baptist Church, founded in 1899 and located in Oak Cliff, Texas, later incorporated into the city of Dallas in 1903. Their relationship blossomed quickly, and by the middle of 1910, Marvin was actively courting Ruth. After graduating from college in 1909, Ruth took a teaching job in the small farming community of Jean, Texas. One of the board members hired her in 1910 to open the new high school. She comments that most of the students were young men in their early twenties, older than her. It was during her employment in Jean that the letters between her and Marvin began. Realizing that Marvin was "the one," Ruth moved to take a position in Lancaster, Texas, in 1911. Living and working in Jean, when Marvin and her family were located in the Dallas area, Ruth realized that long-distance relationships are difficult at best and doomed to fail at worst. Relocating to Lancaster cut the distance in half between Ruth and her beau. Marvin courted her during that year, and by early 1912, they were engaged to be married.

The story constructed from the letters begins with Ruth's writing, not to her beau, Marvin, but to a Mr. McCarter, a man who has behaved improperly. This undated letter reveals the personality of a young woman sure of herself and of one who will not be pushed around by any man. Ruth must have liked what she wrote because she made a copy for herself. It is not clear whether she wrote this letter before or after she had met Marvin, her future husband.

Late 1910

〰 Dear Mr. McCarter,

As I am afraid that I shall not get to have a talk with you soon, and rather that you should not entertain an idea that I am afraid you will, longer than can be helped, I am writing you this note to suppose that you think that I am one of the "fast kind," but I wish to say that I most assuredly am not. It seemed to me that I showed you that I did not approve of the way you have been acting lately. If you had rather get with someone who has a different disposition I wish you would. Of course I don't know whether you will ever desire to come to see me anymore, but if you cannot refrain from being so familiar, I would rather not have you come. Sincerely, Ruth

The conversational letters between Marvin and Ruth that follow reveal the developmental stages of a loving and enduring relationship. As young adults, they were both ready to engage in social contract norms of the early twentieth century. However, we must not discount the significance of the fact that Ruth as a single woman has left home, graduated college, and successfully sought employment! After college, she could have moved back home and taken care of her widowed father. However, an independent woman, she chose to live in a boardinghouse, work a full-time job, and support herself financially. She was a woman ahead of her time.

Marvin found her beauty, personality, and independence attractive. The demure photograph of Ruth taken in 1908 belies her true nature. She faced Marvin, always looked him in the eye, and let him pursue her. However, she did not fall into his arms until the relationship was sealed on their wedding day. After all, as she so eloquently expressed to Mr. McCarter, she was not "one of the fast kind." Martin's surviving letters outnumber Ruth's, but the reader notices that Marvin's letters contain repetitive expressions of passionate desire for her company. He gets "the blues." On the other hand, Ruth's letters guide the relationship forward with witty and humorous accounts of everyday life challenges in small-town northeast Texas. She writes restrained expressions of affection for her beloved. Ruth reveals her independent spirit when she decides not to return home from Arkansas for the Fourth of July in 1911. She frequently visits her sister Kate in Tioga, despite Marvin's pleading for her to "come home." By their wedding day, the relationship has matured, and Ruth and Marvin marry as equals.

The first letter of the Marvin/Ruth relationship, dated September

1910, is written by Ruth to Marvin as she has just arrived in Jean, Texas, a small town in Young County, 14 miles north of Graham and 122 miles west of Dallas. She has been hired to join the faculty of the new high school to teach reading and English literature.

According to *The Handbook of Texas*:

> Jean, at the intersection of State Highway 114 and Farm Road 1769, in north central Young County, was settled in 1875 by rancher S. B. Lamar, who built a schoolhouse and a store there. His son, James Lamar, became the first postmaster and named the settlement after his sweetheart. Jean was moved one mile to the Gulf, Texas and Western Railroad when the line was built through the area in 1903. R. F. Willis donated land for the new townsite and gave the Trinity Townsite Company alternate blocks. G. G. Cantrill built a store that was also used for the railroad station. By 1940 Jean had 300 inhabitants and five stores. In 1980 and 1990 the population was estimated as ninety-one. The population grew to 110 in 2000.[1]

A letter written from Jean, Texas, to Marvin in fall 1910 mentions Ruth's arrival and reveals information about her living situation. Marvin and Ruth are both twenty, born in 1890. After a three-hour train ride from Dallas, she and a colleague hired a livery to drive them the fourteen miles to Jean. Below is Ruth's first letter about her new job.

September 9, 1910

༄ Dear Mr. Dillon,

I left [Dallas for] Graham [on the train] this morning at nine o'clock and reached here [Graham] at twelve. A young man who is to teach near here and I hired a livery man to bring us [the last fourteen miles] across the country [to Jean]. We surely came across some rough country. I know there were rocks on this side of some of those mountains as large as a good sized cottage.

Now I must tell about "Jean". It is a grand place. I have just met several of my "students to be" and other folks of interest. Some of the men said that everybody: trustees, patrons, and all, were going to be at the school Monday morning to hear a big speech from me. You know they'll hear one, do you not? Ha! Ha! Let me tell you, some of the boys who are going to school to me look as if they were twenty-one or twenty-two years old— Think of it!

Sure enough, Jean is a pretty fair little "burg"—It has three drug stores, two black smith shops, about five or six dry goods and grocery stores, a barber shop, a gym, a post office, two Drs. Offices and a lovely high school (with a lovely principal). Better come to Jean!

I am boarding at the Dr. Gris's house. They are very nice people. On the whole I think I shall like Jean fine. I surely did feel the effects of that last car too, for I slept so late I could hardly get to town in time to catch the train. I shall do all in my power to sell an engine. There is one here. I believe I shall go down and get it out of fix "CEE". Please pardon this letter—it is growing dark and I can hardly see what I'm writing. I bought some ink this afternoon but couldn't get the stopper out. Consequently, this "school marm" has written with a pencil. Don't forget my address for you know I shall get lonesome. Your friend. Ruth

Ruth wrote a postcard to Marvin, dated Tuesday, November 22, 1910, and it sounds as if she is recovering from a sore foot. "Was glad to hear from you today, would write you a letter tonight, but I want to retire early as I have taught all day and am tired. I have written you two letters anyway. Felt some better today but have walked none. Better this morning. Ruth"

Sometime during 1910, the friendship between Ruth and Marvin had progressed to the point that he told her to call him "Zeke." His friends called him "Zeke" all his adult life.

The next surviving letter is written from Dallas by Marvin to Ruth, dated Sunday, November 27, 1910, on John Deere Plow Co. stationery.

⟨⟩ My Dear Ruth:

Glad to find a letter from you when I got home Wed. night at 11:59 P.M. and just had to read it before I retired altho I was very sleepy.

Rec'd your card Friday and must say you are very prompt in answering your correspondents if you answer all of them like you did me.

The wind is blowing real hard here and the dust is so bad we can hardly see across the street and I wonder what it is out there where it never rains at all.

Ralph went to church today and insisted that I go also but I came to the store to write to you instead. Dallas is dead as can be it seems since you went away for I miss you so very much and wish every day I could see you and talk to you a long time.

I wonder what you did Thursday (Thanksgiving). I went home in the morning and brought Marianna back with me to a six o'clock dinner at Mrs. Zieglers and did not go anywhere at night.

Haven't been to see a single girl since you left so you see I am being good. Write soon.

As Ever, Zeke

Another letter from Marvin "Zeke" to Ruth written on John Deere Plow Co. stationery, Sunday morning, December 11, 1910, early in their relationship:

⟨⟩ My Dear Miss Gilliam:

I was very glad to get your most interesting letter on my return last night. I found your letter had been at the house since Monday noon but I went away early Monday morning so just missed it two or three hours.

You spoke as if you were not coming home Xmas but that is alright if you had rather stay there than here but I sure would like to see you if you can tear yourself away from Jean that long. I don't know what I'll do Xmas but work as we will only have one day (Sunday, Dec. 25) to ourselves and would like very much to spend at least part of that day with you.

You spoke about the brevity of my last letter but I told you before you went away that I could not write a letter as you must forgive my feeble efforts at communication for I like to hear from you so well that I keep trying to write anyway.

Saw Ralph last night a while and he asked about you and wondered why he did not hear from you as he thinks you should write him first.

You are rather peculiar that way for you are the first girl that ever asked me to write first when they were going away and if it had been anyone but you I would not have done so but I would do most anything for you.

Be Good and come home Xmas if you can. Write me soon.

Your friend, M. D. Dillon

Definitely early in the relationship! In her next letter, written from Jean, Texas, and dated December 18, 1910, Ruth asserts herself as an independent woman, deserving respect. Imagine the hair raising on Marvin's neck as he read it!

ᗗ Dear Mr. Dillon:

Now weren't you ashamed of yourself to bless me out in such a way as you did? You seemed to think that I did not wish to come home Christmas at all. Of course I can tear myself away from Jean, but that is not the question. There are other reasons which I will give you, if I see you any time soon. I have forgiven you, for your censure tho' and shall forget it.

The Jean High School is as fine as ever. We have enrolled about seventy-five to date. I have not had the least bit of trouble in any way.

You said you saw Ralph the other day. Where is he staying
now? Does he not room with you yet? I am glad you thought
enough of me to write first. I don't suppose Ralph cares to hear
from me for he does not write even a postal.

Sunday afternoon, I took a long drive over this country.
There are many beautiful dwellings in some parts of this
world. Oh! My! Do you not wish you could gaze on some of this
beautiful scenery? By the way, I am about to sell a Gasoline
Engine out here to the Townsite Man. I'm talking it up every
day. There was a big fire out here, you remember and I
impressed it on their minds the need of an engine.

I will know in a few more days whether I shall come home
Christmas or not. If I come I will be there on Christmas Eve.
I have promised if I do give vacation, to spend a few days in
Tioga also, but I shall come to Dallas first. [Evidently Ruth
as teacher has the authority to declare and grant Christmas
vacation days to her students.]

I hope you will not have to work too much during the
holidays, for if I come home, would like very much to see you.
Good night. Your western friend, Ruth

A note about Texas public schools in the early twentieth century: In
1911 "legislation initiated county boards of education and rural high
schools to serve the 600,000 rural students across the state." In 1915
"the state enacted a compulsory school attendance law. Texas was one
of five states that did not have a compulsory attendance law enacted
prior to 1915."[2] "In Texas, before 1926, there was generally no twelfth
grade. Once a student finished the eleventh grade, he or she could be
a graduate of the Texas school. In 1926, however, the school system in
Port Arthur added a twelfth grade."[3] The Dallas Independent School
District did not add twelfth grade until 1941."

Here is a letter from Ruth, written from Jean, Texas, and dated March
19, 1911. The writing is so faded I can barely read it.

◌ Dear "Zeke".

Again I am back at my post of duty and by now feel as I had never left it. I have been invited out a great many times since my return and have accepted every invitation except one tonight. I concluded that I had better stay at home and write some letters and make out my report.

There are two more cases of scarlet fever in our beautiful little city which is set on a hill. Some of the people are almost frantic while others are not so alarmed. There is no telling— you may hear that I have it next, for I was with the child who died. Goodness, I hope I shall escape without any serious illness. Scarlet fever is all we can hear now on every side.

I wonder how you are liking dear old Clement by now. No doubt you will fall so completely in love with the place that you'll dread the thought of leaving it. I'm speaking from experience. "C"?

I do not know whether we shall suspend school again or not. If we do, it will be for the remainder of the term. You must be good and think of the Jean School "marm" who may be quarantined any day. News has suddenly left me, so good night. Yours. Ruth

P.S. I caught a brain on the train, a man of not less than 40 summers. Isn't it marvelous!

It was common for schools to close during outbreaks of scarlet fever, measles, or meningitis in the early twentieth century. Besides postcards, Ruth and her beau also communicated via telegram through the Postal Telegraph-Cable Company of Texas. Ruth's first experience was to send a telegram to Zeke. Not dated!

◌ Dear Zeke—Here comes that telegram See I am having a glorious time. I sure wish I could see all of you. I wrote to Otha [friend in Paris, Texas] about the picture the other day. How do you think I do on the type-writer! This is my first attempt as you will readily see. I hope you are having a real good time at home today. Did Miss Hern go with you as you expected! This is a letter and a postal,as comesn with your answer. How is G.Edgar? Your Ark. Friend, Ruth.

The previous letter is exactly as she typed it. Ruth and Zeke were both smitten with each other by now. She was visiting friends and cousins in Fort Smith for three weeks, a long time for them to be apart. They wrote each other every day, so their letters often crossed in the mail.

The next letter is from Marvin, dated June 20, 1911, and written in Dallas, Texas:

የ My Dear Ruth:- Very glad indeed to get your telegram today but am afraid you are rather extravagant in sending such lengthy ones.

I am real lonesome tonight and I don't know of any one I had rather see than "dear little Ruth" but will have to content myself by writing to you and expecting a letter from you real soon. I went home yesterday, and had a real nice time with Miss Shore, did not go out, of course that almost broke my heart.

I have not seen her since you went away so don't know much about her but heard that some other fellow went out with her three or four times each week.

I "tendered my resignation" to Briggs-Weaver Monday to take effect Saturday and intend to begin with another company next Monday so you can send my mail to the house after this week (#315 N. Jefferson Ave. Sta. A).

Talked to Myrtle [colleague and friend of Ruth and Marvin] last night and she told me she had heard from you twice so you must think more of her than you do me to write her more.

No. I am not jealous, sweetheart I just said that as a joke and you know what crazy things I say sometime so you will know what I mean.

I think it real sweet of you to send me your first attempt

on the typewriter and am very glad you thot of me but please, don't sign any more letters with that "Ark Friend" for that sounds too much like you were there to stay and one week of your time is up tonight so I'll be looking for you home in two more weeks. And I think of you as one a little closer than a friend.

I have the blues tonight, Sweetheart, but think if I could sit in our swing a short time with just you I would feel lots better and I have just lots to talk to you about.

We'll have a good time while you are there but don't forget Zeke who thinks of you many times each day and who loves real well to get letters from the sweetest girl in Dixie so write when you can to Your Own Zeke

Almost forgot to say G. Edgar [Marvin's close friend] is OK. Haven't seen him since you left but he phoned me tonight and is coming to town tomorrow night to see me. Z

Briggs-Weaver was founded in 1896 when two men, J. C. Weaver and C. H. Briggs, had a single vision to create a successful industrial service company that would become an industry leader. They opened Briggs-Weaver Company in Dallas. The business provided service for pump installations, lift trucks, and material handling. It quickly gained a reputation of providing the best industrial equipment and services to many industries throughout the Southwest. The company, now Briggs, is still in business. Marvin takes the initiative to advance his knowledge of salesmanship by changing jobs as opportunities present themselves.

As Zeke and Ruth were writing to each other almost daily, his next letter to her is dated Dallas, Texas, June 23, 1911.

My Dear Sweetheart;-

Was delighted to get your dear letter yesterday and it was delivered by a white man too. I am real pleased to know that you are having such a good time but am very sorry that your foot is giving you trouble, guess you will have to come back to your Lobb(ster).

Talked to Mrs. Ragon [Ruth's oldest sister, Eula "Eudie"] last night and she told me about your trouble, and I told her I didn't hope you would have any bad luck, but I did want you to hurry home as I am getting real anxious to see you. Also talked to her again tonight and Miss Rode was there so had a short talk with her and she is real anxious to see you too—you see we all want you to come home soon but want you to finish your visit so you can stay at home for a while with us.

How did you like the Dr. and did you sit in the swing and be contented or did you go out somewhere? I have not been away from home this week except one night when I was down town with G. Edgar a short time, in fact have not felt very much like running around nights but have felt some better for the last two or three days.

Ruth age 18, circa 1908

Phoned Myrtle last night and had quite a long talk with her—talked about you most of the time too, so you see we have not forgotten you yet.

The people next door are singing that beautiful little bullet and it sure seems that way to me since you went away.

Took your picture [taken in 1908] home with me Sunday and Sister and Mamma both thot it real cute and expressed a desire to meet you—wish you could have been with me, we had more good things to eat like pineapple sherbet, cocoanut, chocolate, and banana cake as well as two kinds of pie and lots of other things nice.

You know anyone can always make a hit with me by just giving me lots to eat. Well hurry and get your visit out, Sweetheart and come home.

Write again real soon dear girl to Your Zeke

Zeke wrote to Ruth, who was visiting in Fort Smith, Arkansas, on June 29, 1911, from Dallas.

This same state [I think Marvin is registering displeasure that Ruth is still in Arkansas and not back in Texas.]

  ⟪ My Dearest Ruth;-

I feel lots better after reading your most welcome letter but can't truthfully say that I am shocked at their frequency as this is the first one in just one week but was delighted to get it just the same.

I talked to Alma and Myrtle tonight and they are planning some swell doings for Tuesday July 4 and are counting me in as one of the party for they realize as well as myself that it would be a rotten day for me if you were absent so you must not fail to be home by Monday morning so you can rest one day and be prepared for a big time Tuesday.

Have just been looking at your dear photo and Oh! How I wish I could see your sweet face just now while you are perhaps enjoying a boat ride with Dr. Hal.

But that's alright dearie. You have a real good time while you are there for I intend to love you so hard when you do return that you will probably get tired of me and wish you were back in "Arkansaw."

Well at any rate Sweetheart you hurry home and try to love your Zeke a little bit for he thinks Ruth is just the sweetest girlie on earth. Let me know when you will be here but be sure and be here for a big time Tuesday. Goodnight Sweetheart

With lots of love. I am Your Zeke

Ruth sent a long letter to Zeke on June 31, 1911, in the middle of her three-week trip to Fort Smith, Arkansas, which was stretching into a nearly eight-week trip.

ᗁ My dear "Zeke"—

What a pleasant surprise I had this morning when the postman handed me a letter from you! I was not expecting to hear from you nor Myrtle but I was just wishing I could.

The very idea of Myrtle showing you that letter! I'll fix her for it. It was all foolishness.

I am very sorry that you were disappointed when you did not receive my letter. Forgive me if I say I didn't know you really cared as much as you say.

Listen, I said something about coming home, and John and Lou Eddy think it is preposterous. They say that I am not coming home until the first of Sept. So you see how it is. I am just crazy to all of you, and fully intended to come home next week, however I had not mentioned it to them. I wish I could be there for the Fourth but guess I shall celebrate it here. Please do not blame me, because I hate to jump up and run off when they are making it so pleasant for me.

If I can possibly slip off without hurting their feelings sometime next week, I shall do so. I am not going to stay all summer because I can't do without seeing Lobster [I wonder who this is? A dog or cat perhaps?] that long. If by some chance I find that I can come Monday, I will wire you Sunday. But chances are slim, so don't stay at home to hear from me. See?

John said, "Tell all these folks who are writing to you to come home to come up here and spend the fourth with you." There is to _____ Postman just came and interrupted me. He had a letter from a girl in Paris (Texas) urging me to come on down there and see her a while and she would go home with me. She is going to Weatherford (Texas) from my house and wants me to go to tea. Not I tho' if I came home, because I have enough places to visit. I have got to see Kate yet. [Jean is about sixty miles from Weatherford.]

Be good and write to me when you feel like it, and I will see too. Don't count letters with me. Gracious I am making such an out of this, I'd better quit. I'm nearly asleep is what is the matter. I promised a girl to go to town with her this afternoon, but a nap comes first, as "Good bye Dearie! I must leave you, then it breaks my heart to go." Yours as ever, Ruth.

Hand written P.S.

"Don't think I'll forget you, even tho' I am far away, for Honest dear old Zeke, I'm strong for you."

Letter from Zeke to Ruth written July 1, 1911, "ordering" her to come home to Dallas for the Fourth of July holiday.

⟡ Dear Ruth,

The first thing I did when I got home from work and when I didn't get any thing I couldn't help saying "darnit" and a few more forceful expletives.

Say girl! You know next Tuesday is 4th of July and I am going to insist that you do a charitable act and come home Sunday or Monday if not before for you must be home by Tuesday as your three weeks will be up then and you must not forget that you promised me at the station to be home by then so you bid your physician farewell and come back to your Zeke who loves you better than anyone else on earth.

Now don't forget that you are to be in Dallas Monday night at the latest.

G. Edgar spent Saturday night with me and went on to see his Nevada girl Sunday morning and I have not seen him since but he phoned me last evening and reported a delightful time.

Seems like everyone is having a fine time but me and I can't even get more than one letter a week when I am blue and lonely.

Myrtle told me about your awful dream also about you trying to imagine things with Lou Eddy's ring on. Go ahead and imagine Sweetheart and perhaps it will be more real "some of these days."

I'll confess that this is a very poorly written letter but is the best I can do tonight so will quit now expecting a long, long letter from you immediately. (Had a time spelling that) and expecting you home before Tuesday. With love and kisses. Your Zeke

Ruth's next letter, written from Fort Smith, is dated Sunday, July 2, 1911. Ruth teases Marvin about her decision not to hop on a train to join the "big time" party in Dallas. Ever an independent woman, Ruth does not rush to return to Dallas, even at Marvin's "ordering" her to come home.

 ⟳ My dearest "Zeke,"

Yesterday afternoon I was made happy again when the postman called "mail," and I found a dear letter from you.

Of course I was delighted to hear from you but am so sorry you are expecting me home so soon. I don't know just when I shall be there.

Today is Sunday. This is Sunday morning. I wonder if you are better than I and have gone to church. I hope so.

I know you will all have a delightful time on the Fourth. I would rather be with all of you than any other crowd I know of. I hope you will not be angry with me for not coming but weigh the situation and see I'm not to blame. You remember I told you I might slip away the last of the week. John still vows up and down that I shall not come home before the first of September. He said last night I was crazy to think about going home for he had several trips planned for me yet, way up into the mountains at several summer resorts, namely Winslow, Monte Ne(y), and Mt. Vista.

Go ahead and get you another girl and have a good time and just think that Ruth would like so much to be with you. Write me all about it.

I'm sure I shall have a pleasant time on the Fourth, but it will be a different kind to that of being with my same old crowd, way down in Texas.

I wrote to Myrtle yesterday but doubt whether she will answer or not as I fear she will be too angry with me. At any rate, I hope not, for I do enjoy her letters so much.

There is a great Baptist Revival going on here. There were four thousand people at the service last Sunday Evening and over fifty souls were saved. I am going tonight. Then maybe I'll be better. At least I'm going to try to.

Every little kid in the neighborhood calls me "Aunt Ruth." They hear Marjorie calling me that so they all think I'm their Aunt too. This morning there were about five or six in our swing and they all got to arguing at once, and each one was trying to prove his statement by me.

Did you notice something written on the last envelope you received? Natalie Salls (a charming young lady) wrote part of that and my big brother (John Wyndham Gilliam) wrote the other. They thought they were cute.

Mart wrote me a long letter and told me he would reach Dallas about the middle of July. I answered with a card and told him I was here and didn't know just exactly when I'd leave for home. John says, "Let him come up here, if he wishes to see you. "Yes, I'm sure he would (Nit)"

I'm going to take a nap now. If I can think of more when I wake up, I'll tell you.

I had a rather lengthy nap, for this is Monday morning. I didn't go to church last night as it was for "men only," so I took a stroll instead. Just received a short note from Alma this morning. She too asked me to be home for the 4th.

I guess as I won't be there for them I'll just stay on, as long as they want me to.

Please forgive me for not obeying and write me a long long letter just as soon as you have time. With bestest wishes. Ruth

At the time of this letter, Winslow, was a recently incorporated resort town. Monte Ne was home to a health resort in the Ozark hills, on the edge of Arkansas's Beaver Lake.

A LONG letter from Zeke to Ruth, who is still in Fort Smith, Arkansas:

Dallas, Texas July 5, 1911

My Dear Girlie;-

Rec'd your dear letter today and was very glad to hear from you again but would have been tickled to death to have seen you instead but as you have decided to spend the summer up there we will have to be contented with your letters if you will write real often.

You promised to stay no longer than three weeks but broke your promise so I am not going to insist on your coming home until you get ready for I guess you can have a better time there than here and there are so many nice places to go up there while everything is drying up here.

After all our planning for the 4th there was no one in our crowd but Ralph (Brownlee) and Myrtle and Miss Lora Coston and Mr. Dillon but we had such a nice time that we didn't care if the rest did not go.

We left Myrtle's with the intention of taking the 4 p.m. car [electric trolley in Dallas 1911–1948] to Kirkland park, but missed the car and went to Highland Park instead, arriving there about 5 p.m. We drank "strawberry milkshake" and then sat on the grass near the beautiful water and ate some delicious fudge (something of that kind) made by Miss Harris [Myrtle's last name?] and then we took a stroll and explored the park until about 7:30 when we decided we were hungry so we found a nice shady, grassy spot and spread our lunch while Mr. Brownlee brought some red soda-pop and I enjoyed it all more than I ever enjoyed a picnic lunch before and the rest seemed to have the same opinion as myself. The lunch consisted of fried chicken, ham sandwiches, veal loaf sandwiches, salmon "croquetts" (is that correct, medear?) stuffed olives, two kinds of cake, and bananas, and everything tasted so good that there was a very little left.

The girls [Alma and Myrtle and Lora Coston] were so nice to us and everything went so smoothly that we could not wish for a nicer time.

I almost forgot the best part—After supper we took a long boat ride and sang lots of old and new songs while on the water.

I tried to tell you as near as possible just what we did but guess Myrtle will give a more detailed description of the whole affair when she writes which I guess will be real soon.

I was no better than you were Sunday for I didn't leave home all day until about 7:30 when Ralph and I went to Alma's to see her and Myrtle.

We thot of going to Fair Park but they had a big rain in Dallas late in the afternoon while we had none at all on this side of the lovely Trinity so we went to Lake Cliff Park instead but did not go to the show. Ralph and his mother were here for dinner Sunday as well as Mr. and Mrs. Seals—their third time since the Sunday you and Myrtle were here.

You asked me to cheer up Myrtle but that happens to be entirely unnecessary as a certain Mr. Brownlee seems to be doing very well indeed in fact much better than I could do and I fear (or hope) that it is getting rather serious but you can never tell for sure.

I don't know why I am writing such a long letter tonight but I just got started and if this one tires you, which it probably has already, just tell me and I'll not be guilty again but will be more brief.

Mr. Leiucker left Sunday evening for Philadelphia, so I am now rooming alone, but Mr. Bell is sleeping in here tonight on account of the intense heat in his room.

The last three or four days have been something terrible but a good cool breeze came about ten minutes ago and helped matters wonderfully.

It is now 9:30 and everyone is in bed but me and I just had to write to you before I slept altho' I said I was not going to write you for a week yet I was so (shall I say angry?) yes, angry when I got your letter saying you would not be home to spend the 4th with us but of course I forgave you all that when I got your sweet letter today.

Well, have a real good time sweetheart and see all the interesting places you can and tell me all about them but never forget there is someone in dear old Texas that thinks little Ruth is the sweetest girl alive.

Write me real often for I do enjoy your letters so much. As ever yours. Zeke

Monday Night, July 31, 1911

ᎯᏉ Dearest Ruth;-

I wrote you last night but was so glad to get your letter today that I'll write a little tonight and try to show, or tell you, how much I appreciated it.

I was just a little surprised but not very much as I thot I would get it today, or tomorrow.

I'm glad that you liked my poetry for that was my very first attempt and I don't think I could do it again.

I read your poem about "boyibus Kissibus" to Miss Fannie.
She thot it real cute and wants you to write it for her to put in
her scrap book.

She made some "lasses" candy Saturday so we have been
eating candy and drinking grape juice tonight and wishing for
you.

Claud has had a real sore throat for several days but is some
better tonight.

I guess the wind yesterday made you think of dear old Jean,
didn't it?

It was some windy here and lots of bill boards and windows
etc. were smashed.

G. Edgar, Alto, and Marvin were standing on Akard between
Main and Commerce yesterday when a barrel fell from the top
of the new Adolphus and only missed us a few feet and, believe
me, we went. We didn't even stay to see what else was "coming
our way" . . .

The next letter of record is a partial manuscript from Zeke to Ruth
from Celina, Texas, dated August 2, 1911. He is recovering from an
illness.

    ⌦ My dearest girlie;-

I was some tickled to get your card this A.M. I went to the
post hole office myself, under protest from Mamma, but I told
her that a short walk would do me good. They had the doctor to
see me and he gave me all kinds of dope to take, but I didn't cry
about it for I want to come home.

Of course I enjoy a few days at home but this place is so darn
lonesome that I soon tire of it and long for dear old Dallas and
the interurban. ["C"?]. I guess Miss Boothe and Lera and I will
go to our sister's [Bessie] in Prosper this afternoon and stay a
day or two and we are planning a nice time.

Sis and Miss Boothe went auto riding last night with two of
sister's . . .

A letter from Ruth to Zeke, dated Monday night, August 7, 1911. Still in Fort Smith:

Monday Night, Ten 'til ten

༑ My own Zeke,

I have just finished—not just finished but have been talking to the dearest one on earth to me. Can you guess who it was?

It surely did sound good to hear your voice. Oh, if you could have only been nearer!

Please do not think I do not love you, Dear, because I don't write long letters for the Lord in Heaven and all his angels know that I almost worship you.

Poor boy! I know you were lonesome yesterday. I am so sorry I didn't get to talk to you. Had I known that you called I would have called you, but I knew nothing of it at all.

Eudie is not feeling at all well tonight. I think we have all had a trial at "grunting."

Lora is alright now and they intend to leave town Wednesday to be gone about six weeks. I asked Buckler [must be Lora's beau] what he was going to do while Lora was gone and he said he guessed he would go home when he had the blues, so I told him I feared that it would be the next day then. Some of them are going to Handley [Texas town founded in 1884, dissolved and taken in by Fort Worth in 1946] tomorrow afternoon. They invited me but I am not going. Myrtle and Alto are not going either. They may stop here on their way home tomorrow night.

I don't see how I'm going to wait till stand it for "sake."

I know you are charmed with this paper, but Lo! When I went to the writing desk to get the tablet "The leaves had all blown out!" At any rate they were not there, so I tho't you'd like to hear from me anyway, Sweetheart. I'd like to hear from you if you were to write on wrapping paper.

Goodnight, Dear, here's a big hug and all my love and kisses
Your Ruth

Although Ruth did not make it home for the Fourth, she is coming home to Dallas in time for the start of school at her new post in Lancaster. The telegram is undated; best guess is September 2, 1911.

൭ Dear "Zeke"—Meet me at the depot Saturday night, if convenient. If not that will be alright. I'll be in on the Santa Fe line. [And then I told Alma and Lora about Ralph the other night.]

I said "Oh! Yes. What would Myrtle do?" He (Ralph Brownlee) said "She threw me down on the fourth of July." "C"

You said I must hurry up with letters! I have never written you much, Dear, but I have written some every day to show you I still love you and think of you and long for you all the time.

Remember I love you with all my heart and hurry home to Your Ruth

An interesting fragment (pp. 5–6) of an incomplete letter in Ruth's hand mentions school, not by name but the context suggests that the reference is to her position in Lancaster, Texas, which she took in the fall of 1911. The letter was written on a Monday evening.

൭ My dear Zeke:-

I went to church yesterday morning. I wonder if you did! I walked a mile too. School is progressing nicely. We had two new pupils today. John and Cora Brown. I am very glad that your people like me, and I'm sure I can return the compliment. They made it so pleasant for me while I was there. Poor old Kate, I'll have to disappoint her again, for I see no chance at the present for any migrating northward. The tide will surely have to change a great deal, if we do leave Lancaster.

I had a letter from Lou Eddy [her host in Fort Smith] today. She says she and Jim have given "society a turn". She says he's from Cabell [Cabell County in West Virginia], thinks the "Cabell" girls are the whole cheese now. He has a position as a book keeper for the National Packing Co there, and a chance

for a better position soon. Lou Eddy said she and Jim [James
Betterton Gilliam was born in 1888, Ruth's older brother
by two years; he was a jolly man and evidently enjoyed the
company of a lady, though he never married] took in every
show in town. [Seems my brother is having a fine time.] I am
your devoted Ruth

Gatesville, TX Sept. 21, 1911

◌◌ My Dear Sweetheart:

Guess you are having a fine time now while I'm down here in
this little old jerkwater place fighting for my life. (Mosquitos).
Got here Monday at 2 p.m. but had to wait two days on a car of
steel so cannot possibly leave here before Monday.

I wrote Sis [Lera] that I would be home Sunday and we
would come over to see you, but we will all be disappointed for
once.

We found a very large centipede here yesterday and I
wanted to step [on] it but had to cut it in two to kill it, but I
have some other that looks something like an alligator only
very small that I intend to bring home.

I was so sleepy Monday morning that I almost missed my
train and I didn't have breakfast 'til I got here so you can
imagine how yours truly felt and yours truly can also guess
how you felt Jan. 1st on your way to the golden west.

Mr. West went to Galveston Saturday night and tried to get
me on the phone so I could go with him, but I was down town
with G. Edgar and missed him, also the trip.

Guess I'll have to spend next Sunday in this lovely burgh
and the girl that I knew here has been married two years
so the only thing for me to do is to work with the rest of the
negroes which I'll gladly do in order to get away from this place
one day earlier.

Tell Mittie [nickname for Martha, but we don't know her
full name] "howdy" for me and tell her to take good care of my
sweetheart and not let her run around on her sore foot too

much and don't let some other fellow beat my time. Go and
have a big time, dearest, but please don't forget that Zeke is
always thinking of you and longing to be with you.

There is a show billed here for tomorrow night and if you
were here we would go but as I don't know a human in town
I guess I'll stay home and smoke my pipe and think of you. I
might be home [Celina] Sunday week and drive over to see you
but can't promise anything for sure.

Bye bye Sweet Girl. Will see you when you get home I guess.
Go to see Sis if you have a chance. Write to me real soon at
Dallas. Don't know when I'll get back but hope it will be soon. I
am yours etc. ZEKE

A note about "Mittie": It's a nickname for Martha made popular by
Martha Bulloch Roosevelt (1835–1884), mother of President Theodore
Roosevelt, who ran for the presidency again in 1912 on the Progressive
(Bull Moose) party ticket.

Another postcard from Zeke was written September 25, 1911. The
image: Leon Bridge, probably built in 1910, two lanes spanning a creek.

Gatesville, Texas

Drove out to this place Sunday, also to the state
reformatory [it's now the Mountain View Unit of the Texas
Department of Criminal Justice, which houses the death row
unit for women], about three miles north of town. It certainly
is interesting to go thru it. They have 100 negroes and 182
white boys now. Don't know when I'll get to leave here. There
is to be a circus here Wednesday and I guess I'll have to go to
keep from getting too lonely.

A letter from Marvin written on Hotel Royal stationery (two dollars
per day), written from Waco, Texas, and dated September 27, 1911:

My dearest girlie;-
Well here I come bothering you with another letter and I

guess I make you tired but I think of you so much and want to see you so badly that I can't help.

I got so tired of G—ville [Gatesville] I almost died of lonesomeness and was tickled to death to get to come up here tonight but will have to go back there in a few days.

I drove all over Gatesville and surrounding country Sunday to the reformatory, visited Sulphur wells and other places of interest and got along very well 'til we got home at 5:30 and then I got so lonely for Dallas and you that I had a real case of the blues.

There is absolutely nothing going in Gatesville so you can imagine what a good time I had, being a perfect stranger.

Don't know yet what I will do to kill time tonight but guess I'll go to a show or two after a while.

There is no telling when I'll get home but I surely hope you will be there by the time I am. I hope you are having a fine time but you must hurry home 'cause I am very, very anxious to love somebody and that means you. Good night sweetheart. Your own Zeke

Another postcard from Zeke to Ruth in Tioga, Texas, was written from Waco, Texas, dated September 28, 1911. On the front is the Amicable Life Insurance Building, Waco, Texas, twenty-two stories high and the tallest building in the South.

꙳ Have been seeing Waco today from the top of this building. Saw East Lyme at the tent show last night. Will go back to Gatesville this afternoon.

On October 7, 1911, Zeke wrote a postcard to Ruth with an image of Celina High School.

꙳ Arrived here OK with Mollie Bailey on the same train. Seems like these shows are following me up. Will drive over to

Tioga tomorrow to catch the KATY. Write me at Newark. ZEKE

Sometime during the fall of 1911, Ruth wrote a poem to Zeke, apologizing for slighting him:

"An Apology"
Don't be angry with me, "Zeke,"
And act as if you're "sore,"
I know that I was lazy "Zeke"
I won't be anymore.

Now just you listen won't you please.
And I'll try my best to say
Just why I did not wave at you
As you passed my house today.

I did not wake until I heard
A car come round the bend,
And then I hurried to the hall
But a signal I could not send.

I was as sorry as could be
For I could see you plain,
But I hope you'll not be angry
And will wave at me again.

'tis Newark in the golden west
That charms you I believe,
But tho' you're there just for a while,
I hope you can soon leave.

The Dallas Fair will soon be here
With all its pleasures gay,
But this will be but naught to me
As long as you're away.

So now go at it with all your might
And finish up your work,
And remember what your duty is
And never must you shirk.

The biggest task is before you now
And that is simply this:
Just answer "this here" nothingness
And I'll send to you a _____. "Amor"

(The "Newark" that Ruth mentioned in her poem was a flourishing Texas farming community.)

Many of the letters between Ruth and Marvin have survived as undated fragments, which have been incorporated according to context. Ruth wrote to Zeke from Lancaster, Texas, where she had taken a new teaching position in the fall of 1911. Lancaster, Texas, is a city in Dallas County. Founded in 1852 as a frontier post, Lancaster is one of Dallas County's earliest settlements. Ruth and a traveling companion, "Nellie," arrived in Lancaster on the train from Dallas.

Lancaster, Texas, Monday, October 27, 1911
    ᧁ᧒ My dear "Zeke"
    This is Monday a.m. I promised to write to you tonight but I have nothing whatever to do right now, so consequently I'm writing sooner. However, if you feel like I do, I'm sure you'll welcome a letter.
    Nellie never did find Mrs. Harrison, but Mr. Harrison met her. Mr. Houston met me too. It was dark when we reached Lancaster. Myrtle had phoned Mr. Houston and he was there in a closed carriage with a good heavy lap-robe. I was surely glad to see him. [Transportation options are developing in the early twentieth century. People traveled from Dallas to Lancaster by rail. The automobile is still a novelty, so the horse-drawn carriage seems to be a preferred mode of transportation from

the depot to their final destination in town, especially at night. The lap-robe is certainly welcome on a cool October evening.]

I like my boarding place fine. I have a nice room with everything that I need in it—and more good things to eat, but you know I ate a wondrous lot. Mrs. Houston had a good warm supper for us last night and had my favorite cake (chocolate). Mr. Houston said he believed I was in love—the reason I wouldn't eat, but I told him I was so despondent because of one who did that I lost my appetite.

Listen, you fix Claud Bell the next time you see him, for he's told off on me down here. He never said anything bad, but—Oh well you can guess.

Claud's sister Mamie came to school to me this morning. I think she is a sweet little girl.

You should have seen me this morning as Nellie says, "reading the right (riot) act." I had a very small attendance, a great many of the children did not know that school would commence today, while others are still picking cotton. [Texas did not enact a compulsory school attendance law until 1915.]

My! It is certainly gloomy today. It is growing so dark I can scarcely see. Mr. Houston is going to kill a hog this afternoon. Oh! You spare ribs and sausage!

I hope you made it to Newark alright, and will not get too lonesome, you can just write to me when you get lonely. See?

I have not heard from Myrtle yet but suppose she will phone me this afternoon. I've been industrious this morning. I classified all the children, heard some lessons, and called on a sick lady.

There are two small children here, one four and the other two year's. The youngest is named Edwin A. after Dr. Means. I don't miss little Myrtle and A. C. quite so much, as I would if there were no children.

I know you think I'm crazy for writing on both sides of this paper, but I neglected bringing a tablet, and you see I have to economize.

Be industrious (like I) and write to me. With much love. Box
86 Lancaster R#2. Ruth

Zeke's reply is dated November oncet (Wednesday, 1911), written
from Newark, Texas:

⌒ My Dearest Ruth—

Was very glad indeed to get your dear letter this morning so
will be prompt in answer.

You were very good to write to me so soon and I am very
glad you were for I was some lonesome this morning and was
thinking of you as I dreamed of you again last night. I dreamed
that you and I were in a farm wagon taking a bale of cotton to
town and we lost most all the cotton and I lay down on what
was left and tried to go to sleep but woke up before I went to
sleep. I dreamed some other things too that I'll tell you about
when I see you.

The wind has been blowing real hard today and has made it
rather disagreeable for us by blowing sand and cement in our
eyes, ears and mouth.

Jim Bumpas and Mr. West came up yesterday but Mr. West
left last night and Jim and I are alone here now in this small
burgh. We will finish this job about Friday, I guess, then we will
be in Dallas over Sunday and I don't know where we go then
but hope I will it will be Lancaster.

Sure would like to see you tonight sweetheart and love you
a little bit, or a whole lot, if you didn't get tired and tell me to
stop, stop, stop.

Last night was the memorable Hallowe'en and this burgh
was as quiet and lonesome as a graveyard but I tho't of you and
wished a thousand times that I was with you as I was a year
ago. You must write to me just as often as you can Sweetheart
for I think you are just as dear and sweet as can be and I had
rather have a letter from you than anyone else I know of.

I am going to write to you just as often as I can and if I write too much you must tell me about it. Tell me all that Claud Bell said about you and I'll fix him.

Goodnight Darling. With lots of love and kisses. Your sweetheart. Zeke

Circa November 3, 1911, Zeke writes about buying and selling a car that was marketed at the State Fair of Texas, which had been reorganized in the fall of 1911. Woodrow Wilson delivered a speech, and automobile races and stunt flying exhibitions became the top attractions. Missing the first part, the letter begins in mid thought about shopping for a car.

Dearest Ruth:-

. . . The other is a larger car with the same equipment that has not been run at all, only to the Fair Grounds and back one time. It sold for $2050 and can be bought now for somewhere near $1800 or less.

There is not a better car for the money in the state—The Firestone Columbus—and if we can sell him one of them there will be a pretty nice little sum in it for me as my commission and you can tell Mr. Austin that if he buys either of them, I'll split my commission with him if he will not say anything about it to Mr. Firestone, the salesman. [He is talking about the 1911 Firestone-Columbus Torpedo Roadster and Touring Car. Marvin may have been working for the Columbus Buggy Company at this time.] If he is going to buy a car soon it might pay him to have us show him the car. We can come down to see him most anytime if he wants us to.

I'd like awfully well to see you tonight sweetheart but guess I'll have to be contented at home by myself.

I wanted to stay 'til after supper Sunday but Will had a date with his girl and of course I couldn't say anything.

I'm so cold I'll quit now but remember that I'm thinking of you all the time and love you more than I can tell you. Goodnight dearest. With a car load of love. Your. Marvin

The romance between Ruth and Zeke develops further, as he writes to Ruth from Dallas on Monday, November 6, 1911.

    ❧ My Dear Sweetheart;-

Am going to surprise you with a letter tonight and hope you will be good enough to write me a long letter. I've got the blues so bad but I'm too "dang" mean to cry.

Seems awful lonesome when I get home and can't phone my sweetheart and I'm missing you just lots.

Didn't go anywhere last night only up to tenth street a little while after supper to see Ralph and came home before 8 P.M. while Ralph went to see his girl and poor little me with no girl to go see.

Gee! But I wished for you last night and am still wishing tonight but wishing doesn't do one any good.

I'm going to keep right on wishing tho for I think of you most all the time anyhow. Mr. Bell's mother was here today but I did not see her, think Miss Fannie sent you some word by her. She is better today, has been sitting up some and has been lecturing me tonight as usual.

Guess I expect too much of you but when you are away two or three days seem like a week to me and if I don't hear from you I feel like I am forgotten. Don't be surprised at anything I write but just write to me as often as you can and you'll make me love you all the more.

'Tis only 9:30 now and it seems like I have been at home 6 hours instead of 3. The days don't seem very long but the nights are almost endless to me.

I haven't seen or heard from G. Edgar since I came home, but he phoned here for me Sunday while I was out. Will try to see him sometime this week. Be real good Sweetheart and don't forget to write to your Zeke. What is your phone number? MDD

    ❧ Dear "Country School Marm."

Awfully glad to find a letter from you when I got home tonite so will be prompt and answer to show you that I appreciate it.

It has rained here for two days and the streets as sloppy as can be. Hope it isn't bad where you are.

No. Ralph and I didn't go to the show Sunday night and I haven't been anywhere this week at night and don't suppose I will.

Ralph wanted me to go to town with him one night this week but it is so bad I don't think I'll go. I've been real lonely this week and have missed you more than I thot I would. Sure do wish you were where I could see you once in a while.

Had to run Lex away from the phone just now. Mrs. Ziegler tried to get him to leave and she could do nothing with him so I took a hand and he got real "peevish." [Marvin boards with Mrs. Ziegler, who has a young son, Lex.]

Miss Fannie [perhaps sister of Mrs. Ziegler] has been up most of the day but still has to lie down some but says she feels lots better. She sends her love to you and was real glad you spoke of her in your letter.

I still haven't heard from home so I guess they have forgotten me and don't care enough about me to write and I've written Mamma four times since she was here.

You must be some popular human to get two phone calls in such a short time and are you sure both of them were ladies? I am glad you like to hear from me, dear girl, but don't see how you can enjoy my letters for they seem very uninteresting and badly written, but I am willing to make an effort if you like to read them.

You made one mistake in signing your letter, for the question mark should not have been after "best" but should have been left out entirely. You know, Sweetheart, that you are my best girl and that should not be questioned at all.

Say Girl! Please don't address any more of my mail to "Marvin Davis" Dillon for I hate that middle name something fierce and have tried to forget it but you won't let me. Don't think I am scolding sweetheart for I am not, but I just don't like that "Davis" a little bit.

If you don't come home Sunday you must write me a long letter for I'll be some lonesome and would phone you, but they would tease you so, I guess you had rather I would not.

It certainly looks suspicious to me that little Alto can't miss seeing his darling Myrtle on Sunday. Cousins can be so loving sometimes tho' can't they? Would like to love somebody myself tonight but it certainly isn't a cousin.

Well I didn't think I was going to write much tonight and haven't written very much but it covers lots of paper and you will think you have a long letter 'til you have read it, then you'll think my mind was wandering when I wrote it.

Am going to quit now and retire to dream of you, the sweetest girl in Dallas, County. Will expect a long letter from you real soon. Your best (?) beau. Zeke

P.S. Am sending you some Spearmint. Want it?

This revelation explains why Marvin's middle name was omitted even from his obituary in the *Dallas Morning News* in 1943. Also, every signature that exists outside the letters reads "M. D. Dillon."

The correspondence continues with a letter from Marvin to Ruth dated Dallas, November 9, 1911. Written across the top of page 1 were the words "You got the first letter out of this tablet and you now get the last one from this particular tablet."

ᏽ My dearest girlie;-

It is now eleven P.M. and everyone has gone to bed and to sleep long ago except myself and I've been reading 'til I am almost sleepy too.

I've been retiring early all week and having bad dreams so thot I'd try staying up a while. Had a bad dream last night and you were the most prominent figure in it but will not tell you about it 'til I see you again.

Wrote you last night and carried it in my pocket all day and didn't mail it 'til late this afternoon but will try to be more tho'tful in the future if you will forgive me this time.

Have lots of things to say to you when you come home so get your listeners in good receiving order before you come.

Think Ralph went to see a girl in Oak Lawn tonight but not Miss TJ. She called me up tonite and caught me at home.

Would write more but this is the last of my tablet so will try to sleep a little bit and hope I don't have a dream like I did last night. With lots of love and kisses, Write soon. Zeke

P.S. Wish I could squeeze you just once tonight. Tell Nelle "Howdy"!

Again, considering context, a letter from Ruth written on November 11, 1911. It makes sense for Ruth to write to Zeke on Saturday morning since she was a teacher and worked long days Monday through Friday.

Saturday Morn

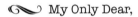 My Only Dear,

How sorry I am that you are not feeling well! I do wish I could do something for you, but I can only think about you continually close and pray for you. We went to church again last night and the lights went out during the service.

Mitt [identity unknown] is looking for one of her beaux this morning at nine-thirty. Rather an early caller isn't he? "Everything's fair in love and war" tho' isn't it, Dear. Do you remember my saying that at the Fair once? I never shall forget how embarrassed I was.

I haven't heard from a soul since I've been here except you, but I had rather hear from you than anyone else on earth.

You said that you had bad dreams Thursday night. I surely did have a bad one that night too. I dreamt that I was shot.

A.C. has just come and is standing right by me. He has been kissing me and is now teasing me so I can hardly write. He surely is an affectionate little fellow—(and kinder reminds me of another little fellow whom I know in Hugo). The evening I came, A.C. saw me coming down the street and he ran to meet me, saying "Auntie Woof" came from Dallas.

You must write and tell me what your mother says about our plans [AH! Ruth and Zeke are now engaged!] I surely am glad Olan [Marvin's brother, maybe his best man] is home now and hope he will stay there.

Get well, my sweetheart and know that my tho'ts are all of you. Love and kisses. Ruth

The month of November was a busy time and the beginning of the holiday season, as it is now. The difference is that Thanksgiving fell on November 30, the fifth Thursday of the month. It was not until December 26, 1941, that Congress decreed Thanksgiving would be celebrated nationwide on the fourth Thursday of November.

The next letter is from Zeke to Ruth, who has not yet come home from Lancaster to Dallas for Thanksgiving.

Wednesday Nite. Nov. 22, 1911

⟲ My dear Ruth;-

Of course I was glad to get your letter today and just had to read it before I ate my supper. It was awfully nice to come home from work and know that I have a letter on Wednesday night from my own dear sweetheart.

Had a card from home [Celina, Texas] today and they are going to have a big turkey dinner and want you and I to come up and help eat it Thanksgiving, so you can come home on Wednesday night, not have any school Friday, and we can go home Thursday A.M. and stay 'til Saturday. I'm going to write them that we are coming so you must make your preparations accordingly.

I intended to write to you last night as I was lonesome but Ralph phoned me and insisted that I go to the Majestic with him and it was most too late to write when I got home tho' I was thinking of you. [Majestic Theater in downtown Dallas was built in 1906, then burned down in 1917. The theater was rebuilt in 1920 and opened again in 1921.]

Part of the show was real good and part of it was n.g. I'll send you the program marked the ones that I liked.

I guess I'll go to Newark on Friday but am not sure so you phone me when you get here Friday and they will tell you if I am eating supper.

I sure did feel bad over the way that happened, but I am sure you are too generous and good not to forgive me.

I'm very glad you did not get real cold Sunday but I did hate to see you go in that crowded carriage in the front seat. 'Twas real cold here Monday morning but has not been cold since and I'm glad to report my throat is OK now tho' I still have a cold.

Have not heard from G. Edgar yet so I guess he has forgotten me entirely. Had an invitation to Miss Scales' wedding in Trenton Dec. 5th, but hardly think I'll attend. She is the girl that I told you about seeing at the State Fair. She is to marry a Mr. Williams and they will be at home after Jan. 1st at 2208 Browder St. Dallas.

If I go to Newark Friday, I guess I'll not see you 'til I'll be home Sat.

You rascal! You wouldn't tell me about not feeling well and your foot hurting you but I found it out anyhow.

When you write I want you to tell me all about your dear self and not keep your trouble from me but let me sympathize with you.

Just talked to Mrs. Ragon and she wants you to come home early Friday so she can go to the show but I guess she will tell you all about that.

If I get back from Newark you and I can go Saturday night, that is if you haven't made other arrangements already.

I am very anxious to know what your dream was but guess you will not forget it before I see you.

Am also anxious to hear more about your beau that you had Sunday night.

Well Good-Night dear. I hope you are feeling fine by now and your foot has quit bothering you. Miss Fannie sends her love to you. I'll close now with lots of love and kisses.

Your Zeke

We can only assume that Ruth and Zeke spent a sweet romantic Thanksgiving with his family in Celina, Texas. She would have returned to Lancaster, probably on Saturday or Sunday, December 2 or 3, to resume her teaching post on Monday, December 4. Zeke wrote to her from Dallas on Monday, December 4, 1911.

My dear Sweetheart;-

News is rather scarce up this way but I'm going to write a little note so you will know I've not forgotten you. I stayed at home and read last night 'til 9:30 and retired early, but thot of you a whole lot.

Ralph and I went for a little ride tonite in "my car," we thot of coming down your way but our tires were rather bad and we were afraid to venture on the country roads.

Guess you will not have to work so hard now as you have an assistant and I am glad for you. I am looking for a long letter from you this week to make up for the one you missed last week so had better get busy and next time don't wait to hear from me first. My letters may be delayed or something might happen that would prevent my writing but I love you just the same and I don't want you to think you are forgotten.

Ralph told me a lot about his case tonight and I believe it is getting real serious out in Oak Lawn from the way he talks.

I have not heard from home yet so I guess they didn't care so much after all whether I came home or stayed in Dallas. They've about quit writing to me and you are the only human that I can depend on to write to me and you are real good that way. See! I'm bragging on you now but you deserve it alright. Just keep it up little girl for your dear letters are very much appreciated by a lonesome boy in Dallas, Texas (This same state)

Guess I'll retire now for I'm getting "Kinder" cold.

Write me a long sweet letter soon. With bushels of love. Your beau. Zeke

Ruth writes about her sore foot on Monday night, perhaps December 4, 1911. She makes reference to the Houstons, so we can assume she is still boarding with them in Lancaster.

꧁ My dear "Zeke,"

I wrote to you last night as promised and mailed it this morning. Mr. and Mrs. Houston persuaded me not to teach today and I'm glad I didn't now. I was so nervous when I went down to breakfast that I was in a perfect tremor.

Am not so nervous now, but I had a chill today, and my foot has not been free from pain very long at the time. The medicine the doctor gave me seems to be too severe. I think I shall talk to him tonight, if I can get him by phone.

Myrtle phoned me this afternoon. She is not strong yet, but taught school today. Alto came down Sat, spent the night, and returned Sunday night. Myrtle said she had received a long letter from Calif. too and there was a message to me but she would not tell me. She also had a long letter from Otha that was written to both of us.

Goodnight Zeke. I hope you'll sleep well tonight and dream of me who thinks of you many times during the day. R__Will go to school this morning.

Here is an undated letter from 1911 to Ruth from Lera, Marvin's sister. I knew her as Aunt Lera. She lived in New Braunfels, Texas. She was always close to my grandmother Ruth. Her daughter, Lera Bess, was a close first cousin/friend of my mother. I played with her son, Vaner, and daughters, Laura and Susie. When Mother died in May 1960, Aunt Lera came to Dallas for the funeral. She stayed with us, slept in my room in the other twin bed, and snored like a banshee all night. She helped me dress for Mother's service. I wore a black-and-white tiny checkered shirtwaist dress with stockings and black patent leather pumps with one-inch heels. Aunt Lera suggested I wear the black belt instead of the red one.

⟨∾⟩ Dear Ruth:-

Will write a few words and send with brother's letter. We are all delighted of course to have him with us—wish you could have come too. I have been quite busy for the last two months. Have given two recitals (piano) and you can imagine what that means.

I rather expect to visit Dallas in a few weeks, don't know just when. Listen, I think you might give me one of your pictures—brother brought his from home and everyone thinks it fine. I'll just keep this one and you can give him another—so—saving the trouble of mailing it. Here's hoping to see you before many weeks. Lovingly, Lera.

Next letter placed in context, Thursday Afternoon, December 7, 1911.

⟨∾⟩ My dear Ruth;-

I've just had a short nap and awoke wishing I could see and love you a little as I am awfully lonesome today.

I started down to see you last night when I had a bad blowout and had to take the car back to the shop. Tried to fix it this morning but will have to have a new tire so guess I'll not come down today. [Dallas to Lancaster is about twenty-six miles.]

I phoned Eudie [Ruth's oldest sister] and she had just gotten in the house hadn't even gotten her hat off. She made quite a long visit with you.

I was very glad to get your letter and glad to know that you liked the candy I gave you.

I went to Newark Tuesday and almost froze when I drove five miles over to Rhome facing wind but thot I'd rather drive over and get to Ft. Worth two and a half hours earlier.

Ralph went to see Miss H —- Sunday nite tho' I tried to get

him not to go. I think he thinks more of her than any of us know about. I was in Oak Lawn last night a little while but not to see her.

Just went over to get a car and see an ex-roommate of mine who is married now. I had a card from Sis [Lera] yesterday insisting that I come home today and am sorry I had to disappoint them.

We had a real good dinner today with no one here but homefolks, wish you could have been here with us. Miss Fannie took her dinner with Gus Brownlee and came home at 3 p.m. with a severe headache, guess she ate too much of the good things.

I am awfully sorry that I couldn't come down today and see my sweetheart but guess I'll see you Friday. If you come on the train I'll meet you but if you drive up, I'll phone you when I get home. I'll close now with a barrel of love for you. Your Sweetheart. Zeke

Letter from Zeke dated simply "Monday night." Though no date is given, it is circa December 4, 1911, and probably the response to Ruth's return to Lancaster after Thanksgiving November 30, 1911.

ᑐ⁓ My dearest girl;-

I surely hope you are feeling better than you were last night and hope you are thro' with the chills and headaches for good.

I would like to be with you tonight and love and pet you for an hour or two and maybe you would feel better and I'm sure I would.

We got home about 11:45 last night and got to bed before 12.

We didn't get cold either as we had the wind to our backs all the way.

Both the other boys had their overcoats but I didn't have anything but got along about as well as they.

I dreamed that I was in Gatesville installing some scales but came home before they were finished because I wanted to see you but had to go on to Sherman without seeing you at all.

I was some mad too but finally awoke and realized it was all a dream.

I'm awfully lonely tonight sweetheart and the nights seem so long and vacant since you went back to Lancaster.

I guess being with you so much last week spoiled me for I want to see you every night now. [Thanksgiving 1911 fell on Thursday November 30. Ruth would have returned to work by Monday December 4, 1911.]

Alto came down for a while tonight and that helped just a little bit. Of course I was glad he came down but it would have suited me much better if I could have seen the girl I love instead.

I worked eleven hours today tho I didn't just exactly feel like it but I guess I felt better at work than I would have had I stayed at home and probably had the blues.

I don't feel real well tonight and I'm "Kinder" sleepy and don't know anything more to write only that I do love you and always will.

Goodnight darling. Wish I had a sweet kiss right now. As ever yours. Marvin

Ruth's reply, though missing, was probably posted on December 19, unless mail service was so frequent that Zeke posted his letter the morning of December 12 and Ruth received it that afternoon. The letters between Marvin and Ruth cross each other in the mail, which confuses the exact time line.

According to Nancy Pope, historian and curator of the National Postal Museum:

> By the first decade of the 20th century some cities saw three to five daily deliveries to business areas, but often no more than twice a day deliveries to residential ones. America's businesses were more than happy with this arrangement. In his Annual report to Congress in 1911, Postmaster General

Frank Hitchcock noted that the policy of reducing residential deliveries in order to increase those to business districts was 'almost universally approved by businessmen, who are willing to have fewer deliveries at their residences in order to obtain more frequent service to their places of business.' By 1950, most cities went to one residential delivery per day.[1]

In a conversation I had on January 30, 2019, with cousin Betty Wortham Rush, I mentioned the frustration of finding so many letters headed by a day of the week rather than the specific month, day, and year. She said, "Yes, that was how it was done back then."

Marvin wrote to Ruth from Dallas boardinghouse on Wednesday night, December 13, 1911.

༄ My own dear Ruth;- Of course I was tickled to get your letter today and read it before supper as usual altho' they were waiting on me.

I am glad to say that I have not been near so blue this week as I have been lately and I am very much pleased to know that "someone" cares.

I am glad that you have Alma down there to help you and be company to you but you just tell her that I'll thank her to let you alone when you are writing to me.

Your letters are short enough when you have no one to bother you and I like to get long letters from you as I never get any from anyone else.

It has rained here most all day beginning about 3 a.m. and it is some muddy tonite in Dallas but I guess it is not muddy down there.

I sure do wish you were here tonight so we could ____ but you are not here so I'll not say it but leave you to guess the rest.

I'm awfully sorry that Myrtle has been sick but sincerely hope she is well by now. You tell her it is too near Christmas to get sick.

I still haven't heard from home but I'm going to write them . . .

I surely hope you did not let the team run into a ditch and turn you over. 'Twas awfully nice and sweet of my girls to meet us at the station and bring us back again. I hope none of you suffered from the drive tho I know it was disagreeable weather for you to be out.

I'm just crazy for your school to be out so you can come home and not worry about going back Sunday but from the way you talked last Sunday it will be worse for poor me than it is now. The way it is at present I get to see you almost every week but if you are going to spend Sunday in Tioga and Fort Smith, I'll be lonely all the time and you will probably forget that you ever cared for me.

I'm more than sorry that you are not here tonight to go see "Graustark" and I would like to see it too if I could go with you but I don't care about going alone or taking anyone else so I guess you will not be the only one without your beau.

There is not one more beautiful than you I saw this afternoon and tonight on the street than I ever saw before in the same length of time, but none of them looked good to me after just leaving you.

You may think some of this is "fiction" but I never was more serious in my life and I would give most anything if things were different with me but as they are now, the future looks dark and gloomy for me.

I don't think it at all fair that some people can have anything on earth they wish for and others can't have just one thing that they want worse than all the rest put together.

This seems like a cruel world to me and if it should ever really happen it would be a blow that I would never get over.

I could tell you a whole lot more if I could see you but I don't know just how to express myself in writing.

I hope you will understand this letter just like I want you to and I think you will know about how awfully miserable I am sometimes and why I have the blues.

Write to me as often as you can dear girl and remember that I love you as well as I love my own life.

Your devoted Marvin I'll retire now just one hour and fifteen minutes late. Zeke

Ruth, an independent professional woman, will not respond at the beck and call of any man.

Graustark: The Story of a Love Behind a Throne was a 1901 book by George Barr McCutcheon. This Ruritanian romance was made into an American silent film in 1915. The reference to the *Graustark* film in Marvin's letter written in 1911 suggests that there was an earlier film made before 1915. Otherwise, the reference in the letter makes no sense. Louise Brooks, in her best-selling book *Lulu in Hollywood* (New York: Knopf, 1982), makes reference to a 1925 film *Beverly in Graustark*. Evidently there was an earlier version, perhaps a play released in 1910/1911.

Here is a letter from Zeke, dated Monday night. There is reference to cold weather, it was likely written in winter 1911, circa December 18, before Christmas.

ᗧ My dearest girlie;-

I suppose you tho't I had lots of nerve to call you last night but I was just awful lonesome so that I'd tell you about Lera's accident.

I was sitting in my room reading when I had a presentiment that I ought to call up the folks at home.

I talked to Mamma at Celina first, then Lera called me from Gunter, Texas and both of them said they wanted you to come up with me Sunday morning and as the majority rules, I don't see how you are going to get out of it.

Lera was real nervous when she talked to me. The train wrecked at eleven a.m. and she, as well as the other passengers, had to stay at the wreck until seven p.m. in the cold wind. Tis a wonder that she was not worse than she was.

I have a call in for her now so I'll tell you more about her after I talk.

I'm sending you a clipping from the Dallas Disgrace [Is Zeke denigrating the *Dallas Morning News*, founded in 1885?] about the accident yesterday afternoon on Jefferson St.

You remember we saw the doctors going up and I met the ambulance just after you left.

I stayed at home last night and read quite a bit but retired at nine forty-five and lay in bed and just thot about lots of things 'til nearly one o'clock before I could sleep at all.

I had quite a long talk with Ralph tonite over the 'phone and he told me lots of things about himself and someone else.

He seems rather changeable for he talked very different from what he told me about a week ago.

I've just talked to Sis [Lera] and she wasn't hurt so bad after all but is still rather nervous from the scare.

They had another wreck this evening at five-thirty just a few miles this side of the one they had one Saturday just a little way the other side so it seems that they are having quite a few wrecks on that road. Three in three days all in seventeen miles of each other is "going some."

Everyone is in slumber land but yours truly and I'm getting cold so I'll quit now.

With much love. Zeke

THE ENGAGEMENT AND WEDDING: 1912

*T*here are no specific references in the letters to Thanksgiving or Christmas, which leads us to conclude that Ruth and Marvin were indeed together and there would have been much back-and-forth between Dallas and Celina. Now we transition to 1912. The reader will notice that Zeke's letter-writing skills have improved. The tone of his correspondence is relaxed and confident. His diction and grammar have improved. It's as if Ruth has been "teaching" her beloved the art of composition through her letters to him. Ruth still holds her position in Lancaster, Zeke still works in sales, and they are apart. She took the train back to Lancaster on January 1, 1912.

Marvin writes on Tuesday night, no date, probably January 1, 1912, after Ruth has returned to Lancaster.

꧁ My dearest girlie;-

I'm a little sleepy but am going to write you a short note before I close my weary eyes in peaceful slumber.

Alto and I went to the Majestic last night and sat down on the fifth row. The show was real good this week. [What was it?] Wish you could have been there with me to help me laugh anyhow.

I suppose you girls had lots of fun on the train. Am so glad you were all together so my sweetheart would not get lonesome.

I wonder if you miss me as I miss you and if you want to see me as bad as I do you tonite.

Somehow you grow dearer and sweeter to me every day and every time you go away it is just that much harder to say goodbye.

I'm going to look for you home Friday night [January 12, 1912] and surely hope I'll not be disappointed.

It's getting cold so guess I'd better quit and say goodnight.

I'll not apologize for this letter for you know sweetheart I always do my best to write you a good letter tho' I most always fail.

With just lots of love and some more kissed. I am still Your Zeke

315 N. Jeff. Ave.

[More on the back] Claud's brother is here tonight and they have already retired and are fussing about the light, but they can just fuss all they want to.

Seems lonesome tonight with you away and I've been with you so much lately that I miss you dreadfully. I sure did hate to see you leave yesterday if you were not going for but the distance doesn't count much when you are away.

Letter from Ruth to Zeke, written from Lancaster, Texas, dated Tuesday, January 2, 1912:

෴ Dear "Zeke",

The old maids reached Lancaster alright. We had a jolly time, as we were all together.

Myrtle's beau met her, but Alma and I had to phone for Mr. Austin to come for us. In the meantime, Myrtle, her beau Willie, Alma and myself went to a friend's house, and whiled away the time. They had us eat supper, and we had some good music, so the time passed quickly.

There was a party up at Mrs. Houston's last night, and we had an invitation but didn't go. I suppose you have a slight idea how sleepy I was do you not? However we sat up until eleven o'clock. I had thought that I would be apt to oversleep myself, and be late for school this morning, but we were good old maids and arose in the early morn and walked our mile in sixteen minutes.

Alma is playing on the piano and singing "Kiss Me." Myrtle and her assistant teacher came up this afternoon and stayed for supper. They went home just a few minutes ago.

Oh! My goodness I wish you could have seen the drove of young men who filed into school this morning.

I was invited over to Mr. Fitzhugh's home to spend the night, one night right soon.

"Excuse me" but I am so sleepy and tired. Goodnight. Ruth

P.S. Had a letter from Mitt. Will tell you about it some time.

Another Monday night, January 8, 1912:

Dearest Girlie;-

Well we got home at just 1 a.m. but were not at all cold so our visit didn't have any bad after effects at all for us and hope it didn't for you either.

Roger spent the rest of the night with me and caught the early train to Cement this morning. I felt pretty good all day and have tho't of you at least one hundred times and dreamed of you last night so you need not think I'm going to forget you.

I forgot to mail Alto's letter last night and again this morning but phoned him and he came down after supper and got it.

He and I are going to Mr. Coston Wednesday night to play "42" and "500". Wish you were going to be there too.

G. Edgar said he was real glad that he went and we are going

to do the "Same Thing Over Again" "Some of These Days" so
you need not be surprised to see us most any time if you don't
come home pretty soon. Claud is writing to his girl now and we
have been telling "yarns" for a long time but have both told out
so we will resume our writing.

I don't know very much to write tonight sweetheart only to
tell you that I still love you a great big lot and I've told you that
so much that you know it already.

Letter from Ruth, written from Lancaster, Texas, dated Monday,
January 15, 1912:

୧୬ Dear Zeke,

True to my word I'm going to write you tonight, tho' I fear
my letter will not be very lengthy. I surely was glad that you
called up tonight for I too was so lonesome. I'll tell you what
that was funny about your call. To begin with Mr. Austin said
at supper, "Miss Ruth, I'll venture to say that you will get a
long distance call before Friday night." He even bet me a "juice
harp". When the phone rang I answered it, and central said,
"You're the very one I'm looking for, Dallas wants you." I said,
"Alright" and while I was waiting I placed my hand over the
transmitter and was talking to Alma when Central said, "Oh!
Now you needn't be bragging so big, I hope you will not get to
talk." About that time Dallas operator said, "Lancaster I can't
find the party who wanted to talk to Miss Ruth now." I tho't
that that operator would never quit laughing. It did him so
much good. Then Dallas operator asked me if I had any idea
what number might be calling and I told her probably 529.
Then our Central heard every word you and I said and teased
me about it. He has been . . . [Pages 4–7 are missing. The letter
picks up mid-sentence on page 8.]

. . . "even asked about "Zeke", [who swore,] "I never saw
the girl before in my life!" You lay old Claud out. He won't do
to trust. You tell him I said, "Never mind, I'll have a little talk

with him if I ever see Dallas again."

Bedford Terry, the young man whose picture I showed you, married Saturday night. Tell Claud he married Jessie Worley.

We went horseback riding Saturday. We wanted to ride to Dallas, but alas. Heard from Kurt today and he has . . . [The letter breaks off here.]

Following is an undated, incomplete letter from Zeke to Ruth, written after a telephone conversation on a Saturday night, perhaps January 20, 1912. Zeke expresses not only love for Ruth, but appreciation for the admirable qualities of her personality. He is apologizing for something he said on a phone call that evidently put her off. He is asking her to soften her heart and to write more loving words to him.

ᐧ My dear Ruth:)

I'm going to play fair tho' and tell you who I love, and you won't even do that when we are together or in a letter either.

I think if you knew how much good those words would do me coming from you that you would write just a little more personal than you do most of the time. I'm so glad to get your letter that I'm not complaining at all, dearest, but I sometimes get awfully hungry for just a few loving words from the sweetest girl that lives.

Of course you can't write these things unless you feel just that way but you are so sweet and good to me that I just think you do love me a "little bit."

You seem to think that I'm just as fickle as can be just because you happen to know the unpleasant particulars about one other girl but if that had been as good as you are I would never have done as I did but of course you can't understand all that for as much as you know you don't know all of it by any means.

But Honest Girl! As long as you treat me as well as you always have in the past you need not be afraid that I'll "drop" you for that is not my nature at all and I love you far too dearly for anything like that.

I've gone with lots of girls in my not very long life and you have meant more to me in your pure, sweet ways than any one I ever went with.

I'll never forget our visit last night and surely hope I'll see you again before long. I may have talked a little too freely on some subjects over the phone Saturday night and if I did I humbly beg your pardon.

I believe you were a little glad to see us but you were not nearly so glad as I was to see you. Write me a long sweet letter real soon and remember that I'm thinking of you all the time and loving you more than you will ever know.

Give my regards to all the folks down there. With bushels of love and some kisses.

Your own ZEKE

Letter from Zeke to Ruth, dated Tuesday night, January 23, 1912:

My very dear Ruth;-

I believe you said it was very careless of anyone to write a letter with a pencil but I am just going to ask you to "Excuse me" and I'll go ahead and be careless as usual,

Gee! But your voice did sound good to me last night and I wanted to tell you how much I tho't of you but one must not say too much over these party lines.

Alto and I walked from the post office in Dallas to the end of Ervay St. and caught a car and came back to town then went to the Dallas Electric power house and from there over the viaduct to Oak Cliff.

When we got to Mr. Coston's [Lora's father] house, Lora was sitting on the porch "All Alone" so we stopped and asked her to play for us and she was kind enough to do so.

She phoned her friend, Miss Roberts, to come over so we went back after supper and spent a very pleasant evening. I was just ringing the doorbell when Mr. Coston hung up the receiver after talking to Alma.

Sure wish I had been just a little bit earlier so I could have gotten in a few words but I'm always just in time to miss the best of everything.

Talked to Eudie last night after I talked to you. She said she tho't it was time you wrote to her. I tho't you would get my last letter Saturday after I nearly froze going to the depot to mail it and was late at work but I guess the train was late going down there to see my own sweetheart no matter what those people have to say.

There is no danger at all in coming home and I think those people are a little bit crazy so if they don't let you come home they are going to have to keep me away with a shot gun or raise the quarantine. [There must be scarlet fever or meningitis in Ruth's school.] Eudie wouldn't tell me just what her dream was but dropped some pretty strong hints, so I think I know what it was. Guess she will tell you all about it when those scissor bills [slang for "an inferior or stupid person"] decide to let you come back to civilization again.

I've had several dreams about you lately but can't tell them very well on paper, but they will keep.

Any old time you feel lonely and think of me just write me a long sweet letter and thereby pass away the time and incidentally help a poor lonesome boy in Dallas who thinks of you all the time and loves you just a whole big lot. Don't wait on me but write as often as you feel like it for a letter from you the sweetest girl in Texas is always very much appreciated by a certain "Mr. Dillon." I'm one letter ahead now so hurry up. Hoping to see you real soon.

I am your affectionate beau.

The Kissing Bug. Wish I had one now.

Here is a letter to Ruth from Zeke dated Wednesday Night. On the back he wrote: "N.B. This letter is to the sweetest girl in Texas. Written from Newark, Texas, on January 24, 1912, at 10:05 p.m." There is no salutation on this letter. Zeke registers awareness of the probability of having missed receiving a recent letter from Ruth.

    ◯◯ My dear Ruth,

If I was at home tonight I hope I would have a letter from my sweetheart but I'm in this most beautiful little hamlet and lonesome as the dickens.

Came up here this a.m. and thot I would get back to Dallas tonight but drove over to Rhome this afternoon and stayed so long I missed the train here so will have to spend my very valuable time here 'til 10:20 tomorrow.

Alto and I were going to Lora's to play "42" tonight but—well we didn't, at least I didn't. I would have phoned you tonight but the phones are so rotten up here I could not have talked or heard you talk so I'll just send a note to you instead.

I drove around over town last night for quite a while but was afraid to venture out in the country. Sure wish I could have seen you, in fact I want to see you all the time but it seems that I don't happen to be lucky enough to see you very often of late.

I'm going to look for you home this week and if you don't come something is liable to happen that will cause those clodhoppers to sit up and take notice.

I told Claud that some geezer from Lancaster was out to see his girl Sunday night and had him going some 'til I told him better.

Guess you were surprised at the handwriting on the letter I wrote you Monday night so I'll tell you how it was.

Claud was writing his girl at the same time I was writing you and we finished our letters at about the same time and he suggested that he address mine and just for fun I did.

Guess you thot you had gotten a letter from "somebody," didn't you?

If you don't come home, write and tell me just what you did think.

Mr. West [Marvin's boss] is going to south Texas on a big

fishing trip the last of this week or the first of next week and has been after me to go with him but I don't think I'll go. Would like to very much but don't see how I can.

I phoned to the bank for your check book on Tuesday morning and hope you have gotten it by now. Am sorry but I just completely forgot it on Monday but hope you will "excuse me" for my carelessness.

I also phoned Mrs. Ragon Monday night and told her that you were OK and just as sweet as ever.

Don't know a blooming thing more to write so I'll close this most interesting epistle from "One who cares". With love, hugs and kisses. Your Zeke

From Zeke to Ruth, letter dated Thursday night, January 25, 1912:

ᘓ Dearest girl;-

Tomorrow is Friday and I keep on thinking that someone will be home but guess I'll just "keep on" being lonesome unless those unreasonable hay-seeds come to their senses and let my dear sweetheart come home.

Just talked to Eudie tonight and she said that she would have to send you some clothes by me. I'll sure be one willing messenger alright.

I'm coming down Sunday if it is pretty weather no matter what those people have to say for I sure want to see my sweetheart.

I talked to Ralph tonight, he says he is going to Duncanville next Sunday to see Miss Horne and I'll gosh-dinged if I stay here and be lonesome all day with you so near (and yet so far). [Duncanville and Lancaster are about 20 miles apart.] I was awful glad to get your letter Wednesday and want to thank you for writing such a long one. I must admit that I was rather agreeably surprised.

I was much surprised at the unusual length of the one I wrote Tuesday night.

Alto came by here a short while ago and wanted me to go to town with him but I tho't I'd stay here and make an attempt at a letter tho' I fear 'twill not be quite so long as the last one.

Honest Girl! If Sunday is as pretty as last Sunday was I'm coming down there unless you come home so you can tell them to have their darn shotguns ready to run me off.

Claud intended to go see his girl [Inez] Sunday but she wrote him that her mother was afraid for him to come so he has the blues too.

I'm glad of it tho' and hope he doesn't see her for six months. I'm getting "kinder" cold so guess I'll quit. I hope to see you real soon.

With lots of love and innumerable kisses. Zeke

Here is Ruth's reply to Zeke, written from Lancaster, Texas, dated Wednesday, January 31, 1912. She is writing diagonally on personal stationery paper embossed with an italicized *G*.

⧉ Dear Zeke;

If I can possibly get my senses together for a few moments, I will also let you know you're not forgotten. It was so nice of you [to] write even tho' you had no news as you said, to tell. That's all right, I was glad to read your letter anyway, and am always "tickled to death" to read them. Honestly, there is absolutely nothing "newsy" down here, either. It seems worse than ever.

Alma started a letter the same time that I began this one. She is trying to write in bed (lazy) and has torn up two or three pages and finally has given up altogether. Probably she doesn't ___Oh! Well ---- care [to] see?

I know you are wondering what in the world I am writing in such a manner as this but I think it must be my "criss-cross" feeling tonight. I don't have the "blues" tho' but poor Alma has, and of course I have to fight catching the same. We had only eleven pupils today on account of the hard rain. The work is so light. I have only twelve students in classes a day now where I used to have about twenty-five.

Wish you and Ralph could have come down. You must bother to come sometime and see these poor old Lancaster school teachers. Be just as careful as you can, for you must not forget what I dreamed. Yours as ever. Ruth Pleasant dreams.

Ralph Brownlee is Alma's beau.

Letter from Zeke to Ruth dated Thursday night, February 1, 1912:

Dearest Ruth;-

Here I come again the third time this week. Don't you get tired of me? I must thank you for your exceptionally long sweet letter received yesterday. If I had had the blues I would have gotten over them at once but I knew your letter was here before I got home so I didn't have them.

Bless your heart! That letter was a part of my dream of Monday night. I think I'm the luckiest human in Dallas if you mean what you wrote and of course I believe you.

I'm awfully sorry I haven't been down to see you this week for I want to see you awfully bad but I've been feeling rather tough this week and have not felt like going anywhere.

Mrs. Zeigler, Miss Fannie [she seems to have recovered her health] and Mr. Dillon walked down to the viaduct to the new ornamental lights turned on last nite. They were very pretty and we enjoyed our walk very much.

I was standing looking over the rail at the river wishing that you were with us when Miss Fannie remarked, "Mr. Dillon don't you wish Ruth was here?" So you see we all think of you very often indeed.

Claud and I didn't get home 'til nearly eight o'clock tonight. I had to work late and he stayed at the office getting used to his new job.

He is working for the Westinghouse Elec. CO now at $10.00 increase in salary.

I phoned Ralph this morning and asked him to go down

to see Alma one night soon but he is so busy he says he can't possibly get away.

Alto phoned me to come up and stay a while with him tonight while Uncle and Aunt had gone visiting but I didn't go for fear they would come back before I left.

I had a long letter from Mamma yesterday with another long lecture and a rather urgent request that I come home on my birthday [Feb. 11] and help eat that turkey but I just can't decide whether to go or not.

You will have to excuse this letter tonight sweetheart for I don't know another thing to write. I hope to see you sometime soon but if I don't I want you to be sure to come home a week from Sunday and help me celebrate my 22nd birthday.

Wish I could kiss you goodnight but I'll have to be contented with writing it. With barrels of love. Your own. Marvin

Here is another letter on the *G* stationery from Ruth to Zeke, from Lancaster, Texas, Monday, February 12, 1912. Ruth, Myrtle, and Alma are all teaching in different schools in Lancaster. Ruth and Alma share a room in the Houston boardinghouse; Myrtle boards with the Austins. They frequently travel back and forth from Lancaster to Dallas on the train together.

༄ Dear "Town Guy,"

I guess you feel your importance because you're in the city this week. Huh? Oh! Well I don't care! What's the use?

Myrtle and I reached here last evening at about six o'clock. She ate supper with me and then one of her trustees, Mr. Austin, came after her. I tried to persuade her to spend the night with me, but she was afraid it might rain and she would not reach her school on time this morning.

I sat up until ten o'clock last night, then I read my Bible, prayed for forgiveness of my meanness, and for you, and retired.

This morning Mr. Houston called at six o'clock, an hour

sooner than usual. He went to Dallas today and wanted to get an early start. I didn't care anything about going with him either. Oh! No!

There is the phone. I'll venture it is for me. Yes, it was, and before I came back upstairs, it rang again for me. One was a lady, Mrs. Denton, and the other was Ina Austin, one of Myrtle's pupils inviting me down to her house Wednesday night. So if nothing happens, Myrtle, Eudie, and myself will spend the night there. I'm sure we shall have a pleasant time, for they are such nice people. Always yours. Ruth

Ruth writes on another Monday night, February 19, 1912:

⟡ Dear "Zeke", Back at dear old Houston's again! Joy to the World! Alma is almost acclimated now. We reached here at about six-thirty last evening. I wonder what you did! I sincerely hope you did not have the blues, as you prophesied.

You must quit having those despondent feelings so often. Just think "Somewhere, somehow, somebody cares." Poor old Myrtle was really sick last night but managed to teach school today. Alma says for me to tell you "hello" and that she wished she was in the land where intellect, knowledge, and wisdom were poured in rather than crammed in. Poor girl! She was so tired this afternoon! She'll soon get used to work tho!

That lady is in a good humor with Alma and myself. She has invited us over to spend the night. Alma is "rearing and scotching" because I won't quit and talk to her. She is singing too so I can't collect my tho'ts. My tho'ts are few tonight anyway.

Be a good fellow and don't forget. Your Ruth. Alma has just finished a solo in bed.

An incomplete letter from Marvin to Ruth, dated Wednesday night, February 21, 1912:

    Dear Ruth;-

I hope you have gotten over those dreadful blues by now and feel better. I know just how you have felt for I've been feeling that very same my own self this week and have not entirely gotten over it yet.

Would like to see you tonight and let you tell me what you could have read in a letter that would make you fall out of a chair. I hope you were not seriously hurt by the fall.

Tell Alma I thank her for doing as I requested and I'll try to do her a favor sometime.

I appreciate your poetry very much and am sorry that I can't write some too but I'm so ignorant that I'll just have to tell it to you in the old fashioned way.

I sure would be glad if you could come home tomorrow and help me celebrate the viaduct opening and George Birthington's Washday [Yes, this is how he put it!] but as you are not coming I guess I'll do my celebrating at work at least in the forenoon if not all day.

Did you see the snow last night? It snowed real hard for a while but the wind blew so hard that it didn't stay on the ground very long.

I'm sorry that you lost your belt and pin. You sure are losing you things lately. Be careful that you don't lose yourself and time tonight for I would hate for you to be as cold and lonesome as I am just now.

About the car. There is a man here from the factory that has two cars brought here for demonstration and as they are last year's models they want to sell them and bring down new cars. One of them—the one I took you home in has been used for some time but I know it to be a good car and in first class condition. It is a five passenger, thirty-five horse power with top, windshield, magneto and speedometer and originally sold for $1800 but can be bought now for $1000 and maybe less. You promised to write as often as I so come on with the letters. Zeke

Another incomplete letter from Marvin to Ruth, dated Thursday Night, February 22, 1912:

My dearest sweetheart;-

I got home at 12 o'clock today and was awful glad to find your sweet letter and a card from Lera.

I wrote you a letter last night and guess you will get it tomorrow. I'm just as angry as I can be tonight and I have enough to make me "cuss." Intended to come down to see you tonight in a car but one of the boys wanted the car to take his girl riding and to keep me from getting it, he hid one of the inner tubes and of course I could not take the car out with only three tires.

Claud was coming down with me and he and I hunted for the tube for over an hour but couldn't find and there was not another one in the garage that would fit.

There is going to be something doing in the morning so don't be surprised if you read in the "Dispatch" of one M. D. Dillon being arrested for fighting. I was simply tickled green at the chance of seeing my darling tonight, and then to be disappointed is enough to make anyone say naughty things which I probably did.

Gee! But I felt good when I read the last part of your letter and if you had been near I 'spect I would have done some hugging and kissing. It sure makes lots of difference to a poor lonely human like myself to show that there is a good sweet girl in the world that he knows really "cares."

I'm glad you girls enjoyed our visit Sunday night [February 18] and can truthfully say that G. Edgar and myself enjoyed it even more than you did.

I hated to leave when I did but I knew I couldn't stay much longer anyhow.

I'm sorry we didn't get to see Mr. and Mrs. Austin again but I thot they had retired.

You must thank them for us for their good supper and the

way they treated us while there.

No one can make me believe that all men are born equal and have an equal chance.

I sometimes think I've done wrong in going with you so much and learning to love you so very dearly when I had nothing on earth to offer you but when I look into my heart I find no regret there.

You have simply been "everything" to me and there is no one on earth that can ever take your place with me and no matter how blue I get I always try to have hopes that I'll someday have better luck and realize my fondest dreams.

I really believe that if I had to give you up, that there would be no more pleasure on earth for me. I remain your Marvin

Marvin's terse comments to Ruth in response to the dinner conversation on Sunday, February 18, registers tension rarely expressed in their correspondence. The politically charged year of 1912 invaded domestic peace with talk of women's suffrage, labor unions, and Negro rights. Theodore Roosevelt was mounting a third-party run for president, and later that year, Woodrow Wilson took the White House for the Democrats from William Howard Taft.

Letter to Marvin from Ruth, written from Lancaster, Texas, dated Wednesday, February 28, 1912:

Dear Marvin,

I was surely glad to hear you talk this evening. I was sorry I was not here last night when you called.

We had a real nice time last night over at Mr. Worley's home. Myrtle, Alma, and I all three went. We have promised Mama Bell to go home with her tomorrow night. I am not feeling at all well tonight tho' and can't say whether I will get to go or not. Surely hope I can.

You, G. Edgar and Alto had better be very careful, where you stand from now on. "A miss is as good as a mile," and I'm truly thankful that the barrels missed you.

Goodness! A new norther has come up. Hope it will not be too bad Friday so that I can't come home. I had heard about the Sanger's home burning. Hope it saved Ravenna. I know the fire looked big to Eudie and them.

I had a card from Mittie this week, and she is as mad as the mischief at me, because I haven't gone up there yet.

Mr. Austin's father is real sick tonight and he has gone to see him. We surely do miss him too, for he is always joking us, especially me. I have played several jokes on him lately and he said he surely was going to fix me, the next chance he got so "I'm just waiting and watching."

Here's hoping to see you Friday night at about 7 or 8:30. Yours lovingly. Ruth

P.S. The letter is so near nothing, that I feel almost tempted not to send it. Guess I will tho'. "Excuse it."

An incomplete letter from Marvin to Ruth, dated February 28, 1912. Marvin ends his letter with the following:

൧ Don't forget that next Sunday [March 3] is your birthday. Let me know real soon what you are going to do about your "celebration."

I hope Nelle came up to see you Sunday and helped you sleep the blues away.

I missed you a whole lot and hope you missed me some too.

I guess I'll have to quit now as I don't know what else to write.

Hark! An inspiration! I love you in mornings, I love you at night. And will always love "you".

Your sweetheart (Am I?)

Marvin

After Ruth's birthday celebration on Sunday, March 3, she and Alma took the train back to Lancaster on Sunday night and evidently the weather did not cooperate. Ruth's letter to Marvin, written from

Lancaster, Texas, dated Monday, March 4, 1912:

    ☙ Dear Zeke,

"The day has been cold and dark and dreary." You know the
rest so I will not repeat it, for fear it might give you the blues.

We surely did have a time getting home last night. Mr.
Austin's father was very low and he could not come for us,
and they were to phone the Man where Myrtle boards to, but
the people whom Mrs. Austin phoned failed to tell Joe for
some cause or other. Consequently we were until nine thirty
reaching here. It was raining too, and by the time we got warm,
it was bed time. So you see I couldn't write last night as I
promised.

Let me tell you one of our trustee's wife remembered that
yesterday was my birthday so she sent the nicest dinner to the
school house for Alma and myself. Wasn't that sweet of her?
Oh! Yes. Alma gave me the nicest embroidered handkerchief,
and Mrs. Austin said she was having something made for me.

Listen here, don't say anything about the awful time we had
getting out here, where Alma's people could hear of it, for they
would "have a fit."

Alma said she thought my dictionary was fine. "I'm simply
wild about dem" as George says. I guess you and Alto both had
a good time last night.

I'm getting so tired of being away off here where we never
see anything or go anywhere and have to go in all kinds of
weather. I'm surely going to change things up before long, for
better or for worse. I mean it too.

I hope you did not happen to have any accident on that
job at the T & P. It was surely nice for me that you got off
yesterday afternoon.

Listen, will you please phone Eudie to take my cuff buttons
out of my waist before she sends it off? I forgot them and I lost
a pair like that once before. I'll surely appreciate the favor.

Alma is in bed, and as it's cold in the room I suppose I had better retire too.

With much love I am Yours as you wish. Ruth

P.S. Mr. Austin's father died last night of pneumonia. Good luck to you.

Fragment from Zeke's reply to Ruth makes reference to her request to secure the cuff buttons from sister Eudie.

ᑐ I called Eudie and told her about your buttons, but she had already thot of them. Please don't be angry because I didn't write more sweetheart but I've "run out" and this is all the paper I have so I'll quit. With a barrel of love and 'steen thousand kisses. Your Marvin.

Ruth wrote to Marvin from Lancaster, Texas, Wednesday, March 13, 1912.

ᑐ Dear Marvin,

Oh! I'm so sleepy I can hardly hold my eyes open, so if I say anything strange, I might per chance be 'a dreaming!'

I spent the night away from home last night. Had a very nice time, but surely was glad to get home tonight, and especially was I glad to hear from you.

Have just finished talking to Nellie. She knew a great deal to tell consequently I am tired and more sleepy.

Myrtle is up here, and we have been playing 500. Mr. Austin and I played against Myrtle and Alma. We won two games to their two. One of the games we made the 200 in two bids. We made all ten tricks once too. How's that? (In another hand: Yes and we did some stunts too. MMM).

We are all simply crazy to come home Friday, and we are coming too, believe me.

I had a letter from Jim [Ruth's brother] today. He is fine. I am so glad that he is getting along so nicely.

That surely was nice of you to fix Claud's engine. Wish I

could have been there to have helped the good work along.

Myrtle and I are both trying to write. _____ grzzzzzzzz

_____

Excuse me, I was snoring. Yours as ever. Ruth

P.S. I have a dandy joke to tell you on Myrtle when I see you. It's raining this morning. If it's too bad we won't come through the country but will be on train if it's not too bad.

Here's a letter from Zeke to Ruth, dated Sunday Night, circa March 17, 1912. Ruth and Zeke are apart because she is teaching in Lancaster and he is working in Dallas and traveling throughout north Texas.

ᑰ Dearest Sweetheart;-

Gee! But I wish you were here tonight for I am awfully lonesome and I find after searching my heart that you are the very girl that I want to see worse than anyone else.

Mamma and Freida [Marvin's youngest sister, age 6)] came this morning and we went to church and then came home for dinner and Myrtle and Alto came down and spent about forty-five minutes with us and after they left we went to town and visited the "Jungleland" theatre and the "Olympian" confectionary then home again for supper and back to the train at seven twenty-five.

I went with Mr. Harrison from the station and have just gotten home to write to the dearest girl in Texas.

Mamma asked about you and said she would like to have you and Myrtle visit them this summer. She sure thinks a lot of you.

I looked for a letter from Saturday but was not very much surprised when I didn't get it for I was real careless and neglected writing you from Monday 'til Thursday but I think you would have forgiven me had you known how I felt all week and I worked overtime three days in succession. I'm not trying to make a lot of excuses but I want you to pardon me this time and I'll try not to be guilty again.

Some things I do may seem rather strange to you, sweetheart, but you probably don't understand and I want to tell you again that no matter what happens I love you and you only and when you don't hear from me right on time don't begin to think that I've forgotten you or intend to treat you mean for there is usually a reason for my conduct. I can't write just like I mean it but I hope you will understand me.

I'm going to look for you home not later than Thursday and would be awful glad to see you sooner tho your two weeks will not be up 'til then.

Honest sweetheart! It seems like you have been gone at least a month now and if you don't come home pretty soon I don't know what I'm going to do for when I get lonely like I am tonight nothing but your presence can satisfy that "longing" feeling down in my heart.

Write to me sweetheart and let me know what day you are coming home.

Give my regards to Kate and Mittie.

With a bushel of love, your Sweetheart. Zeke

Long letter from Marvin to Ruth, dated Wednesday morning, March 20, 1912:

૭ Dearest Ruth;-

I'm awful blue and lonely today. Wish I could see you and talk to you a long, long time and perhaps I would feel better.

I called Nelle last night and she told me all about her trouble. I sure do feel for her and think it the most disgraceful thing I ever heard of and in Dallas County too.

The postman has just come and brot your letter and it surely did help me too. Am so glad you found time to write for I would have felt a little disappointed if I had not gotten it. I've been thinking of you all the morning and counting the minutes 'til time for the postman. I forgot to tell you about the flower that I sent you so will now. (Better late than never.)

Last Wednesday night while I was writing to you Miss
Fannie came in with the flower and asked me to send it to
you with her love and I jokingly told her I wouldn't do it and
tho I fully intended to send it I forgot all about it and left it
on the table where I was writing and found it there and thot
I wouldn't send it because I was jealous of her. After I had
written Sunday Mr. Zeigler told me what she said about it so
I put it in. Of course I wasn't jealous but I simply forgot it 'til
they told me about it.

This is some dismal weather we're having and I surely
hope it will be a pretty day Friday so you can come home. Two
weeks isn't so very long but it seems like a long time when you
are away and I would rather see you now than anyone else on
earth.

Oh let me tell you about my dream last night. I dreamed
that I saved a girl from drowning and when I got her out I
found it was a girl that I went with about three years ago but
she has been married about two years. I don't know what on
earth made me dream of her for I hadn't even thot of her in two
months or longer. I've dreamed of you several times since I saw
you but I've never had the honor to rescue you.

I guess you will be rather lonesome down there after this
week with Nelle and Alma gone and Myrtle without a phone but
you can surely stand it two weeks and then tell them good bye
forever.

I've just been to dinner and told Miss Fannie what you said
about the flower. She asks about every day almost and always
tells me to give you her love when I write.

I'm so glad you got alright without having pneumonia and
hope you will not be sick any more.

I went out at eight and came back at eleven, my usual hours,
but spent the time in a very different way from what I usually
do and I can't say that I enjoyed myself quite as well as I have
lots of other times before. Can you guess the reason?

I shall never forget the very pleasant time I had Sunday

although I didn't get to be alone with you near as much as would have liked I got to love you a little bit and I'm not at all sorry I went.

I talked to Eudie last night and we are planning some things to try to keep you here this summer.

Guess I'll quit now and take this to town so you will get it tomorrow. I love you more and more every day sweetheart and I want you to try to keep loving me if you can. Your Marvin.

P.S. Tell Alma I wish she would please explain what she wrote on your letter last Sunday. Zeke

Letter from Marvin to Ruth, dated Wednesday night, March 27, 1912.

ᠺᠥ Dearest Ruth;-

Was awful glad to get your delightful letter tonight and I'm crazy to hear the rest of the interesting narrative you started but didn't finish. Why didn't you go ahead while you were at it and tell me all about it? You know I haven't any curiosity but I don't like continued stories very well.

I'm sorry you had such a time getting home and wish I could have gone back with you but I guess Mr. A ____ is glad I didn't.

Talk about a de-e-elightful time. We had a glorious time Sunday night waiting for the "Limited." We had to wait about an hour and a half to get to ride fifteen minutes. Yes, I was out on the Interurban Monday night but the attraction was not the same as it usually is. I got the engine running alright but am going back to work on it again Sunday.

Alto came by here last night and tried to get me to go to the Knights of Pythias banquet at Turner Hall with him but I didn't go. Retired at nine and slept 'til seven this morning

That was earlier than I've retired in several months but think I'll try it again tonight and see if I can get a little ahead with my sleep.

Alto said he was coming down here again tonight but it is now eight-fifteen and he hasn't gotten here yet. Claud has retired and wants me to put out the light but guess he will have to wait awhile. G. Edgar called me last night for the first time in over a week. I mean that was the first time I've talked to him. He called two or three times last week but I didn't happen to be at home.

Just talked to Eudie and she says she had a letter from Kate today and has something to tell you when you come home.

I had a letter from Clifford [Marvin's younger brother who died in a plane crash in 1929.] on Monday and one from Mamma on Tuesday. Mamma said, "If you never intend to come home again write as often as you can." I called her up last night and told her about a house they could get on 12th St. She says they will come here if they can get a house in Oak Cliff. I'll sure be glad if they will for I'm getting tired of boarding. The folks here are as nice to me as they can be but I'd rather be at home than at the finest boardinghouse in Dallas.

You must not have the blues even if Alma does but when you feel them coming on just do a Christian act and write me a long letter and forget them entirely. I'm ahead of you now, so you will have to hurry to catch up.

They have had one case of meningitis in Celina and suspended the schools for two weeks but they reopened last Monday.

I'm going to look for you Friday and you can look for me Friday night.

Goodnight Sweetheart. "I am Yours 'til Niagara Falls" Marvin.

I suppose Nelle is glad that they closed her school so she can be at home. Maybe they'll close yours soon so you can come home too.

Do you want to close or had you rather stay down there and teach?

Think of me sometimes sweetheart and write real often for "I love you too" just a whole big lot. With love. Your Marvin.

The Knights of Pythias is a fraternal organization and secret society founded in Washington, DC, on February 19, 1864. It celebrates the myth of Damon and Pythias, the ideals of loyalty, honor, and friendship.

Turner Hall [the event venue mentioned in the letter] is located at 401 North Rosemont Ave. in Dallas, Texas. A historic home in Oak Cliff's Winnetka Heights neighborhood, Turner Hall has been a fixture on Rosemont Avenue since 1912. It is now home to the Oak Cliff Society of Fine Arts and is also a popular wedding and event venue. In 2002, the site was dubbed Turner House in honor of Oak Cliff Society of the Fine Arts founder E. B. Turner. Marvin's parents did move to the house he found for them on Twelfth Street in Oak Cliff in fall of 1912.

Marvin's letter dated Friday night, March 29, 1912, makes reference to a photograph of him and Ruth along with Anna perched in a tree and Marvin's brother Milton. The photo was taken by Clifford. The brothers were likely the photographers at Ruth and Marvin's wedding in September.

Ruth, Marvin, Anna, Miltone, March 1912

 My dear sweetheart;-

Guess you've received my two letters by now so we are even. I'm awfully sorry they are scared of the meningitis so you can't come home.

I am not at all uneasy and don't see why they should be down there in the pure country air. I had letters from Mamma, Clifford [brother 1897–1929] and Milton [brother 1899–1973] today. They said the pictures they had made of the tree were "right good" and they were saving one for you and one for me. Mamma said you sure made a hit with the whole D. family and papa in particular. I knew my sweetheart . . .

. . . don't know what I'll do all day but I'm sure I'll be awfully lonesome for someone. Tell those people that the meningitis is all over and come on home. Write again real soon.

With lots of love, Your Zeke

This letter from Zeke to Ruth is dated Monday Night, April 1, 1912. Zeke has had an accident on the job.

 My dearest girlie;

The day has come and gone and now I'm going to try to write to the "only" girl.

Our train came about 8:40 last night so you see we had quite a wait after you left and we got awful tired and lonesome. Sure wish I could have spent that hour and a half with you.

It's now 11:15 and I've just gotten home from Mr. C. M. Ragon's (do you know anything about them?) where I spent the evening working on an engine still out of order.

I may have to go to Hugo from here before I come home but I don't care if I do if you go to Kate's as you spoke of in your letter Thursday.

If you do go there you must still write to me every day for I enjoy your letters so much.

I stuck a piece of rusty steel in the side of my right foot this evening just about five minutes of six and it is hurting me terribly now but I think it will soon be OK as I put a bandage and some iodine on it just as soon as I could get my shoe off so there is no use for you to worry about me.

I may go up to Otha's Sunday if she asks me to, that is if I can ever get her over the phone. Remember I am always your Zeke.

P.S. Give my best regards to Alma and Myrtle.

Letter from Marvin to Ruth from Paris, Texas, Friday night, 9:20 p.m., April 5, 1912. Marvin has not seen a doctor about the nail in his foot. He boarded a train for Paris, still suffering from the injury.

⟋⟍⟍⟍ Dearest Girl;-

I mailed you a letter at seven-thirty this evening but will write again for if you like to get letters from me as well as I do from you, you will be glad to get this.

I walked to the station and mailed your letter and my foot hurt me so badly I could hardly get back to the house, (only one block). I caught a car and went to town and got some Campho-Phenique and bandaged it to the sore place so it doesn't hurt near so much now. I wish you were here to love me and tell me how sorry you are. I don't think it would hurt quite so badly.

The piece I stuck in was a piece of a rail about two inches long and one-eighth of an inch wide and very rusty and I think it stuck the bone as it went in on the side of my foot back of the little toe.

I guess I've told you enough about my troubles so I'll change the subject.

My greatest troubles, dearest girl, are spending so many lonesome nights all alone. Nobody here but me when I can't even talk to my darling Ruth.

I think I'll get done here Friday or Saturday but if I go to Hugo there is no telling when I'll get home.

There was a band concert on the square tonight and I intended to go but didn't on account of my foot. I got my

"Dispatch" for first time today and was real glad to get it.

I tried to phone Otha again tonight but the line was still down so I haven't talked to her yet but will try again tomorrow. If I don't get to talk to her I don't know what I'll do Sunday, but I know it will be a long lonesome day for me.

They are real nice to me here, I have a big bowl to peaches and a pitcher of ice water on my dresser and all I need now is you to make me satisfied.

It didn't rain today for the first time since I came but it is still cloudy and rain is predicted for tonight but I surely hope it won't.

'Tis 'most ten now so I think I'll retire and maybe my foot will quit hurting so I can go to sleep. Goodnight Darling Ruth. With all my love, I am yours, Zeke

This is the last sheet of a tablet I bought after I came here and it has all gone to you except two short letters to Mr. West. Lovingly, ME

Sat. 6 a.m. My foot is better this morning tho I can't get my shoe on. I'm awful lonesome, my darling girl, for you and you only. Forever yours. M.D.D.

Another letter from Marvin to Ruth, dated Monday night, April 8, 1912. His business travels take him all over northeast Texas and into Oklahoma. He must pass through Paris, Texas, where friend Otha lives on his way to Hugo, Oklahoma, located twenty-six miles due north.

⟨⟩ Dear Ruth;-

I wonder if you are thinking of me tonight. I've thot of you all day today as I had a rather disagreeable dream about you last night and I just couldn't keep from thinking of it all day.

Alto and I got home [to Oak Cliff] at 8:30 and he came by and stayed here about an hour and after he left I read 'til about 10 P.M. and then retired.

I kind of looked for you to come home today for I thot they

might become frightened and dismiss the schools on account of the meningitis scare.

I'm awfully glad that this is your last week down there and surely hope you will not stay another week for we need you in Dallas.

I don't think you would hardly recognize me if you should see my "beautiful" face tonight as I have a lovely stye on my right eye. It is some sore but guess it will not last long.

I had another accident today that came very near being serious but was lucky enough to escape with only a burned arm and my shirt and jumper sleeve torn off at the elbow.

Got my sleeve caught in the lathe and 'tis almost of miracle that I didn't break an arm—but I didn't.

I'm crazy about you sweetheart and want you to remember that I love you and only you.

Don't forget to write to Your Marvin

Marvin's comment about this being Ruth's "last week" teaching in Lancaster and her last day being Friday April 12, and his desire for her to leave Lancaster is wishful thinking. Ruth is probably under contract until at least the middle of May. The Texas school year was about one 165 days, roughly from the Tuesday after Labor Day in September to the middle of May, with a short break for Christmas. The Texas Education Agency was created by the Texas legislature in 1911, so the standardization of the actual number of days per school year was probably gradually implemented across the state. The school year, which was scheduled around planting and harvesting seasons of the agricultural year, began in late April or early May. Harvest happened in June and continued through summer. When I began teaching in Texas in 1969, the school year was about 170 days. In the late 1970s, teachers were given a substantial raise in salary while the school year was extended to 180 days. Each state "raise" in salary was tagged to an increase in the number of days in the school year. Teachers do not now and have never received "paid" vacation.

Letter from Marvin to Ruth: At home Wednesday, April 10, 1912.

᳀ Dearest girl;-

So glad to get your letter tonight as I was not quite sure I would get one today after getting one yesterday. It was awful sweet of you to write both of them.

I mailed you a short letter at the P.O. Monday morning and one Tuesday morning in hopes you would get them the same day but guess you didn't get it Monday as you didn't speak of it in your letter.

I had a card from Olan today, written Tuesday night, and he said Mamma was a little better, able to sit up a little but not much.

Tried to call Eudie tonight but the operator reported the line "out of order" so I guess I'll not talk to your sister tonight.

G. Edgar didn't call me last night so I don't know whether he came to town or not. Don't suppose he did or he would have called.

I dreamed of you last night. Perhaps I'll tell you some of it when I see you but it doesn't amount to anything much so don't get your curiosity aroused.

Claud has a beautiful boil on the back of his neck and I've been trying to help him doctor it but didn't have much luck so he has gone to bed to try to sleep it off.

I'm rather anxious to hear the "rest" of what the Fortune tellers told you as she (or he) must have been pretty wise to tell you so much.

I've been reading every night this week and have found some real good stories in my Blue Book [*The Standard Blue Book of Texas 1912-1914*, a book of advertising principles]. There is one that I want you to read without fail. Can't think of anything more to write so guess I'll quit. With bushels of love, I am your Marvin

Ruth wrote to Zeke from Lancaster, Texas, sometime after Easter

1912, which fell on April 7. She would have returned to her teaching position later that week, so I date the letter about April 12, 1912. Ruth makes no mention of Marvin's foot injury. The paper appears to have come from a Big Chief tablet, now yellowed. The *Titanic* sank on April 15, 1912. Neither Ruth nor Marvin mention it in their surviving letters.

Dear Zeke,

Now don't say a word about this paper. I haven't another sheet and can't borrow any for there is no more on the place.

I taught till eleven o'clock yesterday and then dismissed on account of the funeral of Mrs. Fitzhugh. I didn't have to teach any unless I wanted to but I did.

J.N. (the little boy) and Mr. Fitzhugh are better this morning. Mr. Fitzhugh's brother is now very ill, and they are afraid it is going to develop into meningitis. I surely do feel sorry for that family, for I thought so much of them. They are surely burdened with sorrow.

We are hoping for a change, a nice little rain this morning. They are all vowing that I am to stay down here next week.

I was glad that you and Alto came down with us Sunday. We appreciated it. I must go to school now. As Ever, Ruth

P.S. Hope you are feeling just fine.

A short, not typical note from Zeke to Ruth, dated Thursday, 6 a.m., April 18, 1912:

My very dear Sweetheart;-

I feel just like I would give most anything to see you this morning and squeeze you a little and kiss you some 'steen thousand times.

Looks like rain again this morning but I surely hope it will soon clear up. My eye is better but it is awfully sore yet. With bushels of love. Zeke

An undated fragment follows here, from Marvin to Ruth, but context is not clear, so it is difficult to date. "Down there" refers to Lancaster, Texas, south of Dallas. April 19, 1912.

ᏬᏬ . . . you will not stay down there another week but if you want to stay I guess you will suit yourself so 'twill do no good for me to protest.

Stay if you really want to Sweetheart and I'll love you enough when you do come home to make up for lost time.

I might accidentally go home Sunday if you don't come home but am not sure yet.

I never know what I am going to do tho' 'til the time comes.

Don't think I have forgotten you, Sweetheart, because I didn't write more for I still love you as much as it is possible for anyone to love a girl, and always will. If you do stay there please write to me when you can. With lots of love, Yours forever, Marvin

Letter from Zeke to Ruth, dated Sunday night, April 21, 1912.

ᏬᏬ My own dear Ruth;-

I am going to look for a letter Tuesday from you will write you a little tonight and be as good to you as I want you to be to me.

I came on home after you left and developed a fine case of the blues but had only been home a short time when Mr. West phoned and wanted me to go to East Dallas and get a car and bring to the garage and I was more than glad to have something to do to take my mind off my troubles which are many.

I brot the car in and then got another one and drove all over east and south Dallas with another boy and have just gotten home (10:30).

I sure wish you could have been with me instead of being down there and probably lonely. Am awful sorry you went away feeling so badly but hope you feel a whole lot better tonight.

I wish things were so that I could do your suffering for you as I would gladly suffer to save you if it were possible but someone higher has decreed that we must bear our own troubles and all I can do is offer my deepest sympathy. [Has someone close to Ruth died?]

Write when you can, sweetheart, for the best remedy on earth for my blues is a long letter from the girl I love. With lots of love and a long sweet kiss,

I am YOUR own Zeke

P.S. I counted your letters and I have twenty three letters and thirteen post cards that I can find now. Count up and see who wins. M.D.D.

Here's a letter from Marvin to Ruth, dated Monday night, April 22, 1912. Ruth is still teaching in Lancaster, but the school year is almost over. She is in no hurry to give up her room in the Houstons' Lancaster boardinghouse. She has friends and a social life in Lancaster. She enjoys and values her independence. If she were to return to Dallas, she would live in the house at 1202 South Ewing Street with her widowed father.

 Dearest Ruth;-

I've tho't of you all day sweetheart and wondered if you were very lonesome and who you wanted to see real badly.

I tried to phone you but couldn't hear anything and the operator asked if I wanted it repeated but I told her if I could not talk to you I didn't want any second hand conversations so I'll call you some other time when I can hear.

I sure did some sound sleeping last night. Went to bed at 9:40 and was asleep in about two minutes and didn't wake 'til 6:15. Slept better than I have in six weeks or more.

I hope Mr. Austin was there so you would not have to wait and also hope Myrtle went on with you and you didn't do any spooning on the road.

I guess you are glad it rained today so you would not have so many kids at school but 'tis almost clear now so you are liable to have a full house the rest of the week.

Those kids are foolish if they let a little rain keep them away for if I were near you rain nor hail would keep my from being there.

Can't write much tonight sweetheart so I'll retire now and dream of—The Only Girl—Ruth. With much love. Marvin

Letter from Zeke to Ruth, dated Friday, May 3, 1912. School in Lancaster is out. Myrtle and Alma are back in Dallas and Ruth is somewhere having a "fine time."

☙ Dearest Ruth;-

I surely hope you are having a good time and I want you to have a fine time while there and hurry home. [Perhaps in Tioga with Kate]

I miss you already sweetheart for it seems like I just feel more lonesome when you are not here.

Myrtle and Alto came by and invited me to go to Alma's with them but I didn't go.

You have the best of me for you will probably get "this" Sat. afternoon while I'll not get your letter 'til Monday night.

I'm going home tomorrow (Sat) but Alto has changed his mind and will not go with me so I'll have a lonesome trip. Sure do wish you could go up with me.

The "Holy Rollers" are having a big meeting up on Church St and we can hear them singing and shouting without going up there.

I don't know any news that would interest you sweetheart so I'm afraid this is going to be a short letter but I hope you will overlook it and write a long one and tell all about your good times.

Will write you again Monday night. Don't think I've grown tired of you Ruth for I still love you as much as ever and always will. Your beau. Zeke My best regards to Mittie and Kate. Z

Letter from Zeke to Ruth, dated Wednesday, May 8, 1912:

⟨∿⟩ My very dear Ruth;-

You don't know how sorry I am that my sweetheart is sick and I'm going to scold you for not saying anything about it in your letter of Monday night.

When I got your letter I knew that something was wrong somewhere. You didn't say you were sick and didn't give any reasons for such a letter—if it could be called a letter—only that you had the blues and that is no excuse at all for a letter like that.

I had much rather you had told me you were sick and left out the rest of it than told how much corn you are or who was there for I would have understood then but you just left me to guess and worry about you.

Please don't do me that way anymore Ruth but when you are sick and don't feel like writing a long letter just tell me so and let it go at that and I won't worry half as much as I would if I didn't know what was wrong.

I think you should come home and rest 'til Sunday and if I could get away from the shop tomorrow I would come down and get you but we are three men short and it would be almost impossible for me to get off. [The letter stops here, another of many incomplete manuscripts.]

Letter from Zeke to Ruth, dated Thursday night, May 9, 1912:

⟨∿⟩ Dearest Sweetheart;-

Was real glad to get your letter yesterday and I think it about time that you came home for you have been gone three weeks already.

I've been working hard all week but have thot of you every day.

Went to Mr. Harris on Monday night and played 500 with Alma and her cousin. Had a nice time and Myrtle had some awfully good candy and of course that suited me.

We spoke of you and wished for you but I guess you were having just a good time as you would have had here.

Alto phoned and asked me to come up tonight but I didn't go and he half way promised to come down here but hasn't shown up yet.

Next Sunday is Mother's Day [May 12] and I am looking for Mamma to come down and spend the day with me.

I went to see Miss Wauser and ate too much butter scotch pie and was almost sick this morning but feel very good tonight.

Sweetheart I'm just awfully lonesome for you and want you to come home as soon as you can finish your visit. [With sister Kate in Tioga]

I may go to see other girls sometimes but when I do it always seem like there is something missing and the more I see of them the more I think of you for none of them can half compare with you in anyway.

Have a good time dear girl but try to hurry home and be sure to let me know when you are coming.

Give my best regards to Kate and Mittie and tell them that I want them to take the very best care of my sweetheart while there.

Miss Fannie sends her love. She asks me about you every day.

With all my love. Your Zeke

Letter from Zeke to Ruth, dated Wednesday night, May 14, 1912. The reference to Marvin's having a date with another girl speaks to his humanity. A handsome, gainfully employed young man, Marvin was a target for flirtatious women. It's interesting that Ruth chose to spend Mother's Day with her sister, rather than spending the day with Marvin and her future mother-in-law. She trusts him. Their wedding day is set. Marvin and his siblings are celebrating their mother. Exercising her independence, Ruth chose to spend time with sister Kate on this

Mother's Day, knowing that she would have many Mother's Days with Marvin's mother after their wedding. I wish more of Ruth's letters had survived. She probably chided Marvin for seeing another girl!

⟨∾⟩ Dear Ruth;-

I didn't write before I went to see that girl because I simply could not write feeling like I did. I've gotten home and I don't know over a dozen words she said although she did most all the talking. I guess she thinks I'm an awfully thick headed brute, but it doesn't matter for 'Twas never intended for me to have any pleasure in this life anyhow.

I'm not at all angry with you Ruth for what you wrote tho your letter was different to what I thot it would be.

I can't write what I want to say and am not going to try to tell you what is in my heart 'til I see you but will then if I can.

What you suggest may be hard for you but 'twill be so much harder for me but I'll wait and talk it over with you when you come home. Remember—I love you. Zeke

A gap in the correspondence between Zeke and Ruth suggests that she has indeed given up her room in Lancaster and returned to Dallas. She is living with her father in the home of her childhood on South Ewing. Zeke's next letter is dated from Celina, Texas, Monday, June 17, 1912.

⟨∾⟩ My dear Sweetheart;-

I've been thinking of you constantly since I came home and even dreamed about you last night. I'm rather lonesome for you too. Of course I couldn't be very lonesome with all the kids here but I mean I miss you all the time.

Mamma sure did give me some lecture yesterday but I guess I deserved it alright. She said I looked like I had a long spell of sickness and wants me to stay here and recuperate but I don't think I want to stay away from the dearest girl on earth a whole week unless it is absolutely necessary so I think I'll be back not later than Wed.

They all had a fit over your picture and Lera says she is going to keep it but I'll have something to say about that.

I'm sorry you didn't come with me for we could have such a nice time and stay here all week. There was a crowd of girls here yesterday afternoon and we had all kinds of ragtime music and singing. The girls all had beaux and went to church last night but I went to bed at 9 and slept 'til 7 this morning, more than I've slept in a long time.

Just as soon as I got in the house yesterday morning Mamma asked me if I had been sick and I told her I had not but she know better and says, "You are so sick now that you can hardly stand up" and began doctoring me at once.

I'm not very sick tho' for I ate more yesterday than I've eaten in one day in a long time. I wish I could get a long sweet letter from you today but don't suppose I will be so lucky.

I haven't told Mamma "anything" yet tho' I've dropped several hints but don't think she took any of them seriously. I don't know whether I'll tell her or not. [Zeke is referring to the fact that he and Ruth are now engaged to be married. Mamma already knows.]

I may go down to Bessie's [Marvin's older sister (1887–1967) lived in Prosper, Texas] this afternoon if it doesn't rain any more. Wish you were here darling girl to go with me. If you were here I would be contented to stay all week.

I don't know any more to tell you now sweetheart only that I still think that I have the dearest sweetheart on earth and love her more and more each day and live for you and you alone.

Will see you when I get back to Dallas. With lots of love and some ten thousand kisses.

Your only, Zeke

P.S. Am sending you a program of Lera's recital at her request. Lera may be in Dallas in a week or two.

Letter from Zeke to Ruth, dated July 9, 1912:

❧ My Dearest Ruth,

I haven't the blues tonight, sweetheart, but I'm some lonesome human and the wind sounds so dismal that it makes me even more so.

I'm real glad that you want me to think of you and you know I think of you so much now that I couldn't think of you much more unless I quit thinking of anything else at all for you are on my mind all the time and very often when I'm at work and should find myself indulging in day dreams, of you and building air castles.

Too bad that they have to tumble down and bring me back to earth.

I've been sitting here smoking my pipe and as the smoke curls up toward the ceiling I can see, or imagine I see, your face in it and you appear to be "Kinder" lonesome but I really hope you are not nearly so lonesome as I am.

I was a little surprised to get a long distance call from you last Thursday [July 4] but it was more pleasant than anything else would have been unless it could have been you, your own dear self, at home.

Alto and I went to see the fireworks Thursday night and met Lora and Miss Turner as we were leaving so we walked home with them and they were kind enough to play and sing for us about an hour.

I tho't of you and of course wished that you were with us to enjoy the ragtime music.

I heard "Billie" played at the St. George tonight and it made me think of Christmas [1911] and the good times we had at home.

They also played "Silver Threads Among the Gold" and "Put Your Arms Around Me Honey" and they also bro't back pleasant memories. You can tell Alma, and Myrtle that I'm glad they tho't of me and I "feel" for them but hope they won't have the blues too bad but think of what good time they are going to have next summer when there "ain't no school." You must not have the blues either sweetheart for they are not at all good company. I am your own Marvin

Ruth is away for another Fourth of July, not to visit friends in Arkansas, as in 1911, but to be with Kate in Tioga. Ruth has packed a bag and left home because her father refused to acknowledge that his youngest child and his favorite daughter was indeed a grown-up! She had taken care of him from the time her mother had died in 1906 until she went to college in Denton, Texas. Now an independent woman at twenty-two, she supported herself working as a schoolteacher, has quit her job, and plans to marry! The letter Ruth wrote to Marvin expressing her anger with her father has not survived. Marvin's supportive response to her appears in the letter of July 13, 1912.

The next surviving letter from Zeke to Ruth was written on stationery from Peace Hotel in Wills Point, Texas, "Louis Simpson, Manager. Mrs. Ennis Peace, Propt's." The daily rate is two dollars, and the hotel offers the European Plan (rate is for room only) and the American Plan (rate includes three meals per day). The letter is dated Friday, July 11, 1912.

    Dearest girl;-

I was more than surprised to get your real sweet letter this evening but I was awful glad to be surprised.

We got to this God-forsaken place at 10:45 a.m. and been perfectly miserable ever since. The hotel is the worst I ever saw in a town of this size. The rooms look more like dog kennels than a place for humans to sleep in and it takes forty minutes to get anything to eat after you get to the table. 'tis now eight p.m. and we've just finished supper but thank goodness they put up a very decent table. Enough of my troubles tho' for you don't need to know how much we are enjoying the town.

When you wrote you said you hadn't realized that I was gone but I realize now that I'm not at home to phone to the sweetest girl in the world or perhaps be closer than the phone so you would not miss my goodnight kisses.

There is a picture show here but I hardly think I will attend tonight for I need the sleep.

I haven't been very sleepy today but am beginning to be now tho I doubt if I sleep any for several hours on account of the intense heat. The perspiration is dripping from my face and arms as I write so don't be offended if I don't write very much.

I'm very lonesome for you sweetheart and don't see just how I'm going to stay away from you 'til Tuesday. There is an excursion to Dallas Sunday for $1.50 for the round trip and if I don't get lots of letters from you I may be home Sunday but don't know for sure. Of course I want to see you awfully bad and will want to see you lots worse Sunday but I may decide to stay for "our" sake. (understand?!)

Lizzie and Billie want to go to the show but I don't believe I care to go tonight.

Write as often as you possibly can, darling, for your letters help me to tolerate a very undesirable place for a few days.

I love you tonight dearest as no boy ever loved a girl before and the only reason I'm staying here is to try to hurry up the time when I'll be the happiest mortal on earth.

With all the love my heart summons. Your. Zeke

A note about Wills Point, Texas, from Wikipedia:

Founded in 1873, Wills Point gets its name from an early American settler, William Wills, who had arrived in the area *circa* 1848. Wills eventually purchased a cabin from Adam Sullivan in 1852. The name "point" may also derive from the shape of the original timberline near the cabin, though there have been unsubstantiated arguments that the name relates to the area's elevation. The layout of the city was the work of engineer General Grenville M. Dodge of the California Construction Company. The downtown streets were laid with

red bricks upon packed sand in the 1920s by locals and remain
in use. Downtown Wills Point has many of its original buildings
that are over one hundred years old including the Wills cabin, a
drugstore, a dry goods store, and a law office. Governor George
W. Bush officially named Wills Point the Bluebird Capital of
Texas in 1995.[1]

The Majestic movie theater was opened in 1926 by Karl C. LyBrand
and was still family operated by Karl C. LyBrand III until its closure on
October 4, 2010. It had been the oldest continuously operated movie
theater in Texas run by a single family. The Bruce & Human Drug
Company, located on the corner of Fourth Street and James, was built
in 1879 and is the oldest family-owned drugstore in Texas.

Wills Point is also the final resting place for Trailblazer, the first
commercially operated monorail system in the United States.

The romance continues to blossom with another letter from Zeke
to Ruth, written from Peace Hotel in Wills Point, Texas, Saturday, July
12, 1912.

     My darling girl;-

I have to sit around here and wait on a phone call to Dallas
so I'll occupy my time by writing.

This is some swell town but thank goodness I won't be here
all summer and there are six trains each way daily.

I almost had the blues last night, but after I read your letter
I felt lots better so you had better keep them coming as often as
you can. Your letter came just as I came up to supper.

'Twas so warm we didn't get to sleep very much, and
Lizzie declared he murdered 'steen thousand bzbzs [must be
mosquitos] and I know there were that many there.

I'm going to hunt a place to board today where we can have
a clean bed if we don't get quite as much to eat.

Will write again tonight sweetheart if I get another letter
from you today.

I would give lots just to see you awhile this morning. I

wonder if you longed for me as much as I did you last night. I
love you dearly sweetheart, so don't forget to write to me "heap
much." Very lovingly. Zeke

Evidently, Zeke did receive another letter from Ruth, telling him
about the argument with her father over her engagement. Zeke wrote
again from the Peace Hotel in Wills Point on Sunday, July 13, 1912.

   怀 My very dear Ruth;-
    Well I'm still here but can hardly say that I'm in love with
the town or anything in the town. I've had my supper and a
fine swim and feel first rate but am awfully lonesome for a dear
little girl out at "Hillside on the Urban."
    Looked for your letter last night but didn't get it 'til this
morning about 8 o'clock but was just as glad to get it.
    I guess I will not come home tomorrow for I would have to
leave at 8 p.m. and I would not get to be with you enough to
justify me to spend the money as bad as I need it just now.
    I'm sorry sweetheart that I can't be with you tonight and
tomorrow but guess I'll sleep most of the day if it is not too
warm.
    I started this letter about thirty minutes ago and I wrote
about two or three lines when someone says something to me
and stops me but I'm going to finish now and not let any of
them bother me again.
    Lizzie and Billie kept persuading me 'til I went to the show
with them last night but I've been sorry ever since and I think
they have been too. [Among the films released in the summer
of 1912 was *The Musketeers of Pig Alley*, the world's first
gangster film.]
    The Wolcott-Norfleet Concert Company [a concert company
that performed at Chautauqua events] were here last night
and tonight but they are showing tonight without us to hear
them. Their music was very classical so you can imagine how
we enjoyed it.

I don't think we will be able to get away from here before
Wednesday as we have had a little bad luck and it has been so
awful hot that we could not do very much in the afternoon.

I'm sorry that your father [O. A. Gilliam, Confederate
veteran] doesn't want you to marry but I don't blame him very
much still I hope you will not change your mind without better
reasons than that as he hasn't a right to say anything about
it. I love you so dearly that I can't even think of you changing
your mind so we will not even say anything about it anymore.

Sweetheart I enjoy your letters so much and I wish I could
get two or three every day, but I guess you are so busy you
don't have time to write so much.

I'm sorry Lora is sick and hope she is well by now. Think I'll
quit now dear and write again tomorrow, so good night darling.
Write and tell who you love.

With Love and 'steen thousand kisses. Zeke

Judging from context, tone, and paper quality, the following letters
were written by Ruth in the summer of 1912. Written across the top
of the page: "Excuse me for writing on both sides of the paper." The
lengthy gaps on Ruth's side of 1912 correspondence—only two letters
in March, only one letter in April—are attributed to the fact that as
Marvin was traveling all over north Texas, he just didn't save her letters
as diligently as Ruth saved his. We know she wrote faithfully because he
mentioned having received letters from her. By now Ruth has resigned
her teaching position in Lancaster and is preparing for their wedding,
scheduled for September 21, 1912.

Tuesday, July 16, 1912. Tioga, Texas
൭ My dearest Sweetheart,

Wish I could see you right now. Hope you are not
working hard this afternoon, for it is so warm. I am not
feeling at all well this afternoon, Dear, Think I have a little
fever and my head aches "pretty much." It is just this cold,
tho', and I'm still taking medicine, so I'm in hopes that I'll

soon be OK.

I may go home this Saturday, or probably before then if
I don't get well because you know if I were to need a doctor,
there would be no one like Dr. Means.

I didn't receive a letter from you yesterday afternoon, last
night nor early this morning, but it reached here about noon
today. I surely was glad to hear from "My Sweetheart" too.
Mrs. McDonald [sister Kate's mother-in-law] went to church
and came by the office and brought me a letter from Myrtle,
one from Eudie, and Edna, and yours. I told her that I would
send her again.

Myrtle said she was going out to Oak Lawn to stay till Friday
with a crowd. Aleq Sparkman came after her in his car. He
has a Buick. She also said that Mr. Harrison had called her up
twice since I left. She has heard from Clyde again too, Dear, but
I'll have to tell you about that when I see you.

By the way, Eudie said that Mr. Bush had called up again
and she told him that I was in Tioga, and that if he'd call up
here he would most assuredly find "Miss Gilliam." He told her
he was so sorry I was not there. Oh! Me! I wonder what he
wants now.

Mrs. Glass has bought a farm in Michigan and says she's
coming home right away and take papa [O. A. Gilliam, 1846–
1938, Civil War Confederate veteran, now age 66] back with
her. I doubt very seriously whether she will persuade him
to leave Dallas tho'. [An indication that O. A. has not yet
remarried]

I have a lot to tell you about Mitt and Chas when I see you,
sweetheart. I fear that when I do see you it will take a good
while for me to tell you all that I know.

Eudie said in her letter that she may come down here as
soon as I come home. That being the case, I guess I'll be house
keeper for a while. Anna will be with me tho'. [Anna Thornton—
her grandmother's maiden name—Ragon was born April 5,
1897; her parents, Claude M. Ragon and Eula T. Gilliam, were

married December 19, 1895. This is "Cousin Anna" who called
my grandmother Aunt Ruth, which she was, even if she was
only seven years her junior.]

Kate has the "cookbook" and is lying down here on the bed
beside me asking me if I am going to cook all of those good
things, where oh, well when "C". [Cabbage]

I am sending you all my love with lots and lots of kisses.
Yours only, Ruth

Within the context of this and other letters, Ruth seeks refuge from
her tiresome father in Tioga with Kate. O. A. Gilliam did marry a woman
named Abbie sometime after Ruth and Marvin's wedding in 1912. Was
it Mrs. Glass from Michigan? Whoever it was, Ruth was relieved that
her father had a wife of his own to look after him. Abbie Gilliam did
outlive O. A.

From Marvin to Ruth, dated: "At home, Sunday 11:30 p.m., August
4, 1912":

☙ Dearest Sweetheart;-

I've just gotten back from Celina and will write you a note
before I retire.

Arrived at Celina Saturday at 5 p. m. and found Mamma
very sick. She had been in bed since Friday a.m. and was not
much better when I left her this afternoon.

The rest of the folks were all well and doing fine. I think they
will be living in Oak Cliff real soon.

They all asked about you and said some awfully nice things
about you and wanted to know why I didn't bring you home
with me.

I'm just writing this to tell you that I still love you and to let
you know that I've been thinking of you ever since I left you
down town yesterday. You certainly did look sweet and I was
almost tempted to steal a kiss.

Will write again tomorrow night and tell you some more.
Very lovingly, Marvin

Following is a letter to Marvin from E. P. West of West & Company, shortly before the wedding. Marvin and E. P. West seem to have been "buddies" after a fashion.

൭ Dillon—Friday, August 9, 1912.

I regret very much that on Sept. 21st you must shuffle off this mortal coil, but I will keep it in mind so that you can be at the killing.

Here enclosed find cards.

Keep me posted about the automatic & if necessary I will run up and help you out. Bear in mind that all SAABS [Marvin is driving a 1912 Swedish SAAB] are alike with 3 point bearing, as to the automatic earlier I think you can study it out by keeping quiet, say nothing, but think much.

Look your work over and see that it looks finished on top in sight and one of the things to make your work please is to make it meet the eye of others pleasantly, and pleasing in the finishing touches that pays most of all, in settlements and in prase [sic] to the man in shape of the work.

This for your information we remain as one in haste. West & Company. E P. West

From the website of Dillon Equipment Company.

In 1911, M.D. Dillon, walked into the West & Company machine shop to learn the scale business. Eight years later he resigned his job, had his letterhead printed and sent letters written in long hand by his wife, to scale users over the state. Thus began Dillon Scale Company.[2]

"The following photo was made in 1937 at 4151 Commerce Street, then the location of Dillon Scale Repair Company. The name was later changed to Dillon Equipment Company in order to more accurately reflect our present activity. Dillon Equipment Company, Inc. is located at 3907 Elm Street and has been in the same location since 1948. Our Deep Elm location assures you of convenience and availability of your material handling requirements."[3]

Photo of Dillon Scale from 1937.

The two men wearing panama straw hats in the photo above are M. D. Dillon, CEO, and his business partner, Ernest Buck. The woman on the left is Marvin's daughter, Sue Dillon Bussard.

Following is a series of four letters from Ruth to Marvin. The first is dated "Sat. Morn 10:30 a.m., August 10, 1912."

   ◦◦◦ My own Marvin,

See how bright and early I am writing to my Dear! Today is busy, don't you know. I dreamed about you last night. Goodness. How I wish I could see you this morning.

I hope you have talked to Otha [Paris, Texas, friend] before now, and you are going to see her tomorrow. I talked to Nell last night and told her what you said. She is still having beaux every night. I think Grover and Jess are running a race for her. I haven't heard from G. Edgar since I talked to him the other day.

I noticed in the paper where a Mr. Pleasant Proffit of

Cennent got killed the other day. He was an aged man so the paper stated. I thought maybe you might have known him. A heavy piece of machinery weighing about two tons fell on him. [There is no record of a town called Cennent, Texas. I wish she had saved the clipping.]

I came home yesterday morning. Don't know just what day I will go to Kate's.

Grover went with Ralph to Duncanville a good while ago, and Miss Horn told Grover about a young man who jilted her. That was the first time she had seen Grover too. I wonder if she meant you.

You should have seen Anna and myself sewing yesterday afternoon. I am feeling very well Hon. Don't worry about me, for I'm alright. [Ruth and Anna are sewing the wedding dress and trousseau!]

Be sure to remember that there is one who loves you dearly and longs for you all the time. Write often to Your Ruth

Following is the second in the series of four letters from Ruth to Marvin. This one is dated Monday at Hillside.

August 12, 1912

◌ My Dear Marvin,

Anna is talking to Rollie over the phone. Oh how I wish I could talk to you even though I can't see you.

I was so lonesome I could hardly see last night after you left and am weepy yet as far as that is concerned.

I am in hopes that I will not be so terribly lonely after I get to Tioga, not that I want to think any less of you, Dear, but you understand.

Last night when I went back to the buggy Mr. Buckelew was sitting in there talking with Myrtle and they both began to smile and said, "Look at the tears in her eyes." There might have been some trace there, for my heart surely did ache. Here I am talking about my troubles again—I'll try not to any more.

I have decided to go to Kate's tomorrow [Tuesday] so you can write to me there at Box 27. [Kate, Ruth's older sister, lives in Tioga, a small town in Grayson County, part of the Sherman-Denison Metropolitan Statistical Area. The population was 803 in 2010. The town was named for the Tioga tribe in New York.]

I told Nell what I knew and she surely did laugh. I didn't tell her how I found out. [I wonder what Ruth knows.] I am in a hurry to mail this, so will have to bid you farewell.

With all my love. Your Ruth

Letter number three from Ruth to Zeke is dated Wednesday, August 14, 1912.

❧ My dear Zeke,

Am in Tioga once more, enjoying its sights and church. I reached here yesterday afternoon at four thirty. The trip was rather pleasant as I met up with three girls whom I knew and Mr. and Mrs. Hooper and two children. Mrs. Hooper had been to Farmersville on a visit. She begged me to get off the train and stay with her, but I couldn't. I told her I might stop on my way home. They asked me all about "Marvin," and said, "Ruth I don't know whether I want you to marry or not—I'm afraid you won't love me anymore." I told her that you and I would visit her sometime.

I wonder how you are liking Hugo, OK by now. Hope you are feeling fine.

Mitt has been telling me about all of her beaux. I'm afraid that other is about to fade away. See, that is a long [illegible words]. We're not going to let our love fade tho', are we, Dear.

I talked to Olan the other day. He passed through Dallas on his way home. He had been to Gainesville and had stuck a nail in his foot. He said it was so painful that he could not wear his shoe. [Hmm. Marvin did the same thing.] He was talking about you and me and our affairs and made me tell him about Sept. 21 [Marvin and Ruth's wedding day]. He said he and Lera would surely be there. He also said your mother told him she thought it would be a good thing for you to marry.

Sweetheart, Mrs. McDonald [Kate] is going to the office now, and I want to send this to you.

Remember I love you with all my heart. Yours only. Ruth

Letter number 4 from Ruth to Zeke, dated Thursday Morn, August 15, 1912:

〇〇 Dear Zeke,

Here comes letter number four. You'd better hurry and send me some. I've had only one card from you so far.

Myrtle and I are up at Maud's house this morning. About four o'clock they phoned for them to come after Mrs. Harris so Albert and Maud left early and we are staying with children. I think Mrs. Harris has been taking too much of her medicine. That's the trouble.

Listen, Dear, I think I shall go up to Kate's in a few days. She is not well and I think I can better go now than a little later. Don't you? The next time you write address it the same as usual, and if I go, I will leave a forwarding card.

I called G. Edgar the other day and he said he had been real sick but is better now. I told him that you said you would write to him, and he said he surely hoped you would, so remember now. Myrtle and I went to town yesterday afternoon and we were like two "rubes," sure enough. It was the first time I had been to town since before the fourth of July.

I wonder if you have heard from Otha yet. Hope you have, as it will keep you from being so lonesome.

I had a long letter from Mrs. Weems yesterday. She told me of several of my pupils who had married and one girl who is going to teach this year. She [Mrs. Weems] has something made for me. Here's all my love and a great big kiss. R__

Zeke wrote to Ruth from Same Place, Thursday, August 15, 1912.

ᏀᏂ Dearest Ruth;-

Was as glad as could be to get your letter today for I didn't get one yesterday. 'Twas awful hot again today and I sat around in the shade most of the day.

I'm not any nearer being done than I was yesterday and unless we get some material tomorrow, I'll be here all next week.

It has been very hot here 'til last night when I didn't sleep very well and couldn't eat anything for breakfast but one egg and I didn't want it at all.

I feel now just about like I did last night but hope I will sleep much better and not have such bad dreams. I'm awful glad Olan (age 17) is back home so Mamma will not be so worried and hope he will stay there now.

I wrote Mamma last night and told all about our plans and told her to write and tell me what she tho't about them so I guess I'll hear from her in a few days.

Goodnight and pleasant dreams, Darling. With much love and many kisses. Your Marvin

Friday 6 a.m. Didn't sleep very well and don't feel like eating breakfast. Have a terrible toothache and may go have it pulled this morning. Very lovingly. Zeke

Zeke wrote to Ruth from Hugo, Oklahoma, on Friday, August 16, 1912.

ᏀᏂ Dearest Sweetheart;-

I had begun to think I was not going to get a letter from you today but I finally got it at 8 p.m. and was awful glad to get it.

I surely hope you got a letter Thursday for I wrote to you Monday night but sent it to Dallas and have written every night since.

Please don't doubt me Honey for I love you all the time and

am not going to neglect you in any way if I can possibly help it.

They have a new piano where I'm boarding and the newly married lady plays so I've been up there singing with her and her hubby. They are awful nice people from Temple, named Patterson.

I'm sorry I wrote you such a mournful letter last night, Dearest, but I did feel real badly and no one to tell my troubles to and I knew my Sweetheart would sympathize with me but am sorry now that I caused you to worry. I feel much better so you need not worry any more.

My foot is just about well and bothers me a very little and my shoe doesn't hurt it now.

I've almost got the blues tonight but am trying hard to drive them off and am going to sleep pretty soon and hope I will dream of you. I am glad that you dream of me, Sweetheart, for I know you think of me lots or you wouldn't dream of me.

I think I would feel a hundred percent better if I could see you tonight but will try to keep my spirit 'til I can get home.

With a heart full of love for you. Your Marvin

A letter from Zeke to Ruth from Hugo, Oklahoma, dated Monday, August 19, 1912:

My Dear Sweetheart;-

Today is the first time I've failed to hear from you since I left home and I just can't keep from feeling bad about it and I'm a little worried too about you.

If you feel too bad to write a letter I think you might send me a card and tell me how you feel so I won't be worried.

I'm not angry, honey, but I hate to feel this way and not hear from you at all when I'm so just awful bad, honey, but you go on to Kate's and get your visit over with just as soon as you can. I saw your fortune teller on the train the night I came up here, the one on Commerce St., and she sure is some swell human. Her hair looked like it had never been combed. The man that sat by me on the train knew her and told me all about going to a séance at her house one night.

I'm glad you talked to G. Edgar but am sorry he has been sick.

I sent him a card but have not heard from him yet.

'tis about train time you sweetheart so I'll hurry to the depot and mail this.

With lots of love and kisses. Your Marvin

You can write to me at Paris (same address) 'til Sunday and then send my mail to Hugo again.

I'm getting awful tired of this place although I've made quite a few friends here but all of them could never begin to take your place so I want to see you worse every day.

I may go up to see Otha Sunday if I am in Paris but don't know yet what I'll do.

I know what I'd rather do but am afraid I won't be lucky enough. Can you guess what it is? Goodnight Sweetheart! Write as often as you can to one who loves you very dearly.

With much love and lots of kisses. Marvin. C/O Paris Cotton Co.

Otha is an enigma in the correspondence between Marvin and Ruth. She evidently lived in Paris, Texas, and is first mentioned by Ruth in the telegram she sent to Marvin from Fort Smith, Arkansas, in June 1911. Ruth would have visited Otha in Paris, when she travelled by rail between Dallas and Fort Smith. Ruth has already introduced her to Marvin. Otha's friendship with both Ruth and Marvin stands out, as she is mentioned a total of seven times, the last three in letters exchanged in August 1912, the month before the wedding. Surely, Otha would have been invited.

What follows next are two letters dated September 18, 1912, just three days before Ruth and Marvin are to marry. Ruth writes to Marvin, Wednesday morning, September 18, 2012.

Ᏸ My Only Dear,

Just a few words to let you know I love you more than anyone on this earth. I spent the night with Lora and Alma last night and am still here this morning. Eudie is coming by this a. m. and we are going to town.

G. Edgar is in Paris now, Hon. He has gone to work for Arrow & CO. Maybe you can see him in route home. I am so sorry he did not get a position in Dallas. I miss you so much so hurry on home to Your Ruth.

Zeke replies to Ruth from Hugo, Oklahoma, September 18, 1912, the last letter between them before the wedding. The letter is written on business stationery for "WEST & COMPANY Machinist and Garage, Corner Magnolia and Caruth Sts. Phone: MAIN 4264." The WEST in the letterhead is E. P. West, owner of the company. Marvin is employed by them, and he and Mr. West are friends as well as employee/employer.

Ᏸ Dearest Girl;-

Have just talked to Mr. West and he said I could go to Leonard next week instead of coming back here and he would finish up here himself so you can tell those that are anxious to know that we will go to Leonard next week.

We will be married Saturday evening about 7 p.m. and catch the KATY Limited for Greenville at 7:55 and stay in Greenville 'til Monday or Tuesday, if we want to. [Wow! What a quick ceremony! No reception or celebrating after! A kiss for luck then hop a train!]

We will be in Leonard about all week but will go to Galveston Saturday [the 28th] if you care to go. I'm sorry I didn't get a letter from you today but was real glad to get your card.

I'm feeling fine and dandy and haven't had any serious accidents so far and am going to be very careful.

I almost froze last night as we had a rain about 8:30 and it turned real cool and I only had a sheet to cover with but didn't take cold and I have a quilt tonight.

Am awful lonesome but am happy because the 21ˢᵗ is so near and I have at last decided what I'm going to do.

I wonder if you are as anxious as I am for the 21ˢᵗ to come. I love you a whole carload and a little bit more. Yours and yours only. Marvin

Ruth and Marvin did marry on September 21, 1912. There was no reception after. Here is the wedding announcement mailed by Ruth's father, which reminds us that her mother is not alive. (Ruth's mother had died in 1906, and O. A. had not yet remarried.) The announcement reads:

Mr. O. A. Gilliam

Announces the Marriage of His Daughter

Ruth Collier

To

Mr. Marvin D. Dillon

on

September Twenty-First, Nineteen Hundred and Twelve

at Oak Cliff, Texas

At home after October first in Oak Cliff,

Station A, Dallas Texas

Ruth and Marvin were married in her father's Oak Cliff Dallas home at 1202 South Ewing at 7:00 p.m. It seems it was a family/close friends affair. O. A. gave away the bride. Marvin's parents, William Jasper Dillon and Laura Turner Dillon, would have attended, as would the Dillon siblings in town. The youngest ones living at home were Frieda, age six; Bernie, age nine; Milton, age thirteen; Clifford, age fifteen; Olan, age seventeen; and Lera, age nineteen. Older sisters Bessie, age twenty-five, who lived in Prosper, Texas, and Cora, age twenty-nine, who lived in Ardmore, Oklahoma, may also have attended.

Ruth and her niece Anna had sewn her trousseau together during the spring and summer of 1912. All members of Ruth's and Marvin's families who were within traveling distance would have attended.

Eula, age thirty-eight and mother of Anna, would have been there. We don't know if Ruth's brothers Jim, who lived in San Antonio, or John Wyndham attended. Ruth's close friends Myrtle and Alma would have been there, as well as Ralph and G. Edgar, Marvin's best friends. Otha, the enigma friend from Paris, was surely invited. Lera, Marvin's sister, probably played the "Wedding March" and other selections on the piano. The ceremony was intimate and informal. If the bride and groom had attendants, I believe Marvin would have asked his brother Olan or his best friend, G. Edgar, to stand with him. Ruth might have asked her sister Kate Gilliam McDonald, age thirty-two, or perhaps her niece Anna Ragon, age fifteen, to stand with her.

The photo session on the wedding day had to have taken place in the afternoon, before the nuptials at 7:00. Perhaps a light supper, dishes lovingly prepared by the bride's sisters and the groom's mother and sisters, was served before the ceremony. Was there even a wedding cake? If there was, it had to have been served before the ceremony, since the couple took the 7:55 train to Greenville after. There is no mention

Wedding Day, September 21, 1912. Left to right: *Kate, Ruth, Anna.* Seated: *Olan*

of who officiated. However, recalling conversations with relatives, I believe Dr. George W. Truett, pastor of the First Baptist Church of Dallas, married Ruth and Marvin.

The photo of Marvin and Ruth standing on the train as they departed for their Galveston honeymoon had to have been taken on the platform in Greenville, where they spent their wedding night. It appears that Ruth is wearing her wedding dress. The kiss for luck on September 21, 1912, began their life together as a married couple. Upon returning from their honeymoon, Marvin resumed his career in sales, and Ruth took on the role of wife and homemaker.

Ruth and Marvin boarding train for Galveston honeymoon

THE DILLON CHILDREN,
SUE AND EDGAR: 1913–1943

*A*fter returning from their honeymoon in October 1912, Marvin and Ruth took up residence at 1222 South Ewing, Dallas, Texas, next door to Ruth's father. The couple resided at this address until 1934. Marvin's parents had moved to a house on Twelfth Street in Dallas in 1912 with their school-age children. Marvin resumed his job as a sales and service representative for West & Company. Marvin wrote to Ruth from Waco, Texas, on Thursday, March 27, 1913. By now they have been married six months, and Ruth is pregnant with my mother. She conceived on their honeymoon.

In this letter, Marvin registers his concern for the health of Ruth and the child she is carrying. After all, the health challenges of pregnancy were formidable and life-threatening for both mother and child in 1913. The newlyweds were living only a few blocks from Marvin's parents. It would have been incumbent upon Ruth to forge a strong and amicable relationship with her mother-in-law. As a mother of eight, Erman Laura Dillon at age forty-nine would have had much to teach her young daughter-in-law about surviving pregnancy, about raising children, and about maintaining a peaceful and efficient household. The Dillon children living at home and attending school between 1913 and 1920 were Clifford, Milton, Bernie, and Frieda. As the children grew up, they left home to make their own way in the world. By the time Marvin and his partners had founded Dillon Scale & Equipment Co. in 1920, Frieda, now fourteen, had entered high school.

March 27, 1913
 Dear Sweetheart;-

I've been looking for a letter from you all day but have given up hopes now (9:45) and am going to bed to dream about my own darling girl.

This is the first day since I've been here that I haven't heard from you and I miss it so much I don't know what to do. [Of course Ruth wrote to Marvin when they were apart; the letters just didn't survive his job as a traveling salesman.]

Mr. West went to Dallas this afternoon and I told him to mail you a check for ten [$10] as I was afraid you would not have enough money to get over to Kate's on . . .

Shea and I went to two shows tonight. I get so lonesome if I stay at the house that I get the jimmies. I want to see my girl so very bad and love her and "little Zeke" that I can't be still. [Of course, Marvin is hoping for a boy!]

I do love you darling and want you to take the very best care of yourself so you will feel well and not have the blues.

We will be in Waco 'til about Wednesday I guess so you need not look for me Sunday but give all of them my love and think of me a whole lot.

'Twas real cold here with frost and ice everywhere this morning but after the sun got up good it turned out to be a very pleasant day.

My eyes were almost stuck up this morning but I think it was on account of the cold wind yesterday as they haven't bothered me today and I think they are doing fine.

Write to daddy every day dearest girl and tell him all about yourself and "little Zeke" and if you need me just phone me at the Crouch Grain Co.

Daddy loves his darling more than anyone else on earth.
With 'steen thousand kisses for you.
Your loving husband, Marvin

Ruth replied immediately to Marvin's letter on Friday, March 28, 1913. Evidently, she is visiting her sister Kate in Tioga.

ᏏᎳᎧ Dear Sweetheart,
I tried to phone you today, but you were in Strawn. [Strawn, Texas, is located in Palo Pinto County, population about 1,500 in 1913.]
I was so glad to hear from my Dear today, for I haven't been feeling so well tonight I may come home.
The reason I called you this morning, I wanted to see when you were going to Waco. I thought if it would be a good while before you leave I would come on home. I have been in bed almost all day, and am taking medicine, but I believe your face would do me more good than anything else.
Be sweet darling and still love
Your wife,
I am crazy to see you.
Ruth

This is the last surviving letter exchange between Ruth and Marvin as a young married couple. A total of seventy-eight letters from Marvin to Ruth have survived, while only twenty-seven letters from Ruth to Marvin have. Why is there such a discrepancy? From 1910 to 1912, Ruth resided in three towns: Jean, Lancaster, and Dallas. From 1910 to 1912, Marvin crisscrossed northeast Texas, staying in hotels and boardinghouses in at least a dozen towns. At the end of Marvin's business day, he went to his room after supper and wrote a letter to Ruth, which he posted the next morning. Just as faithfully, Ruth wrote regularly to Marvin, often after teaching all day, even though she probably worked on lesson plans and graded papers. Many of Ruth's letters were written on the weekends, which was also the time that she and Marvin would meet.

If they met, then no letter was written. Ruth saved Marvin's letters diligently. Marvin may have even missed some of her letters, owing to his transient existence. Marvin probably returned Ruth's letters to her when they met during their time of courtship. It is nothing short of miraculous that any letters survived at all.

Marvin continued to advance his career and provide for his family between 1913 and 1920. Ruth fulfilled her roles as wife to Marvin and as mother to their young children. My mother, Erman Sue Dillon, Ruth and Marvin's first child, was born on July 26, 1913. She was named for her paternal grandmother, Erman Laura Dillon and for her maternal grandfather's sister, Sue Gilliam. A son, Edgar Marvin Dillon, followed on January 21, 1915. He was named for G. Edgar, Marvin's best friend, mentioned in the letters, and for his father, Marvin. The Dillon family managed to survive the Spanish flu pandemic of 1918–20 untouched, and Marvin did not serve in the armed services during World War I. He worked for West & Company through World War I, then resigned in 1919 to start his own business.

Edgar, age 2; Sue, age 4, circa 1917

By 1920, Ruth and Marvin's children—Sue, age seven, and Edgar, age five—were starting school. Ruth read to her children and taught them piano. The children were raised in the faith community of the Baptist Church. Ruth also was a watercolor artist, she produced beautiful needlepoint, and she wrote poetry. She crocheted baby booties with matching hats and sweaters. She also cooked, kept house, and managed household finances. While Ruth was a stay-at-home mom, Marvin was the breadwinner. Due to his business acumen, Marvin was able to raise the funds to start a new business, and he and partner Ernest Buck founded Dillon Scale Company in 1920. Ruth and Marvin established themselves as a couple and as parents. William Jasper and Erman Laura Dillon settled into the role of beloved grandparents to their eldest son, Marvin's, children. Only Marvin's youngest sibling, Frieda, remained at home with her parents.

In 1926, Marvin's father died at age sixty-eight. Meanwhile, Dillon Scale had become a thriving business, and Marvin was making a good living for his family. Marvin, Ruth, Sue, and Edgar still lived at 1222

Dillon Family circa 1924. Top row, left to right: *Marvin, Cora, Olan, Bessie, Milton.* Middle row, left to right: *William Jasper, Erman Laura, Lera and daughter Lera Bess age 4,* bottom row: *Clifford, Frieda*

South Ewing. Mama Laura Dillon, now widowed and age sixty-two, still lived on Twelfth Street, only a short distance from her oldest son and his young family.

As all white middle- and upper-class families did at this time, the Dillons hired black workers as gardeners, cooks, housekeepers, and nannies. Marvin and Ruth hired Willie Mae Johnson, about age thirty-three, to cook, clean, and help Ruth look after the house. She worked for the Dillon family until she retired in 1960.

To the largely white population living in the Southern states that had been the Confederacy, the War of Northern Aggression had ended "only yesterday." The bitter rawness of not-so-old wounds informed the cultural ethos of the post–Civil War South, including Dallas. Civil War veterans, even though they were indeed traitors to the United States, vividly recalled battles in which they had fought. Robert E. Lee and Jefferson Davis were iconic cultural heroes, and adult blacks were only one generation removed from slavery. Blacks in Dallas lived in segregated neighborhoods with clearly understood boundaries. They worked for their white employers for meager wages. The term "civil rights" applied to white men. Everyone knew their place in the cultural hierarchy of the new South.

Within that culture, Sue and Edgar matriculated public school, graduating from Sunset High School in 1929 and 1931 respectively. Sue started college in 1930 at Mary Hardin Baylor in Belton, Texas. Edgar also enrolled in college after high school, but no record of his having earned a college degree has survived.

A TREASURE FOUND

Sue kept a scrapbook: a leather-bound rectangular volume titled "Stunt Book: Record of My Favorite Good Times" (designed and illustrated by Elizabeth Colborne, Publishers: The Reilly & Lee Co., Chicago, copyright 1914, The Reilly of Britton Co.) She kept this record of her life through high school, updating it as time allowed. Her family gave her the scrapbook for her fifteenth birthday. The enclosed card read: "With a heart full of love for our Susie. We hope you have many more birthdays. Mother, Dad, Edgar." Into this gift thoughtfully chosen by her mother, Ruth, Sue relocated her childhood treasures—notes, photos, cards, party name tags, theater tickets — previously stored in a box under her bed. Now, she had a depository fitting to memorialize her teenage years in the 1920s. The first event recounted is Sue's thirteenth birthday, July 26, 1926, celebrated in Amarillo, Texas. She was attending a B.Y.P.U. (Baptist Young People's Union) summer camp. Her cousins and friends gave her a birthday party. Sue received a red crepe de chine handkerchief from Ermie Olive, a linen handkerchief from John White, and a cute vanity from Frances Hancock.

> ℭ𝒻𝒪 Mother and Dad sent me a pink mesh bag, hose, and some pearls with this on it: "With love for your birthday from Mother and Dad." All these things I received on my 13th birthday. After I received all my presents, we all went to the Fair Theatre and came back and had ice cream and cake. The show was Colleen Moore in "Ella Cinders."

Ella Cinders was a 1926 based on the story of Cinderella. Sue thought it was "awfully cute."

Those present were: cousins John E. Gilliam and Charlie Gilliam (sons of John Wyndham Gilliam), Ermie Olive Sherwood, Frances Hancock, and Hugh Chesnutt. There seems to be some confusion as to which birthday, thirteenth or fifteenth, is being celebrated or if she spent both in Amarillo. John Wyndham Gilliam was Ruth's only brother with children. His son John E. Gilliam was very handsome and a contemporary first cousin of Sue and Edgar. He married a woman named Billie. They had two daughters, Anne Louise and Billie Irene, born in the postwar 1940s. Just as Sue and Edgar grew up with their cousins, Dillon and I grew up with our cousins. When we were all children, we spent time together as families. John E. even worked for Dillon Scale for a time in the 1950s. I served in the house party for Anne Louise's wedding in the 1960s. Her father, John E. Gilliam, lived to be nearly one hundred.

There is a photo in Sue's Stunt Book of a church steeple belonging to Central Presbyterian Church in Amarillo, Texas. The caption reads, "Every Sunday with Rochelle, Mary, Irene, Eric (in the choir)."

Mother wrote the following summary about the summer of 1926 (she was thirteen) when she was fifteen. The voice of the narrative is that of a young person.

> *ℭℌℌ* The summer of 1926, I was in Amarillo, Texas visiting
> my cousin, Irene Gilliam [daughter of John Wyndham
> Gilliam, Ruth's brother, and sister to John and Charlie].
> I met more nice kids and just had oodles and gobs of fun!
> The kids were Frances Hancock, Ermie Olive Sherwood,
> Ruth Brandt, Mary Alice Griggs, Hugh Edward Chesnutt,
> Bill Bynum, and I don't know how many more. Oh yes! John
> White. She [Cousin Irene] gave me a birthday party, and I
> received lots of things.

> *ℭℌℌ* The Summer of 1927
> Ruth (37), Sue (14), Edgar (12), Miss Alma Coston (30+)

True to her independent nature and sense of adventure, Ruth and a woman friend loaded the two Dillon children into the family vehicle, which was probably a late-model Ford, and headed down the road to Arkansas. By now the main roads and highways would have been paved and well marked. Father Marvin had become a prosperous businessman in Dallas. He probably owned more than one vehicle, so he provided a Model A Ford for his wife, Ruth. Although there are no surviving letters exchanged between Ruth and Marvin during this trip, she would have written to him about the sights and events on the journey. Perhaps this was the very automobile in which Sue learned to drive a year or two later.

Imagine the conversation over supper between Ruth and Marvin in early June before departure. Road trip!

"Marvin," Ruth said, "Alma and I want to take the children to visit John and Lou Eddy in Arkansas for a few weeks this summer. It's time for them to meet. I have already written to Lou, and she said August is convenient for her."

Marvin asked, "How will you get there? Shall I book train tickets for you and the children?"

Ruth answered, "Oh no, dear! Alma and I will drive. With the car, we can travel through Arkansas, see the Ozarks, and visit craft shops."

Marvin countered, "Oh, Ruth, that's over three hundred miles! I'm not sure you should drive all that way alone with the children!"

Ruth answered, "Don't worry. We'll be fine. Besides I won't be alone. Alma will help with the driving. We'll be home before school starts in September."

Sue wrote her own account of the trip in her Stunt Book.

Mother, Edgar, Miss Alma Coston and I drove through to the Ozarks. The first night we stayed in a little town in Oklahoma. Boy! And talked like it wasn't hot that nite! We had one little old room with one window in it! The next morning Mother went down to the car, and she had a tag for parking wrong. It was written on a piece of an old envelope, which said, "You are parked rong. Report to the sheriff." Well, as the sheriff's office was next door, and there was no sheriff to be seen, we lit out of that burg at 5:00, and believe me, we surely stepped on it. We ate breakfast in Alma, about fifty miles from there. The next nite we went to Winslow, Ark, and rented a little camp cottage for a few days. On the way to Winslow, we passed by the summer home of some friends, and had a lot of fun. We stayed in Winslow for a few days, then we went on up to Fayetteville, Bentonville, Rogers, Bella Vista, and then to Cave Springs where we stayed a few days. We next went to Siloam Springs to Forest Park and stayed one night. The next night we stayed at a hotel at Muskogee. Well, to make a long story short, I took the tonsillitis and we stayed there for a few days, as I was sick in bed. We then came home and my vacation ended by having my tonsils yanked out! Some ending, I should say! My throat was still sore when I started back to school in September.

August 5, 1928. Sue was visiting in Amarillo. She attended Central Presbyterian Church with her cousin Irene and her friends Ermie Olive Sherwood and Mary Nye. What follows is a note exchange between Sue and Mary. The notes were written on offering envelopes and passed during worship. In her Stunt Book, Sue labels the envelope that holds them "In memory of a certain Sunday."

℘ Olive: Hey dere! What time is it for pity's sake? Who writ this?

Sue: It's fifteen (15) min til twelve (12), Olive. I'm sleepy. What are we going to do this p.m. 'Lil Susie wrote this. Thanx.

Mary writ this! I suppose we'll play or go riding. Come over. We'll go riding if Johnnie hasn't already spoken which I guess he has. But we'll see, we'll see. Well we might eat, but we can't do that all afternoon. Don't you wish we might go on a bike to the canyons? We might go on a bike when it gets cool and take our supper or we might cook supper out tonite over grills. P.S. This ain't a letter.

℘ Sue: We're going to church tonite so we can't go on a bike. I don't think Shelly will cook out. I guess we'll just fool around and look dumb. We've got to take Emmet and Mom to the train. Other than that we might come got our Henry (Ford Model A) That's nice. We'll just act natural. Susie

Mary: When are they leaving? That'll be hot. K.O.?

℘ Sue: I said this P.M. for Topeka and Colorado.

Mary: What come over for. I will but What'll we do? I've got a creek in my neck. It ain't from necking either.

℘ Sue: Does it flow, the creek?

Mary: We'll find something to do, if nothing but eat.

Sue: Let's go riding if we can.

These youthful teens lived a care-free, sheltered existence in 1920s Texas. Sue does not mention "current events" in the stunt book diary. Neither she nor her friends seem to have noticed that Charles Lindbergh flew solo across the Atlantic in 1927. In this decade of the Roaring Twenties, Sue was a flapper and danced the Charleston, even though she was raised Baptist.

The Stunt Book contains some yellowed newspaper clippings, probably from the *Dallas Journal Morning News*. The dates are missing, but it's clear that the events Sue included in her book took place while she was a student at Sunset High School, 1927–1929.

From Sue's Stunt Book:

ⓒ⤰ How Sue Spent Hallowe'ens
  −1925 (age 12). A party at Ottamies Longmire's house, with friends
  −1926 (age 13). Down town at the show with Mother, Dad, and Edgar
  −1927 (age 14). A party at my house with a whole tribe of kids
  −1930 (age 17). A dance at school, Mary Hardin Baylor in Waco, TX, with Jim

ⓒ⤰ How Sue Spent Christmases
  −1926 (age 13). In Hattiesburg, Miss with the Thompson family and ours
  −1927 (age 14). In McKinney, Tex with My cousins, aunts and uncles. [Likely the Andersons: Marvin's sister Bessie married an Anderson]
  −1928 (age 15). At home with Uncle Jim [her mother's brother] and family
  −1930 (age 17). At home with Uncle Jim and family

The following is a newspaper article recounting the "Cadets' Banquet" hosted at the homecoming of Sunset High School, 1928

Cadets of Sunset Guests at Banquet 1928

More than 100 students of Sunset High School attended the home-coming dinner-dance Monday night in the Jefferson Hotel roof garden for R. O. T. C. cadets of the school who have returned from Camp Dallas in Mineral Wells.

The entertainment was given by parents of the cadets, the Parent-Teacher Association and Dads' Club of Sunset High School.

Honor guests were Col. James Ronayne, Col. And Mrs. A. C. Burnett, Capt. H. H. Ransom, Mrs. John Knott, president

Erman Sue Dillon, age 15, dressed for banquet performance, circa 1928

of the PTA, and Mr. and Mrs. J. A. Wilson, principal, was the
toastmaster.

The banquet program included music by a string trio
composed of Mary and Ruth Jenkins and Irma Sue Dillon.
[The paper got Sue's name wrong; it should be Erman.]
A vocal solo by Patsy Evans and short talks by the honor
guests. The string trio played an original composition of
Miss Dillon. [Sue played the cello. Her father gave her the
instrument for Christmas in 1926. I never heard her play.]

Music for the dance, which attracted additional students,
was furnished by the Seven Deuces.

About the time Sue turned thirteen, Ruth and Marvin gave her a
cello for Christmas, 1926. Mother told me, "Mother and Daddy hid
my cello behind the piano in the living room on Christmas morning.
It was the last present opened that day." Mother was an accomplished
musician. She played cello, piano, and organ. How I wish I could have
heard her play the cello!

THE SUMMER OF 1928
Sue is fifteen, almost sixteen.

⌇⌇ During the month of June, I spent all my week-ends
at Camp Dallas. Irene came June 10, and we had a good time
together going out to camp, visiting Dolly and Bud, etc. Then
about July 7, I went home with Irene.

Boy! Talk like the good times we had! First, we had a
scrumbuncsious [sic] time on the train. We left at 8:30 in
the morning and arrived in Amarillo at 9:30 that night.
Then is when the fun began. Of course, Irene couldn't think
of going to bed until she had seen all the kids, so Eric came
by and took us over to get the rest of the kids. I never shall
forget that night. I met more nice kids up there. They were:
Rochelle Doud, Ed Doud, Mary C. Nye, Eric Nye, Hermes
Nye, Mignon Nye, Gail Bivins, and I can't name them all.

Every evening, Irene and I would either go to the Country
Club, play tennis, go to a show, or do something of the sort.
Then I had a birthday on the 26th of July, so Irene, Mary,
Rochelle, and the rest proceeded to surprise me with a
Kid party, although it wasn't much of a surprise. There
were about thirteen kids there, and they were dressed
like kids, too, by the way. The ones there were: Irene,
Eric Nye, Mary C. Nye, Charlie G., Rochelle Doud, John E.
White, Gail Bivins, Bill Bynum, Charles _____, Mignon
Nye, Hermes Nye, Ellen May and myself. [The friendship
between Sue and the Nyes lasted until her death.]

A few days after that, Irene, Mary, Rochelle and I got up
at 6:30 a.m. and went out to Weisman's to go in swimming,
however, I didn't swim 'cause it was too cold. About 8:00
a.m. we came back and got some Coney Islands [hot dogs],
and by the way, Mari's and mine were "with" and then got
some Eskimo Pies (or Divinity Bars, I believe they call
'em). This was our breakfast. Two nights before I left, Mrs.
Nye, Eric, Mary, Rochelle, Irene, and I went out to the
Palisades to go swimming, and then we had some eats. Boy!
I never et so much in my life! And then I got a telephone
call to come home, so thus I ended a very pleasant vacation
in Amarillo, Tex.

Headline in the *Dallas Journal* published sometime in the summer
of 1928 or 1929:

After Saving Boy and Girl, Clois Roberts, Senior at Sunset, Perishes in Lake Worth

Sacrificing his life in saving two friends, Clois Roberts, 18,
senior at Sunset High School and fullback on the Bison
football squad, drowned Sunday afternoon in Lake Worth,
near Fort Worth.

Roberts went under after rescuing Miss Claritta Raney,
16, sophomore at Sunset High School, and Ted Johnson, 18,

who were members of an outing party from Dallas taking a
pleasure ride in a motor boat.

Miss Raney was riding a surf board being towed by the
motor boat, operated by J.B. Johnson, 2806 Astor street, Oak
Cliff. In the boat with Johnson were Miss Lucille Johnson,
Roberts and Ted Johnson. When about 300 feet from the
pleasure pier at the lake, Miss Raney fell from the surf board
and began swimming about in the water toward the boat. She
became tired and called for help.

Johnson Tries First

Ted Johnson dived in after her. "Put your arm around my
neck and I'll take you in." he told her. She did, and he began
pulling her toward the boat.

A short way from the boat, he also became exhausted.
"I can't make it; I'm going under," he cried, freeing the girl.

"Hold up, Ted. I'll get you," Roberts answered and dived
in. He reached the girl and the youth, holding the girl until
the surf board could be pushed to her. She seized it.

Roberts then went to the aid of Johnson who was
struggling in the water. He pushed him toward the boat.
Johnson grabbed the side of the boat and Roberts sank.

When Roberts came up, the boat was some distance from
the youth. Johnson circled around him three times in an
effort to reach him, but without success. He sank a second
time.

Calls for Aid

Johnson then sped in the boat to the pier at the bathing
beach and called for aid. A diver accompanied him to the
spot and recovered the body in about twenty minutes with a
grappling hook. In the meantime an ambulance had arrived
and a pulmotor was sent out in a second boat. It was used
while Roberts' body was being brought to shore, but without
success.

About 300 persons who had gathered on the pier cheered
when Roberts was brought ashore, believing that the

pulmotor would be able to revive him.

The outing party had left Dallas about 1 o'clock Sunday afternoon for Lake Worth for a swimming and boating trip. Mrs. Johnson who went with the party remained on the pier.

Roberts lived at 126 Grady street, Oak Cliff, and is survived by his parents, Mr. and Mrs. J. J. Roberts; a sister, Miss Dorothy Sue Roberts and two brothers, Earl Roberts of Oklahoma City, and Morris Roberts of Dallas. Miss Raney lives at 2547 Grafton street, Oak Cliff.

What a tragic, sad, preventable accident! Were there any life jackets on the boat? Sue and Edgar probably knew these young people.

Sue and Edgar grew up in Oak Cliff, Texas, across the Trinity River from Dallas, Texas. They attended grammar school and junior high school at W. E. Greiner, and both graduated from Sunset High School: Sue in 1929, Ed in 1931. The photos in Mother's scrapbook show happy

Edgar, age 14; Sue, age 16, circa 1929.

children enjoying their youth. They grew into young adults during the Great Depression and the Dust Bowl days. Sue enjoyed Sunset High School, where she excelled academically and socially. Her photo in the 1929 yearbook *Sundial* is that of an attractive young woman who was admired by her peers. The photo caption read:

ERMAN SUE DILLON
Sundial, '29; Orchestra, '27–'29; Scholarship Club; National
Honor Society; Variety Show, Senior Play '29
Find us a sweeter girl and we will show you an angel.

Her senior English teacher was Miss Agnes Taylor. I know this because I inherited a textbook in which Mother had inscribed Miss Taylor's name. Ironically, when I entered Woodrow Wilson High School in the fall of 1963 and found an Agnes Taylor on the faculty, I stopped by her classroom after school one day and introduced myself. I thought it too

Erman Sue Dillon, age 16

amazing to be a coincidence. She remembered Sue Dillon, my mother, and was saddened to learn that she had died in 1960. Miss Taylor retired from teaching at the end of the school year in 1964 after a long career that spanned at least from 1929 to 1964, some thirty-five years.

After graduating from Sunset High School in 1929, Sue enrolled as a freshman at Mary Hardin-Baylor University, chartered by the Republic of Texas in 1845 in Belton, Texas. I remember Mother's mentioning tea dances held on Saturday afternoons for young men and women to socialize in a "properly chaperoned" setting. She attended a performance of *The Merry Wives of Windsor* on Saturday, May 24, 1930.

After one year at MHB (1929–1930), Sue enrolled as a sophomore in North Texas State Teacher's College, located in Denton, Texas, where she met the man who would become her husband and father of her children, James "Jim" Layton Bussard. They both graduated in 1935. Mother earned a bachelor's degree in English and music education; Jim's degree was in biology and music education. He played the trombone. Both Jim and Sue excelled academically and socially at NTSTC. They made the dean's list. Sue was tapped to join a selective women's service organization on campus called "Green Jackets." She was also a *YUCCA* (the yearbook) beauty. Jim, along with his twin brother, Bob, lived in the band hall and played in the marching band under the direction of Professor "'Fessor" Floyd Graham. I took music appreciation from Professor Graham in 1966. He remembered Jim and Bob Bussard. As a consequence of the Great Depression of the 1930s, which forced the separation of the boys from their parents between 1931 and 1935, the twins were charged with looking after their younger brother, Bill, age fourteen. They found him a place to board and saw to it that he finished high school in Denton. More details of this story appear later in this memoir.

*Sue and Ruth at Mary
Hardin Baylor, 1930*

*Erman Sue Dillon, age 22,
YUCCA beauty NTSTC,
circa 1935*

STRONG FAMILY TIES: 1920s AND 1930s

*A*s noted earlier in this book, Ruth Gilliam and her niece Anna Thornton Ragon were very close. Anna and her beau, Jester James "Jess" Wortham, married on December 16, 1916, just four years after the wedding of Ruth and Marvin. Anna was nineteen. Jess worked over fifty years as a salesman for Dillon Scale & Equipment Company, founded by Marvin Dillon and Ernest Buck in 1920. Anna Ragon Wortham gave birth to daughters Dorothy Virginia Wortham on December 14, 1920, and Betty Jane Wortham on January 21, 1929. Also worthy of note, Betty and Edgar, Sue's brother, had the same birth date, but fourteen years apart, Edgar's in 1915, and Betty's in 1929.

Betty recalls a sixth birthday party given for her by her aunt Ruth and uncle Marvin in their Kessler Park home on January 21, 1935, which fell on a Monday, so the party was probably held the Saturday or Sunday before, on January 19 or 20. Also in attendance were Ruth's sister Eula (aka Eudie); her daughters, Anna, age thirty-eight; and Myrtle, age twenty-five, with her daughter Patsy, age four. Ruth warned Dorothy and Myrtle not to go upstairs to Edgar's room, as he wouldn't like it. She said, "Edgar doesn't even let me into his room!" Of course, such an admonishment is all a teenager needs to enter forbidden territory.

Betty recalls that she and Patsy, along with Dorothy and Myrtle, did in fact sneak upstairs to Edgar's room and have a look around. Betty says she noticed a cute little red table and chair set in Edgar's room. Later, that same red table and chairs set showed up under the Christmas tree for Betty. (This memory, of course, is hazy to Betty, now ninety-two. More likely, the sighting of the red table and chairs happened in the previous year, maybe around Thanksgiving before Christmas 1934.)

Betty remembered the closeness between the Worthams and the Dillons. During a visit to her home in June 2018, Betty recalled a vivid childhood memory. She recalled, "In the summer and fall, we would go to Aunt Ruth's house after she had bought baskets of fresh fruit and bushels of black-eyed peas at the farmers' market. We would all sit on the back porch, shelling those peas and telling stories." In the year 2020, Cousin Betty recalled that her mother, Anna, would put up the peas in mason jars and share them with the various households of the family. The Worthams and the Dillons gathered often in each other's homes.

I remember Sunday dinners at Cousin Anna's house. She was a true Southern cook, which meant we feasted on baked ham, fried chicken, collard greens, black-eyed peas, boiled okra, mashed potatoes, yeast rolls, and corn bread. Dessert was often chocolate icebox pie or coconut cake served with Grandmother's homemade peach ice cream. One Sunday, Mother reminded me about Sunday dinner table manners: "Say nothing about what is on your plate, whether you like it or not." She knew I did not like boiled okra. However, that Sunday, when boiled okra appeared on my plate, I ate it. I will never forget Mother's incredulous expression! I remember that throughout my childhood, in the 1950s, before Grandmother got sick, she used to make homemade peach ice cream on the back porch. Dillon and I minded the electric powered ice cream freezer, gradually adding the ice and salt to keep the dasher turning. When Grandmother died, the delicious peach ice cream recipe died with her.

Edgar had been given an airplane trip to New York for his twentieth birthday from his parents. After that trip, probably later in the spring or summer of 1935, his parents hosted a belated birthday party for their son and all his friends in their new, well-appointed home in the Kessler

Park neighborhood of Oak Cliff. The festivities included dancing on the balcony patio, lots of food, and pretty girls dressed in the fashion of the day. Edgar had his pick of dancing partners the whole evening. Cousin Patsy recalled, "We thought that the Dillons were rich and that Edgar was living like Jay Gatsby!" F. Scott Fitzgerald's novel *The Great Gatsby,* published in 1925, portrayed the excessive opulence of the Jazz Age of the 1920s.

My uncle Edgar aspired to live that "Gatsby" lifestyle—nearly bankrupting his father's business in the years after World War II. When I was a child in the 1950s, I remember Uncle Ed's wearing monogrammed shirts and designer suits. Edgar enjoyed a comfortable, middle-class childhood until he contracted tuberculosis in his twenties. Could he have contracted it while on the trip to New York in 1935? His symptoms would have been a persistent cough, fever, chills, body aches, fatigue, poor appetite, and weight loss, which would have come on gradually. He probably had a chest X-ray, although the technology was not yet widely available.

Edgar always lived with his parents, except when he was married for a brief time to a woman about whom no details are known. I have deduced that Edgar's marriage ended when he contracted tuberculosis—the couple would have been in their twenties. Neither Edgar nor his young bride were mature enough to sustain a marital relationship when one of the partners had contracted a debilitating if not fatal illness. They divorced. The family never talked about it. Edgar moved back home so his mother could take care of him. Edgar's wife probably appears in some of the photos that have survived, but she remains to this day an unknown woman. Edgar at age forty-three was still living with his mother, Ruth, when she died in 1958 at age sixty-eight. More of that story later.

THE WEDDING OF SUE DILLON AND JIM BUSSARD, 1936

Jim Bussard and Sue Dillon married on June 21, 1936, at First Presbyterian Church in Denton, Texas. Dr. Wallace Bassett, Sue's pastor from Cliff Temple Baptist Church, Oak Cliff, Dallas, officiated.

According to the article published in the *Dallas Morning News,* the bride, who was given in marriage by her father, wore an orchid jacket dress of pink alpaca with pink and dubonnet accessories. Her corsage bouquet was made of pink and white rosebuds and sweet peas. Miss Mary Frances Gardner, Sue's college roommate in Denton, attended the bride as maid of honor. She wore a yellow and orchid frock with yellow accessories and a corsage bouquet of sweet peas.

Herbert "Bill" Bussard, brother of the bridegroom, was best man. The wedding music was given by Mrs. Louise Hutcheson, from Denton, who sang, accompanied by Miss Mary Anderson, organist. Miss Anderson also played the "Wedding March," and Floyd Graham played oboe during the ceremony.

Sue's family attended the wedding in Denton. Her father, Marvin Dillon, gave away the bride. Ruth and Edgar were seated in the front row. Sue's grandfather, O. A. Gilliam, accompanied by his second wife, Abbie, probably made the road trip from Dallas to witness his granddaughter's marriage. Cousin Anna and family would have attended. Marvin's mother, Sue's namesake and paternal grandmother, Erman Laura Dillon, was probably there also. By this time, her youngest daughter Frieda, age thirty-three, had married Carl Lewis. The couple was living in Wichita Falls, Texas. Laura, aka Mama Dillon, was also living in Wichita Falls at this time. Laura's husband, Marvin's father, William Jasper Dillon, had died at age sixty-eight on March 12, 1926, when Sue was thirteen. Mamma Dillon lived to age seventy-five and died in Wichita Falls of a heart attack and pneumonia on July 10, 1940. Sue was twenty-seven. No photos of Sue and Jim's wedding have survived.

The couple honeymooned in Cheboygan, Michigan, where Jim Bussard had enrolled in a summer program at the University of Michigan Biological Station. In the fall of 1936, Jim and Sue both took teaching jobs at the high school in Groom, Texas, a farming town located on the high plains of the panhandle, east of Amarillo. Sue taught English and music; Jim taught biology and served as band director. Considering the Great Depression of the 1930s, it was surely an economic decision that brought Sue and Jim back to Dallas after only one year. Not to mention that life in the Texas panhandle must have been bleak when compared to that in Dallas. The newlyweds returned to Dallas in 1938. Jim went to work for Dillon Scale & Equipment Company under the mentorship of his father-in-law, Marvin Dillon. Edgar joined the company at about the same time.

An interesting letter written by Sue Bussard to Katheryn Brown, the fiancée of Bob Bussard, Jim's twin, has survived. Sue and Jim were living in an Oak Cliff bungalow at 1313 Hollywood Avenue. Edgar was recovering from a life-threatening infection, most likely brought on by the tuberculosis, which would have weakened his compromised immune system. Sue's 1938 letter to Katheryn Brown, cited below, makes reference to Edgar's being seriously ill from an "infected arm" and that he is not strong enough to survive amputation. A handsome, intelligent young man with a bright future, Edgar was plagued by ill health for the remainder of his life.

Sue and Jim rented the house and lived there only a short time. Daddy was working for Dillon Scale. The letter is addressed to Miss Katheryn Brown, 404 N. Monroe Street, Tallahassee, Florida. Bob was working as an elementary school principal in Tallahassee, Florida, where he met Katheryn Brown. Sue writes:

August 6, 1938

⟨∾⟩ My dear Katheryn,

I'm not sure whether we are to call you that or "Kay." I believe Bob calls you the latter when he writes.

I am so ashamed that I have not written you sooner to tell you how very happy both Jimmy and I are for you and Bob. The main reason I haven't written sooner is that my brother has been very dangerously ill with an infected arm. We were terribly concerned about him as they thought they might have to remove his arm, and he is not strong enough for anything like that. He is getting along fine now, I am glad to say, but he has surely had us scared. So much for that. [In 1938, Edgar would have been only twenty-three.]

We surely are looking forward to your visit with us, and we're going to try to make you feel at home in the Bussard household. I know Mommy will be disappointed that you couldn't come to see her and Dad first. I couldn't begin to come up to Mommy when it comes to entertaining and such, for to my way of thinking, she is the perfect hostess, but I shall try to be a fair substitute.

All of which brings me to this thought. Kay, she is positively, without exception, the noblest, sweetest, most courageous woman ever. She is really a good sport, too, as is Dad.

Jimmy and I are going to Denton to spend the day tomorrow. Bill and Nita are "swell" people too. [Bill is Jim and Bob's younger brother; Nita is Bill's girlfriend.]

Don't you hope we can all go out to see the folks Christmas! We would really have a wonderful time. They do get so lonely for their family, and especially so at Christmas.

Jimmy and I do want to remember you with a wedding gift, but we shall wait until you get here if that meets with your approval.

We appreciate your invitation to the wedding so much, and there's nothing we would rather do than to be there, but it is impossible, since this is Jimmy's "busy time" at the office.

We're counting the days until you kids arrive! Lovingly yours, Sue

P.S. I have some darling baby pictures of the twins to show you when they aren't around! It "hacks" Jimmy to death for me to show them. Ha! S

"Mommy and Dad" mentioned in the letter are Jim and Bob's parents, Grace and Bill Bussard, who lived in Tucson, Arizona. Sue's assessment of Grace's character refers to the fact that she had married Bill after his first wife, Ruth Layton Bussard, nee Flook, had died of sepsis at age twenty-six on May 3, 1911, at home in Elkhart, Indiana, three days after delivering twins James Layton Bussard and Robert Earl Bussard, named by her on April 30. According to Ruth's obituary published in the *North Manchester Journal* on May 10, 1911, "The two sons will be cared for by the parents of the father L. J. Bussard and his wife as their own children." The Bussard grandparents raised the twins until they were six years old in North Manchester, Indiana, which is located sixty miles south of Elkhart.

After the new widower signed over custody of his infant twin sons to his parents, Bill met Grace B. Neu in May 1911 in Elkhart, less than a month after the death of wife Ruth. They both worked at the local bank: Bill as a teller, Grace as a bookkeeper. Much to the scandal of their families and friends, Bill and Grace began "keeping company." They married in the fall of 1912, about the same time Ruth and Marvin married. When the boys returned to live with their father and step-mother in Elkhart in 1917, Bill and Grace had a home ready for them. Since twins Bob and Jim had never known their biological mother, one can only imagine how their relationship with Grace developed. About the same time the twins came to live with their father and Grace, she gave birth to son Bill in 1917. A baby afforded the family a new center, as Bob and Jim took on the role of "big brothers." Another son, Francis, was born in 1927. He died from scarlet fever at age two. My father only had sweet things to say about his stepmother Grace. He told me, "We called her Mommy."

When the stock market crashed in 1929 and the local bank failed in 1930, Papa Bill lost his job and the family lost their home in Elkhart. In the winter of 1930–31, Papa Bill developed tuberculosis. He left the dampness of Indiana for the dry air of El Paso, Texas, to recover his health. Grace stayed behind in Elkhart with the boys and returned to her bookkeeping job to support her family. She also made a plan to secure a college education for her sons and to join her husband in El Paso. In the summer of 1931, Grace loaded the three boys and all their possessions into the family Model A Ford and drove southwest from Elkhart, Indiana. She settled the boys in Denton, Texas, to go to school. Twins Bob and Jim (both age twenty) enrolled in North Texas State Teacher's College, and brother Bill (age fourteen) enrolled in Denton High School. Then Grace drove the rest of the way to El Paso by herself to join husband Bill in El Paso. The boys grew into young men in Denton. In 1932, Grace and Bill moved farther west to Tucson, Arizona. Jim and Bob earned their degrees, graduating in 1935. The twins lived in the band hall. Bill took a job waiting tables in a boardinghouse, where he himself boarded. He finished high school in Denton in 1934 and enrolled in NTSTC that fall. In 1936, Bob moved to Tallahassee, Florida, Jim married Sue, and brother Bill continued at NTSTC for a time, then moved to Waterloo, Iowa.

Bob and Katheryn married in Tallahassee, Florida, on August 21, 1938. For their honeymoon, the newlyweds drove west to Dallas to meet Bob's twin, Jim, and his wife, Sue. The twins had a history of playing tricks on people who could not tell them apart. One evening, Bob and Jim donned identical dinner jackets and made Katheryn choose which one of them was her husband. Bob and Katheryn continued west from Dallas to visit "Mommy" Grace and Papa Bill in Tucson, Arizona. The next month, September 1938, Sue's grandfather and Civil War veteran O. A. Gilliam died at age ninety-two.

RUTH'S FATHER, O. A. GILLIAM

After the September 1912 wedding of his youngest daughter, Ruth, O. A. Gilliam married again. (Was it to Mrs. Glass, the woman who had bought a farm in Michigan, mentioned in Ruth's 1912 letter? If only Ruth had included her Christian name!) At age sixty, he had been a widower since 1906. His second wife, Abbie, appears in a photo of O. A.'s ninetieth birthday party in 1936. She also accompanied Ruth and Kate on the road trip when they drove O. A. to the Battle of Gettysburg Seventy-Fifth Reunion in the summer of 1938. The reunion attendees slept in bivouac tents on the battleground. Abbie is listed as a survivor on O. A.'s obituary. The grand patriarch of the Gilliam family, Oscar Augustus (O. A.) Gilliam died on September 21, 1938, the same day as Ruth and Marvin's twenty-sixth anniversary. Sue was twenty-five. She and Jim had been married two years. Ruth, his youngest and favorite daughter, was forty-eight. Ruth wrote O. A.'s obituary, which appeared in the *Dallas Morning News* on Thursday, September 22, 1938.

Death Calls Confederate Who Guarded Lee's Horse

O. A. Gilliam, 92 years old, who guarded Traveller for Gen. Robert E. Lee in the Civil War joined the bivouac of the dead Wednesday. On the wall opposite his deathbed at 1202 South Ewing, where his eyes could rest upon it before they closed at last, was a picture of his idol, General Lee.

Mr. Gilliam will be dressed in his Confederate uniform when the Rev. Wallace Bassett will conduct the service at the Ed C. Smith & Bros. Chapel at 2:00 p.m. Thursday. The cane he had carried for years will be placed beside him. He never needed it, but he said it kept him from getting lonesome.

He ran off and joined the Confederate Army when he was 15.

His old blue eyes would fairly dance when he found a hearer for one of his stories about the fights at Fort Harrison, Malvern Hill, Fairfax Courthouse, and Sailor Creek. At the Sailor Creek fight, the last of the war, he was left for dead. A passing group of Union soldiers found him. "Give him this bottle of whiskey," a Union doctor said, "he can't live anyway."

That was just one more time that Mr. Collins [typeset error; should read Mr. Gilliam] fooled the Yanks. He was one of thirteen men of his company to survive, though he left most of his teeth and a part of a jaw on the battlefield. Many years later, when he had retired and was living in Dallas, Mr. Gilliam would meet a visitor with "Where air ye from?"

If the visitor happened to be from the North, Mr. Gilliam would laugh uproariously and say, "Well, you tried to get me, but you didn't."

Fifteen years ago, he went back to Virginia for the first time since the war and walked unhesitatingly to the stump where the enemy had felled him.

He liked to boast because it had fell his lot to guard Traveller while General Lee was asleep, and at Dutch Gap on the James River, he was Lee's attendant. The General used to call him "My Boy," and Mr. Gilliam thrilled even at the memory of it.

The white-haired old soldier was never ill until that final illness. At the recent Gettysburg reunion, he danced with the girls and cut a pigeon's wing for the news reel.

He is survived by three daughters, Mrs. M. D. Dillon (Ruth), Mrs. C. Ragon (Eula), and Mrs. W. A. McDonald (Kate) of Denison; two sons, J. W. Gilliam of Denison, and J. B. Gilliam of San Marcos; his wife, Mrs. Abbie Gilliam; a brother John Jennings Gilliam of Farmville, VA; eleven grandchildren and six great-grandchildren.

O. A. Gilliam's 90th birthday, 1936. Top row, left to right: *Abbie, Ruth, Eudie.* Bottom: *Patsy, O. A.'s great-granddaughter (age 5) and O. A.*

Top, left to right: *Ruth, Eudie, Abbie, Anna.* Bottom: *O. A.'s great-granddaughter Betty age 9, circa 1938.*

WORLD WAR II AND THE DEATH OF MARVIN: 1941–1945

With the outbreak of World War II, Ruth and Marvin were not quite empty nesters, as Edgar resided at home, living with the long-term effects of tuberculosis. Ruth's father, O. A. Gilliam, had passed in 1938; Marvin's father, William Jasper, had died in 1926; but his mother, Laura Turner Dillon, survived until age seventy-six, dying in 1940. In 1934, Ruth and Marvin moved into a well-appointed Art Deco house at 705 Kessler Parkway in the Oak Cliff neighborhood of Dallas, Texas. Sue and Jim had been married for five years, no children. Edgar, age twenty-five, and Jim, age twenty-seven both worked for Dillon Scale.

Sue and Jim resided only a short time in the bungalow on 1313 Hollywood Ave. They bought a rancher house on Purdue Street in the University Park neighborhood of Dallas. Since their marriage in 1936, they had joined Highland Park Methodist Church. Sue had been raised Southern Baptist, and Jim had attended the Lutheran church as a child. The Methodist church was a compromise. When Pearl Harbor was attacked on December 7, 1941, Sue and Jim were decorating the Christmas tree. The announcement of the attack interrupted the Christmas concert playing on the radio from Carnegie Hall in New York City. Their world changed forever on that day.

Europe had been at war since 1939, and by then the world knew that the United States would eventually come in on the side of the Allies. Even so, the young couple decorating the Christmas tree must have registered horror and profound dismay at the report of the Japanese attack on Pearl Harbor. Jim knew he would have to serve. Sue and Jim were hosting his brother Bill and new wife, Ruth, in their home on Purdue Street. for Christmas Day 1941. Bill would not be drafted due to health issues. Surviving photos of that Christmas Day place their father, Papa Bill, the photographer, also at the house, but there is no record of Mama Grace's being there.

In spring of 1942, Bob and Katheryn also visited Sue and Jim in the Purdue house. The girls wore identical outfits. Sue and Jim also took a road trip out west. They stopped to see the Grand Canyon, then drove south to visit his parents, Grace and Bill, in Tucson, Arizona. Jim had decided to enlist in the Army, as World War II was already raging. He thought it best to visit his parents before going off to war. He would have been drafted soon anyway, as he was only thirty-one. He worked for Dillon Scale through the summer of 1943 until he reported to boot camp. Furthermore, since Jim and Sue had not yet conceived a child, they decided to postpone starting a family until after the war. Jim enlisted in the Army of the United States of America, and Sue enrolled in a master's degree program at Teachers College of Columbia University in New York. Jim received orders to deploy overseas in the summer of 1943. Before Sue's enrollment in graduate school but after Jim received his deployment orders, they sold the house on Purdue and for a short while moved into the Kessler Park house. Proceeds from the sale of the house financed Sue's graduate school expenses and left a nest egg for the couple with which to start over after the war.

As president and CEO of Dillon Scale & Equipment Company, Marvin took a business trip to New York City in the fall of 1942. Now age fifty-two, he has been diagnosed with an enlarged heart and had probably been suffering periodic episodes of angina and other symptoms of heart disease. Marvin wrote to Ruth, whom he now called "Mom," from New York on September 19, 1942. After having been married for thirty years, the tone of Marvin's letter is that of a middle-aged man, comfortable with himself and emotionally secure in his marriage. He says he "feel[s] fine."

> Hotel St. George, Clark Street Brooklyn, NY, September 19, 1942
> ꙮ Dear Mom—
> Mr. Riehl came in this a.m. but I have not seen him as he and Mrs. R. went up into Conn. to spend weekend with her folks.
> He insisted that I go on to Rutland and remain there several days.
> Most of the branch managers will be there for an important conference next Thursday. They have hired several high powered men and will immediately launch a program of expansion and improvements. They have Warren Hern, ex-chief engineer for Toledo Scale Co. who will re-design many of the scales, etc., also have an Ex-VP and Sales Manager from Toledo and the Ex-Pres from Kron Co. whom I met in Howe's N.Y. office Friday. There has been no time at all to do any sightseeing or rubbernecking except Thursday p.m. late when we drove by and saw the big ships I wrote you about. I have not been to a show or away from the hotel at nite except the nite I went up and had dinner with Travis and Margaret. They live several miles "uptown" and I went up on the subway. There was a Miss Smith there from Dallas who went to Baylor with Margaret. She works here in the W.P.B. office. I left their place about 9:30 p.m. and came back to the hotel and to bed. While I have greatly enjoyed every minute since I got here I have not been playing. Woody has been so good to take me any place I wanted to go.
> Yesterday we went to Rerdoaton Co. in North Bergen, N.J. and then to Howe Scale Co. and back to Jacobs Bros where we were 'til 6:00 p.m. Today we went to Jacobs first then to Hillside, N.J. to see Trombaund Box and Lumber Co. who are making some skids we sold to the Army flying field at Hondo, Tx. We got back about 3:30 p.m. and stopped at one of the

big public markets a few minutes and then to the hotel and
got Carrie to go with us on short "shoplifting" trip [Marvin's
humor]. She and Woody leave Monday noon for a convention
in Scranton. Pa and Carrie will mail some stockings to you
Monday. Should reach you by Thursday. She looked all over
and had to pick up what she could find at each place. The
nylons are about all gone in your size. We bought all they
had today at one store (about six times as large as Sangers)
except some black ones which I didn't think you would like.
Also bought a little trinket for you and Sue which I didn't want
to mail but will bring with me—not much—just some costume
jewelry like you get at the dime stores. [Is Marvin "cheap" or
what? Why not shop at Tiffany!] I would like to have time to
just loaf and see some of the big shows but will not take the
time now. Will leave early Sunday a.m. for Albany, spend the
day with Hartzells and on to Rutland Monday.

I surely wish you were here with me, but I doubt that you
would have enjoyed this trip since I have been too busy to
play or go sightseeing. It has rained for the past two days and
is very hot here now. I have made some very pleasant and I
believe profitable contacts so do not feel the time and expense
are wasted.

As far as I remember, this 21st is the first one we have not
been together in 30 long years. You have been wonderful and
I don't see how you have put up with me so long. I guess our
love has helped you overlook my many faults and blunders. I
surely regret being away from you and know you believe me
and understand.

I'm real tired so will get some sleep as I will get up early
Sunday morning to catch a train to Albany. With lots of love—
Goodnight Sweetheart—Dad.

P.S. Phone Jess & Chas & Buck that I'm OK—feel fine and
will write or wire when will leave Rutland. Write me by Airmail
C/O Bardwell Hotel. Do you remember it? [Bardwell Hotel is

located in Rutland, Vermont. Ruth and Marvin must have
stayed there on an earlier trip!] Love, Dad
    Woody sends love.

When the stock market crashed in October 1929 and the Great
Depression of the 1930s devastated the economy, Dillon Scale thrived.
All through Sue and Edgar's teenage years, Marvin afforded them an
easy lifestyle. Sue and Edgar wanted for nothing. The business grew
during the war years. In the winter of 1943, as the war was escalating,
Ruth and Marvin made another business trip to New York and stayed at
the St. George Hotel in Brooklyn. They are wearing winter coats in the
photo, so we can assume the trip occurred in January or February 1943.

My father, James Layton Bussard, enlisted in the Army of the United
States on April 18, 1942. He told me when I was a child, "I enlisted in the
Army so I would not be drafted and placed in the infantry. I did not want

*Marvin and Ruth
in New York City,
winter 1943.*

to become cannon fodder." As a man with a college degree, Jim entered the ranks as an ordnance/supply sergeant and was discharged as a master sergeant at the end of the war. He was even offered a commission to reenlist. Soldiers were required to serve in the armed forces for the duration of the war, plus six months. Jim was deployed from the fall of 1943 until early November 1945, a full two years. He was stationed in North Africa in the fall of 1943. In 1945 he completed his deployment in Rome, Italy. I remember his telling me that he had made friends with an American priest from the Vatican who took him on a tour of the Vatican Museum. In the spring of 1929, Jim's parents had sent him on a grand tour of Europe for his eighteenth birthday. Bob was supposed to go on tour in 1930. I don't know how it was decided which twin would go first; perhaps Jim had better grades or they drew lots. Bob did travel in Europe as an adult in the 1970s and 1980s.

As an ordnance sergeant working in an office several miles from the front, with time on his hands, Jim composed a letter to his father-in-law, M. D. Dillon.

No. Africa, Monday, Oct. 4, 1943

   Dear M. D.—

It has been some little time since I last wrote you but I knew you could get what little news I had to relate thru my letters to Susie.

The past six months have not been without considerable interest for me, nor have they been difficult. The work which has been placed on us has caused the time to pass quite rapidly for which I am most thankful. I only hope that the rest of the time necessary for us to spend overseas will pass quickly also as I never thot I would miss my folks at home as much as I do.

Undoubtedly many changes have taken place since we left the states. I know business conditions are different and I am wondering how long it will take or will business ever get back to normal after the war. I have not yet received the July issue of the Scalesman which you mentioned in your letter of August 4th. However, I'm not surprised as it sometimes takes weeks for publications or packages to be delivered over seas. I am very much interested in our company and the future in store for it and I'm sure looking forward to getting back on the job with the rest of the boys.

Charlie and Joe both have been gone for some time. I have an idea where Charlie might be but as to Joe's whereabouts, it would be a wild guess. I have little doubt however that Joe's outfit might see some fireworks before this mess is over. As to our immediate future I wouldn't even make a guess. We've handled a big job with the French Lend Lease and I'm still on it. There are some radical changes in the making so we don't know what we are going to do. Time will tell.

Just rec'd Sue's letter of Sept. 13 where she mentions the advisability of selling the car at this time. I have thot the same but forgot to mention it in any of my letters. It's probably true that this car won't be worth much after the war so anything that you can do for Susie in this connection will be okay and deeply appreciated by me. The extra denaro will also give her something to fall back on in case she needs it this winter.

It made me quite proud of "the ole man" to note that Uncle Sam thot enough of him to offer a commission in the navy. Without a doubt there are any number of good jobs you could handle in either the army or navy but unless you are absolutely needed I think you are smart to pass it up the time being at least. Being the efficient business man that you are, I'm afraid you would "blow your top" if you had to put up with some of the regulations, red tape, etc., that all of us are exposed to. Good old sound business is a dream in comparison. [Marvin, age fifty-two and with an enlarged heart, would never have passed the physical to join the US Navy, and son Edgar was chronically unwell.]

Give my regards to all the boys, Ed, Buck, and Jess. It would be interesting to know what your personnel is now. I recall, in a letter from Ed, that Sully is with you no longer, and I believe that several months ago Joe said his brother might enlist in the navy. I almost forgot Mr. Humphreys. I guess he and Mr. Lynn are giving the books "the works". It was quite a surprise to learn that Joe Humphreys had quit Deere John [sic] and gone to work for the government.

Every once in a while I think of old Hobgood [Gordon] and his wife, who as you will recall, was quite a special friend of mine. I am quite well acquainted with a close friend of Hobgood's who came very near getting his "everlasting" about four days previous to our unexpected arrival in Bermuda. He is Ed Kissinger, a fellow in Charley's outfit and a darn nice chap.

What is the latest news concerning Harold Beadles? They are sending the men across quite rapidly now so I'm wondering if he hasn't left the states.

By the way, I got quite a kick out of that post card you sent me from St. Louis. You and Mom and Sue really had a swell time this summer. I don't think Sue could have asked for a nicer summer and I was especially glad for you that you could make the trip. I don't recall that you saw the folks in Virginia but you might know whether or not Buddy Gilliam [another son of John Wyndham Gilliam] is still at Camp Lee. In case you or Mom write the Hughes be sure to tell them hello for me. I wish I could have visited with them longer but Uncle Sam was running my affairs then so I had little choice in the matter.

Enclosed is a sample of some of the money we use. Wish I had one of the new five or ten franc notes to send you as they are printed by a bank note firm in Philadelphia.

I wrote Susie yesterday but will drop her another line along with this letter so that you can forward it on to her. Give Mom and Edgar my regards and write as when you can.

Sincerely, Jimmie

When Jim received his orders to ship out on September 11, 1943, Sue accompanied him to New York, where she had enrolled as a graduate student at Teachers College of Columbia University. The following letter written to her parents set the context of this stage of her life. Tucked in the envelope with the letter was a newspaper clipping sent to her from Dallas by her mother. The clipping shows photos of Mrs. Wallace Bassett and Reverend George Bassett with the headline "Death Claims Two in Family." No date. Dr. Wallace Bassett had married Sue and Jim in 1936. Reverend George Bassett must have been the son, and Mrs. Wallace Bassett was George's mother and wife of Dr. Wallace Bassett.

Friday, October 22, 1943
〇〜〇 Dearest Folks,

Received your letters this morning and was so glad to hear from you. I'm sorry that I haven't written as much, but I have been pretty busy doing this and that. I have had to go to the doctor three times this week, which takes quite a bit of time, and I took the tour of Radio City one afternoon, which was wonderful, then incidentally I have a little studying to do, though my work is not at all hard. On top of that I have been helping Lora and some girls a little to get a party up for the third floor. We had it last night, and it was a howling success. Lora was chairman for it, which certainly proves her popularity with all the girls. Everybody is just crazy about her. I am so happy for her, as she is just a different person. I wrote the little poem for the bulletin boards which went like this. It took me all of five minutes to write! To Lora she was amazed as if I had stirred up a little cake.

> We're having a party, or hadn't you heard;
> For all of the gals who dwell on the third.
> Now don't say, "I haven't a thing I can wear,"
> Or "Heavens, I can't go. I shampooed my hair."
> Just come in your house coat and bobby pins too,
> For that's what we want—to know the REAL YOU.
> It's all just ad lib, so come one and all
> At ten o'clock sharp atop Whittier Hall.

Each floor is having a party, then we will wind it up with a big party for Hallowe'en. There are 49 girls on our floor, with 380 in the whole dormitory.

I have tried so many times to get Mrs. Faison, and I finally wrote her a note. She called me when I wasn't in, and I just can't seem to get her by phone. I shall keep trying. I was watching the ice skaters on the Rockefeller Plaza the other afternoon, when I saw two girls from Dallas who went to school with me in Denton.

My hand is improving for the time-being. I think though I still can't wear rings. We found that Dura Gloss to be an irritant. Revlon doesn't bother, thank goodness, as I hate to go without at all. I'm not going to use it though until my hand is completely well. Still can't use soap on my hands, either.

I must tell you about my good luck. Yesterday the 21st, which has been quite an important day of the month for me all my life [her parents were married on September 21, 1912; Sue and Jim were married on June 21, 1936], I decided to try my luck at job-hunting, not really caring whether I found anything or not. I decided I would rather not apply here at Teachers College, as I am here all the time for my school work, so I went over to Riverside Church to try my luck. I got only as far as the information desk, and when I told the man what I wanted, he said for me to be seated, and since he had to go up to see the manager on some business, he would ask him if he would like to talk to me.

Well, I sat down and waited for forty minutes. He finally returned and said he was very sorry to keep me waiting, but the manager was so busy that he couldn't even get in to see him himself. He advised me to come back this morning. I gave him my name, only saying that I was a student here. I hadn't been home more than an hour when they called me on the phone, (I hadn't even told them where I lived), he introduced me to the manager on the phone, who asked me to come over this morning at 9:00. He was lovely to me. His office is on the 17th floor and was beautiful. He said one of the ministers there needed a secretary. I told him I could work only three days, Tuesday, Wed,. and Thursday, and he said that was fine. When I told him I was an organist he said, well, you can play this organ sometime if you would like to. I just about fell over. Then he gave me a [subway?] ticket good for the year, which are usually given to just members and service men. I have been having to go about an hour early, now I won't have to. You can imagine how thrilled I will be to get to play that organ. It possibly will work into something better, while at present I will get $5.00 per day to begin on. That church is an institution within itself, and it must employ about 200 people, though I don't know. It is certainly a busy place. It has several kitchens, club rooms, a swimming pool, bowling alley, and all kinds of special classes in art craft, Red Cross, etc. Dr. Fosdick [Harry Emerson] said Wednesday night there had been 38 weddings in that church that day, so you see why he has several assistant pastors. I think it will be quite an adventure to even be around a place like that. I know it won't work me too hard, as I will still have a lot of free time, and my work isn't very hard. I can go to some plays, opera, etc. now.

I still haven't received any more mail from Jimmy. I just wonder where he is. Dad, it was sweet of you to write him, and Mom, you certainly sent him a lot of things. I just sent him my picture, as there just didn't seem to be anything left to send him. I did try to get shaving lotion, but there was none to be had.

I am having my coat sent out from Russells. It still isn't a bit cold here. The weather has been beautiful.

I too certainly hate to see Edgar go to Houston climate, but I hope he will be all right. [Dillon Scale had a branch office in Houston. Suffering from long-term effects of TB, Edgar was always sensitive about the state of his health and was reluctant to talk about it.] I just haven't felt that I should write him after all. You still think I should?

Yes, I got Doris' letter, and it is such a foolish request from

her that I don't want to do it. She wants to give her sister
a brown kid purse for her birthday to match the shoes she
bought at Neiman's. Said to pay between $20 and $40 for
it. She didn't send the money either, so I'm not going to too
much trouble. Juanita probably pays that for her gifts, as her
husband is a gambler, but I think it is utterly crazy for Doris to
do it too. Some people just don't have a brain cell working.

I must stop now and go eat. Lora has gone on a trip up
the Hudson today with a friend from California. She is really
having a good time. The twelve o'clock whistle is blowing now,
and you know what that means. If you don't ask Mary, if she
still is with you, is she?

Am enclosing a letter I received from Aunt Lena (sister of
paternal grandparents William or Laura) just to show you her
handwriting. She is 88 years old. Imagine. In the meantime
I had written her and sent her the money for the packing of
things.

So sorry you have all been under the weather. I haven't had
a cold or anything. Thank goodness. Take vitamin shots every
Monday afternoon.

Mother, I did not want you to tear up that check! I still
think the eyes in these pictures are very queer, and I guess we
shouldn't have paid them until I was satisfied with them.

One of the girls just came in to go to lunch with me, so I'll
sign off for now. Did I ever give you my phone number? Can't
remember whether I did or not. It is University 4-7000, room
344. Lots of love. Susie

Sue wrote to her parents again on November 1, 1943, on the Riverside
Church stationery, which was printed with the words "The Riverside
Church, Riverside Drive at 122nd Street, New York."

Dear Ma & Pa—
Have just finished letters [of condolence] to Christian,
Bassetts, Mead, and Doris. Sent Dr. Bassett a $20.00 check

for the Tub offering—Couldn't exactly "afford" it I guess, but I believe the Lord takes care of his own, so . . .

Had a few extra sheets of this stationery, but no envelopes— Just wanted you to see it.

Gee, you were certainly good to write this week. I enjoyed your letters so much, ever Ma's bonus.

Yes. Flicka [pet donkey] looks very pretty from the rear view. So glad you have had her all "fixed up." The pictures were pretty good; but I don't think any of them did you justice, Ma. By the way, I don't have a decent picture of you with me. Won't you send me one of those good ones of you to show the gals? Now don't forget.

Mother, will you get Lois Maxine's baby something for us together, and please let me know how much it is so I can pay my share!

I also wrote Gloria Green the other day. Poor child! It is hard to know what to write her. Will try to write Edgar this week. [It is possible that Gloria was Edgar's first wife.]

As to the box from Jimmy, go ahead and open it, as there are things in there for all of us and his family. Just keep the things there and write me a description of them as I have no desire to see them. I don't want to see them until after I start hearing from him again, as it has a queer effect on me that I can't describe. You remember how it upset me when I received his pictures about three or four weeks after he sailed and I wasn't hearing from him. I'm not worried yet, as it has been only three weeks, but I just plain wouldn't want to open it now. I want you to, though. Understand? [If Sue heard from Jim three weeks ago, that was October 11, 1943, and three or four weeks before that was about September 11, 1943, when he sailed from New York.]

Today is a rainy day and I came in from classes at 11:00 and went to sleep. Have been writing letters about two hours now. Imagine me!

When you see Mr. Tankersley, Lucy, or any of the others

please tell them I send my love. Tell Katy [Katy Buck, wife of Marvin's business partner, Ernest, and Ruth's best friend] I'll try to write her too, though I know she hears through you.

Did you have my telephone number to give Mr. Riehl, Pop, or shall I send it to him?

Had a wonderful dinner at the St. George Thursday nite with Woodlands. They leave tomorrow and send their love.

Ma, I have two tickets for Dec. 18 for "Oklahoma" just in case you are here! How about it! They are so hard to get that I got two when I could.

My hands have flared up again, and I'm going to the Dr. again tomorrow. I don't know whether they are helping me or just taking my money. I'm in hopes that when we have a freeze it might be better. It is in a "rheumy" stage now—not like you have ever seen it.

We had a grand Hallowe'en party last night here at the dorm. I went as a senorita and Ann Krim, a friend of mine, was the senor with my serape over her shoulder. Lora was a little Dutch girl and looked darling! It was oodles of fun.

I'm too "written out" now to tell you about the Hawaiians. Don't worry about me, now, kids. They were lovely, and there were six of us. I'll write you in detail about it sometime.

You don't need to send the money, Mother, unless you just want to stick it in a box with something else sometime.

You asked for Buddy Crockett's address. It is W. G. Crocket, Phm/3c. C.A.S.U. 13, F.P.O., San Francisco. Haven't heard anything from him or his mother.

You might call Mildred and Austin sometime and see if he's still there or not. I wrote M.C. and Hermes or rather Hermes and haven't heard from him. Do you know anything about Mr. Nye by now?

I told Mr. Bashart [?] what you asked me to, Pappy. He is really sold on Edgar. If you can do half as well as Mr. Pearl has on the East Coast you will do all right, Zeke. They are positively wealthy!

I must stop now and go eat supper. I love you lots, Susie
P.S. So sorry Aunt Eudie is sick again. Give her my love.

Sue's father, M. D. Dillon, died at home of a heart attack on November 11, 1943. Ruth and her friend Katy Buck (wife of Ernest Buck) were on a train headed to New York to visit Sue. According to Cousin Betty, her father, Jess Wortham, called the railroad company to have them notify Ruth that Marvin had died. Anna Wortham was with him at home, as Marvin had called her when he felt ill. The railroad company pulled Ruth and Katy off the train in St. Louis, Missouri. They had to wait a good while before boarding a train back to Dallas, as most of the seats had been allocated to soldiers deploying to the war. Sue left school to come home for the funeral. She did not return to New York to complete the master's degree at Teachers College of Columbia University. The December 18 tickets to *Oklahoma!* were given to a friend in the dorm, Whittier Hall. Ever a dutiful daughter, Sue came home to be with her mother.

It was the Kessler Park home that had been Ruth and Marvin's dream house, the fruit of his labors as a traveling salesman and successful businessman. It was also the home in which Marvin died of a heart attack on November 11, 1943, in the bed that his parents had moved to Texas in the covered wagon from Kentucky in 1892. Now, Sue would have to return to lend emotional support to her suddenly widowed mother and to await the return of her soldier-boy husband from the perils of World War II.

On Sunday, November 14, 1943, the *Dallas Morning News* published the obituary notice of Marvin Dillon's death on Thursday, November 11, 1943. The funeral was held on Saturday, November 13, 1943. Sue's husband, Jim, was stationed in North Africa at the time. When I was ten, Daddy told my brother and me, "I received a letter of condolence from someone who did not mention the name of the deceased. I worried mightily for several days, not knowing who had died! Was it your mother, a friend, or a parent?" Finally, Jim found out that it was in fact Marvin D. Dillon, his father-in-law, who had died suddenly. In the obituary, notice his age is given but not his date of birth *or* date of death! Just as she had done for her father in 1938, Ruth wrote the following obituary for Marvin.

M. D. DILLON Is Buried Here

Funeral services for M. D. Dillon, 53, founder and president of the Dillon Scale Company, were held Saturday morning at the Ed C. Smith Funeral Chapel.

Dr. Wallace Bassett, pastor of the Cliff Temple Baptist Church, in which Mr. Dillon had for many years served as a deacon, conducted the services.

The scale wholesaler and retailer died at his home, 705 Kessler Parkway, early Thursday of a heart attack. Mr. Dillon came to Dallas thirty-two years ago from Celina, Collin County. While he had been in the scale business since 1920, he was also known among Texas oil, rail, cotton gin and grain and feed people.

A member of the Masonic Lodge, he was also affiliated with the Dallas Purchasing Agents Association, the Society of Aeronautical Weight Engineers, the Texas Association of Weights and Measures, and the National Scale Men's Association.

Mr. Dillon was born in Burnside, KY, and lived in Trenton, Fannin County, before moving to Celina.

Survivors are his wife, Mrs. Ruth Dillon; a daughter, Mrs. J. L. Bussard [Sue], Dallas; a son, E. M. Dillon, Dallas; three brothers, Bernie Dillon, New Braunfels; M. C. Dillon, Los Angeles, CA; Olan Dillon, San Antonio; four sisters, Mrs. Don Brown, [Cora], Ardmore, OK; Mrs. Earl Lewis [Frieda], San Francisco, CA; Mrs. Joe Anderson [Bessie], McKinney; and Mrs. C. A. Shelander [Lera], Bryan.

Pallbearers were Charles R. Moore, G. M. West, Lin Gower, W. G. Hobgood, Charles A. Humphreys and J. J. Wortham.

The pallbearers were business associates and friends of Dillon Scale. W. G. Hobgood was Gordon Hobgood, friend of Jim and Edgar; G. M. West was the son of E. P. West of West & Company for whom Marvin had worked from 1912 to 1919; and J. J. Wortham was "Jess," senior salesman for Dillon Scale, Anna's husband, and father to Dorothy and Betty.

Jim's letter of condolence, dated December 4, 1943, written to Edgar, his brother-in-law, speaks of devotion to the Dillon family.

    ◖❧◗ Dear Ed:

It is hard to write a brother-in-law under these circumstances for losing Pop has been a terrible shock to me as it must have been to you.

I loved him, Ed, just as tho he were my dad and I want you to know that I share your grief. Being so far away like I am I can't help you, but I hope and pray, Ed, that this war will end soon so that we all can come home and be with our loved ones again.

Since I know nothing of the details or future plans I cannot write you very intelligently. Just remember, Ed, that it is my sincerest desire to help you and to work and cooperate with you to the fullest extent possible. Sincerely, Jimmie

At Marvin's death, Sue withdrew from graduate school and returned to Dallas. Jim remained overseas in North Africa and Italy, serving in the Army of the United States. Sue got a job with the help of Grandmother's friend, Lora Coston Bridges, as assistant director of the Oak Cliff Civic Chorus. A notice in the *Dallas Morning News*, from late 1943 or early 1944, reads, "Mrs. Bussard, an accomplished musician, received her degree from North Texas State Teachers College, where she served as the college organist. She is now organist for Ed C. Smith Undertaking Company."

While Jim was overseas, he remained faithful to Sue despite the Army culture of temptation, which often caused lonely soldiers to succumb to any number of vices. Daddy used to tell us, "The women scared me and the liquor tasted awful, so I grew a mustache and smoked cigars."

He suffered from PTSD. He was blessed to come home in late 1945 to a wife who adored him. One can only imagine what it took to reestablish the marriage.

After Jim was discharged in November 1945 from the Army of the United States of America, he returned to Dallas to resume working for Dillon Scale, though in what capacity it is uncertain. Before the war, Jim had learned the business from his father-in-law and was a valued employee. The company had to be restructured after the death of its founder and CEO Marvin Dillon. The Board of Directors and shareholders in the company were Ruth Dillon, Ernest Buck, Edgar Dillon, and Sue Dillon Bussard. As son of the founder, Edgar was named president of the company. Jim was hired back as a sales representative. Having been out of the business for two years, he had to relearn everything. Also, he had no idea what he would have to do to help his sickly brother-in-law keep the business afloat.

In early 1946 Sue and Jim purchased a rancher house on San Fernando Boulevard in the Forest Hills neighborhood of east Dallas with the proceeds they had saved from the sale of their house on Purdue. At the same time, Ruth and Edgar sold the well-appointed house on Kessler Parkway in Oak Cliff and purchased a rancher-style home on Tokalon Drive in the Lakewood neighborhood of east Dallas. In 1945 and 1946, Sue and Jim were tasked with reestablishing their marriage. At the same time, Jim returned to work for Dillon Scale. It was also time to start a family, and Sue's biological clock was ticking. No stress! She suffered a miscarriage in 1946 before I was born in July 1947. Sue was thirty-four, Jim thirty-six. When brother Dillon arrived in June 1949, Mother was thirty-six, Daddy thirty-eight. The story of *The Crossings* had already leapt across the Atlantic by the time Ingrid Jaensson sailed to the United States of America from Sweden in September 1948—a Swedish Mary Poppins.

PART TWO

The Story of
Ingrid Eva
Linnea Jaensson
and My Family:
1948–2012

*A*ccording to the story, on October 31, 1948, Ingrid Eva Linnea Jaensson entered the life of my family. She arrived in Dallas, Texas (probably on a Greyhound bus) after having docked in the port of New York City, on the MS *Gripsholm* on September 8, 1948. After spending about two weeks in New York, she toured the Midwest visiting Swedish relatives who had emigrated in the 1930s. Ingrid came to Dallas to visit her cousin Harold "Johnnie" Johnson (Jaensson) and his wife, Mildred. Johnnie worked as a warehouse manager for Dillon Scale (later, Dillon Equipment Company) founded in 1920 by my grandfather Marvin "Zeke" Dillon. As noted earlier, Marvin died of a heart attack in 1943, leaving the company in the charge of a board of directors, composed of Marvin's founding business partners, along with my grandmother Ruth Collier Gilliam Dillon, her son Edgar Marvin Dillon, and my mother, Sue Dillon Bussard. Mother ceded her seat on the board to my father, James Layton Bussard in 1947. Between mid-September and October 31, 1948, Ingrid made her way from New York City to Dallas, Texas. She crisscrossed the United States via bus and train, with a stop in Boston, then on to Minnesota, where she visited relatives who had emigrated from Sweden during the Great Depression. About one third of Sweden's population had emigrated to midwestern America in the early twentieth century. While visiting relatives in Minnesota, Ingrid contacted the Swedish hospital in Minneapolis, where she had planned to work as a floor nurse and to take courses in American nursing techniques and hospital administrative procedures through the University of Minnesota. Her job and studies were supposed to begin in early November 1948.

Many of the details of this personal account come from my recollection of stories I was told by my parents and Ingrid. I have been fortunate to receive from Ingrid's niece Susanne Lundqvist Sköld excerpts from letters that Ingrid wrote home to Sweden from 1948 until her departure from the United States in October 1950. Susanne hand copied in Swedish the passages that referenced my family, which a friend from the First Presbyterian Church Choir in Colorado Springs, Sam Zettersten from Uppsala, Sweden, graciously translated, pro bono, into English for me.

As in Part 1 of this memoir, the story that follows has been constructed from letters. It begins with letters written by Ingrid to her family back in Sweden between fall of 1948 and fall of 1950 and continues as members of my family wrote to Ingrid from 1950 until 1967. I began writing to Ingrid in the 1970s. The letters to Sweden written by Sue were circulated among Ingrid and her friends after their respective visits to the United States. It was Ingrid who kept the letters to pass on to me. Ingrid died at age ninety-seven on March 8, 2012. Letters written and saved by both Ingrid and me between April 10, 1985, and January 11, 2012, chronicle our friendship as adults, which spanned the last twenty-six years of her life. Ingrid's letters to my mother and father were not saved. However, I know the story and can imagine Ingrid's side of the correspondence. I have reconstructed details of events from shared experiences and remembered conversations.

THE ATLANTIC CROSSING: SEPTEMBER 1948

*A*t age thirty-four, Ingrid Eva Linnea Jaensson began her own story in the first two letters she wrote home to sister Ann-Marie. The first was written from the MS *Gripsholm*, dated September 2, 1948; the second was written from the Henry Hudson Hotel, New York City, dated September 9, 1948. These early letters are filled with youthful exuberance and enthusiasm at the prospect of spending two years in the US, pursuing her career dream of learning American medical practices and of becoming a hospital administrator. The crossing started well but soon deteriorated into a nightmare of rough seas and turbulent weather. Much of the first letter contains a graphic account of seasickness among most of the passengers and crew.

The MS *Gripsholm* set sail from Göteborg on September 1, 1948. Boarding was uneventful. Sam Zettersten translated the letter, originally written in Swedish. Ingrid wrote, "I will never forget how beautiful the archipelago was. We went with a ship's pilot out to Vinga Lighthouse then full speed on our own engine into the North Sea." When Mother and I arrived at the port of Göteborg in early June 1959, also on the MS *Gripsholm*, we passed by the Vinga Lighthouse as the ship sailed through the Swedish archipelago!

Ingrid continues: "In Göteborg, through a colleague that I met at the ship, I was introduced to a Swedish-American with a 20-year-old son. Very sweet too, but not fun. Unfortunately, I'm sitting at the same table, and I have to sit there the whole journey, they reserved a seat for me. I would have preferred to sit with my cabin companions, instead. But nothing I can do about that." Ingrid's cabinmates were three Canadian ladies. She traveled tourist class (third class), the equivalent of steerage in the early twentieth century—simple, basic accommodations. She remarks that she will try to get cabin class (second class) for the voyage home.

After passing from the North Sea into the north Atlantic, the ship encountered terrible storms, with very cold rain and wind. She continues: "The Atlantic is like a boiling caldron, the waves hit with thundering noise over the bow. It is a strange feeling to only see heaven and the sea day after day. The storm is 'awful and beautiful'. The waves look like white mountain tops. All night it has been so noisy that I thought the ship would break up into pieces, the bow under water most of the time. I will never forget this journey!" Some brave souls stayed "on deck and took movies of the spectacle." The storm delayed arrival in New York by two days. The sea calmed, but the ship had to slow down. "At night we came into fog, the fog horns were sounding and we were close to collide with a warship. The engine stopped for a while, a strange feeling." Next day was fine weather. "We passed Cape Race [off the Avalon Peninsula of Newfoundland]. If the weather stays good we will be in New York Tuesday morning. The Atlantic is azure blue and calm." At the end of the voyage, the ship was "open" to all passengers. Ingrid visited first class and saw "millionaire ladies."

ARRIVAL IN NEW YORK CITY

Ingrid's letter to Ann-Marie, written from New York City at the Henry Hudson Hotel in Manhattan [opened in 1941], twelfth floor, at 237 Fifty-Eighth Street, is filled with enthusiasm and amazement at having just arrived in the US after the horrendous crossing, with a two-day delay in arrival due to the heavy weather. Ingrid writes:

9 September 1948

❧ It's almost beyond imagination that I am in the biggest city of the world. Early last morning we caught a glimpse of land, a wonderful feeling, little by little the outlines became distinct and we could see how the cars in a long parade slid forward on Long Island. After a wonderful farewell lunch, the skyline of New York appeared, and we passed the Statue of Liberty, in verdigris green color she stood there and welcomed us. We saw the sky scrapers so much clearer, the Empire State Building, etc. HMS *Queen Elizabeth* had passed earlier in the morning, now we passed this great giant with 3,000 passengers.

The letter continues with Ingrid's vivid description of a Danish American Red Cross worker who plucked her from the queue in the immigration line and whisked her through customs and immigration into the US. After a taxi ride to the hotel and dinner with her Danish American friend, Ingrid is on her own in New York City. She continues:

❧ I am with Britta's friends from Göteborg. The first evening we walked on Broadway. It is impossible to describe: like an amusement park, sky scrapers with advertising lights in all the colors of the rainbow, and a swarm of crazily dressed people of all nationalities of the world, masses of colored people [Negros and Negresses] in a new look. We laughed at first, but now my eyes had gotten used to it. The avenues are very wide and filled with cars to the breaking point, street lights, when you are allowed to cross there is a tight mass of people going. All taxis are yellow, red, and green. At first, I thought they were fire trucks. Cars honking are deafening. The light advertisements are more impressive than the skyscrapers, you get blinded everywhere. Negroes sell different things and shine shoes. Late we began going home and went into stores at 1:30 a.m. and shopped for whatever we wanted, nylons or food.

Tired I staggered to bed, took a bath first to clean up from the
New York dust. My own bathroom and toilet. The next morning
I called the Backlunds, friends from Sweden. We met at the
Swedish consulate at noon for election.

Ingrid had visited a lunch counter earlier and was fascinated by the
variety of food choices. Later that week, Ingrid joined her friends from
the MS *Gripsholm* for an outing that became an all-nighter.

◠◡ We began at a restaurant on Broadway, big and fancy
and beautiful customers. Had a drink and danced, saw a ballet,
and then went by car to the Waldorf Astoria, the biggest and
fanciest hotel in New York, where the movie "People in a Hotel"
was made. [This movie is *Week-End at the Waldorf*, released
on October 4, 1945, staring Ginger Rogers, Lana Turner,
Walter Pidgeon, and Van Johnson, based on the novel *Grand
Hotel* by Vicki Baum.] I kept close to my companions. People
were seated in the lounge on small round tables crowded close
together with low lighting. The American women seemed to
be dressed in almost nothing with long wide skirts and giant
heels. A famous actress probably of racial mix sang with a
deep and theatrical voice. Very suggestive, she has been to
Sweden and performed with success. After that a ballet [night
club dancers], time was now 4:00 a.m. and life was going on
full speed. In all the venues there was cold air, so it never got
smoky and bad air. After a while we had had enough of this
and continued out to 5th Avenue. I never get tired of walking
on this enormously wide street with the most exclusive
store in the world. By day or night the same enchantment.
At 6:00am I arrived home to the hotel, tired but it had been
very interesting to study New York at such a late hour. After
a few hours of sleep, I was up at 10:00 a.m. the next morning.
Shopped at the huge warehouses "Bloomingdales" and "Macy's"
the last one the world's largest. I understand that it is almost
10 floors high and the area is like 8/4 of the city of Växjö.

[After asking Ingrid's niece what this 8/4 reference means, she replied, "8/4=2. I think she means that Macy's department store on ten floors would be two times bigger than Växjö city.] There is everything to buy. I wish I had you with me Ann-Marie! That evening we went to Radio City Music Hall and saw the Rockettes, fantastically well-trained. I am tired. I like it here and all people are so friendly. Today, a month ago I left Hagavik. I am melting, soon it is over 30 degrees C. I am sitting in the Boston train station. Will travel more in the USA. Will write more later. Bought nylons for 98 cents to send tomorrow. Food is terribly expensive, but clothes are inexpensive. Fruit is cheap. It's the season for peaches now.

Ingrid Jaensson 1948

ARRIVAL IN DALLAS AND TRAVELING IN THE USA: 1948–1950

*I*t happened to be Halloween the day Ingrid set foot in Dallas in 1948. Her cousin, Harold "Johnnie" Johnson [Jaensson anglicized], and his wife, Mildred, had no children and did not live in a neighborhood with children. "Johnnie" worked in the warehouse for Dillon Scale. He was a personable man with a lilting Swedish accent, and he and Daddy were friends. Daddy invited the Johnsons and Ingrid to our home on San Fernando Way in the Forest Hills neighborhood of Dallas, Texas, so Ingrid could see "spooks." Ingrid remarked to me in 2004, "When I walked into the San Fernando house, I noticed immediately the blue and yellow upholstery on the chairs and sofa! Sweden's colors! I felt at home in your house."

Grandmother Ruth, now widowed for five years, had moved to a house on Tokalon Drive in the Lakewood neighborhood of Dallas. Edgar was living with her. My mother, Erman Sue Dillon Bussard, was pregnant with my brother at the time, and I was a toddler of fifteen months. Ingrid and Sue became friends immediately. I believe there was a divine plan at work here.

I have gleaned from family stories and Sue's letters that she was unhappy and unwell at the time. Sue and Jim had married after their college graduation from North Texas State University in Denton, Texas, on June 21, 1936. Like everyone's, their lives were shaped by the Depression and World War II. Jim enlisted in the Army of the United States of America in the summer of 1942. You will recall that they were decorating the Christmas tree when war was declared after the attack on Pearl Harbor on December 7, 1941. Jim waited as long as he could to enlist. He served in North Africa and in Italy from 1943 until six months after VE Day, May 8, 1945. Upon his return to the US, Jim suffered from PTSD even though he was an ordnance sergeant and did not see combat. His twin brother, Bob, recalled, "After the war I was sitting in a Dallas restaurant with Sue and Jimmy, when suddenly, Jimmy burst into tears for no apparent reason." Bob had enlisted in the United States Navy, but the war ended before his unit deployed. He spent the entire war in Miami, Florida. Sue suffered a miscarriage before I was born in July 1947. She was pregnant again with my brother in October 1948 when Ingrid arrived. Ingrid was a nurse. The eyes of these two women met, and a bond forged between kindred spirits.

As mentioned previously, Ingrid was supposed to spend only a short time in Dallas, then move to Minneapolis, Minnesota, for two years to work in the Swedish hospital and take courses in nursing and hospital administration at the University of Minnesota. After spending Halloween weekend with Harold and Mildred and meeting my mother, Ingrid returned to Minneapolis in early November 1948. She was met with the disappointing news that there was, in fact, no job waiting for her at the Swedish hospital and no university study program in which she was eligible to participate. Left with no prospects in Minneapolis, Ingrid contacted Jim and Edgar in Dallas to seek their counsel about what to do. Jim contacted Boone Powell, the head administrator of Baylor Hospital in Dallas. In fact, Boone and Ruth Powell were friends of Sue and Jim. Boone declared, "Bring Ingrid back to Dallas. We will give her a nursing job at Baylor Hospital and let her take any nursing or hospital administration classes through Baylor University that she wants." Ingrid references this time in a letter to her sister, Ann-Marie. She wrote, "I really like it here and people in Dallas are so nice to me. I change my travel plans and stay in Dallas a while longer. I got a job at

Baylor University Hospital." Ingrid also remarked, "Sue is my age and is married and lives in a beautiful house. They have a 15-month-old daughter."

In her letters to Sweden written in 1948 and early 1949, Ingrid recounted Edgar's role in helping to get her a job at Baylor Hospital in Dallas. Then she makes an interesting remark: "Now Edgar Dillon calls and we are going by car to Houston, a beautiful town close to New Orleans together with a brother-in-law and spend a weekend there. I like small surprises and nice people."

For a few years, 1943 through 1952, Dillon Scale & Equipment Company had an office in Houston. The brother-in-law she refers to is in fact Jim's twin, Bob Bussard, who had relocated his family to Houston in 1946 to manage the Houston branch of Dillon Scale.

After the weekend in Houston, Ingrid wrote to her sister, Ann-Marie, about American Thanksgiving on November 26, 1948:

> ᏀᎲᎠ Yesterday, we celebrated Thanksgiving Day. We had a great dinner with turkey. Harold and Mildred were also invited. It was very nice of the Bussards to remember them.
>
> If I had all of you here, I wouldn't hesitate a minute to live here in USA. It will be interesting to celebrate American Christmas. Tomorrow I will bake cookies, my Swedish cookies and then make meatballs. Went by car to the Mexican Bay [Gulf of Mexico] for 2 weeks and then with Edgar Dillon and his brother-in-law [Bob Bussard]. We had a nice trip.

The story develops in a letter Ingrid wrote to her parents, dated 28 December 1948.

> ᏀᎲᎠ Now is the American Christmas over. It is different than the Swedish. It has been very interesting to experience the holidays. They eat turkey on Christmas Day. Early on Christmas morning we gathered in the living room where is the fireplace, stockings were hanging filled with small gifts and goodies. Later came Santa Claus and passed out his gifts.

I received a nightgown and a slip from Jimmy and Sue [my parents], a brown satin blouse from Mrs. Dillon [Ingrid always referred to my grandmother Ruth as Mrs. Dillon], and from Edgar a travel iron and French Perfume, and from Susibeth 17 months I got a lipstick and handkerchiefs. I was allowed to set the Christmas table in a Swedish way, as good as possible. To Mrs. Dillon and Edgar I gave a lovely brass crown using candles and other Christmas decorations with green napkins, it turned out nice. Susibeth opened all her Christmas gifts and tried all the toys. Mildred called and said that Anna's granddaughter had died and would be buried 26 December. I was there.

The reference to Anna's granddaughter is the first child of Anna's daughter Dorothy. Ingrid would have attended the burial with my parents.

I include this letter for the sweetness of it. Ingrid dropped into my family's life and bonded quickly. I became one of "Ingrid's babies." She was surrogate mother to me from the time I was a toddler until her death in 2012. Ingrid was ninety-seven. I was sixty-four.

After the debacle in Minneapolis, Ingrid moved back to Dallas. She lived with my grandmother for a short while and then moved into the nurses' dormitory near Baylor Hospital. By now, Ingrid and Mother were great friends, kindred spirits. She looked after me, helped Mother with housework, and she was present in the delivery room when my brother, James Dillon Bussard, was born on June 4, 1949.

Ingrid stayed connected with Mother most of the two years of her visa. However, she did take time to travel throughout the United States. I have her photo album of Colorado Springs' Garden of the Gods park, the Grand Canyon, and San Francisco, as well as Minneapolis and New York City.

I moved from Dallas to Colorado Springs in 1999. When I spent a week with her in Malmö in October 2004, Ingrid had just celebrated her ninetieth birthday. She said one evening, "I think I will make a hundred." When I invited her to visit me in Colorado, she replied, "There I have been." During that week with Ingrid in Malmö, I told her about a new man in my life, Ron Ruiz. Ingrid declared, "You do not have to marry him." I did marry him the following September. That statement was followed by the account that she did, in fact, have a lover. She said, "He is younger than I, in his seventies. He has a wife. She goes to her knitting circle on Tuesdays, so that is when we meet. We are never too old for love." Then she added, "Do *not* tell any of this to Ann-Marie."

Ingrid shared with me that she had received proposals of marriage, two from Swedish men when she was in her twenties. When she became engaged after the second proposal, her fiancé presented her to his mother as his betrothed. The mother proceeded to instruct Ingrid on how to set up her household and how to be a good Swedish wife to her son. Ingrid returned the ring and broke off the engagement. Each evening during that visit in 2004, we sipped martinis and ate bruschetta made with morel mushrooms we had gathered in the local woods, as Ingrid told me stories about her life in Sweden, her friendship with Mother, and my childhood.

When Ingrid lived in Dallas from October 1948 until October 1950, she introduced my family to Swedish food—mostly cookies, saffron bread, and Swedish meatballs. In December 1949, Ingrid taught us how to celebrate Santa Lucia Day on December 13, a pre-Christmas festival of light to illumine the dark days of winter. Under her direction, my parents hosted a Santa Lucia party at our home, complete with glögg, pronounced "gloog"—an aromatic winter punch made from port wine, burgundy wine, raisins, spices, and sugar. After the wine and spices are blended and brought to a slow boil, a tower of sugar cubes assembled on a mesh tray is set atop the stew pot holding the brew. The punch is then flambéed to make the sugar melt into the mixture. Ladle the glögg into cups, garnish with an orange slice, and sip. Of course, there were also assorted cookies—all made by Ingrid. She wore a white robe made from a bedsheet and tied at the waist with a belt scavenged from a gold cord drapery pull. A wreath of lit candles rested on her head. It was so warm in Dallas that December evening in 1949, the candle wax dripped into her blonde hair. She had to use ice cubes to dislodge the melted candle wax. I am sure the candle wax was not the only thing that melted on that warm Texas night! I have collected Swedish recipes and Christmas decorations from Ingrid.

Even though Ingrid came to love her life in Dallas, she did experience feelings of homesickness. Of course, she missed her family. She wrote to Ann-Marie in March 1949: "I am longing for you and wish we could meet and just talk, talk. Hope I can return home by next Christmas, but I think it behooves me to stay yet. I want to see America really well and learn the language perfectly. I might have use for that."

Ingrid did travel throughout the United States—probably by train and bus—cheap transportation that goes everywhere! She wrote to Ann-Marie from Dallas on April 6, 1949:

> My trip to Florida was a success. From Dallas to Houston along the gulf to New Orleans, I took a trip up the Mississippi and on to Tallahassee where I visited a good friend of Sue Bussard, a professor at Florida State University who was an art teacher. Then I travelled along the coast and arrived in Miami. In Miami, I loved the salt ocean water.

Ingrid's favorite response to me when I mentioned visiting a place in the US—"There I have been!"—certainly rings true when she writes about her travels.

I can imagine Ingrid's eagerly writing letters back home to her parents, sister Ann-Marie, brother Bernth. She wrote late into the night as she was always busy in the day, never wanting to miss anything. Also, she kept urging her family to come to the US. Her enthusiasm for America comes through clearly in her letters.

In an April 8, 1949, letter to her mother, Ingrid wrote:

> Heard that Yngve [Harold's sister] soon will travel to Dallas. Here in Dallas we have summer [in Sweden, April is still wintry]. Last night I was over at the Dillon's for dinner, stayed overnight. They have gotten a TV [RCA eleven-inch screen] which is common here and we enjoy it a lot. It is good program all day, but at night mostly movies. Mildred makes her yard beautiful so it will be nice when Yngve arrives. I will

remain here in Dallas all summer. Heard that Bo Giertz has
been named Bishop. [Bo Harald Giertz was appointed Lutheran
bishop of Göteborg. He was a noted Lutheran Bible scholar,
theologian, and novelist. His appointment made him an official
of the Swedish government, as the state church is Lutheran.]
Elisabeth Giertz [Bo's second wife, not the mother of his
children] wants me to come home for the "installation" in May.

That same week, Ingrid wrote to her brother Bernth, dated 11 April
1949.

⸎ The first nylon shirts have arrived in Dallas. A thousand
thanks for all the newspapers. It makes me very happy. I
assume the Giertz family will be mentioned in the magazines
Veckojournals after his [Bo's] promotion to bishop. I received
a letter from Bo and Elisabeth Giertz. They are afraid that
I will stay here in America for the future. They want me to
come home for the inauguration in Uppsala Domkyrka. I would
love to, but it is impossible unfortunately. Bernth, you should
in some way come to America on a tourist visa for 3 months
and study architecture. Here is much to teach you about that.
Think about it. Saturday afternoon something happened in my
room at 1:00 pm. Police was called. I'll tell in my next letter
since it is 12 at night.

By now Ingrid had secured a nursing position at Baylor Hospital in
Dallas, and she had moved into nurses' housing adjacent to the hospital.
She wrote to Ann-Marie on 12 April 1949, Easter Sunday: "Here they
don't celebrate Easter, only Easter Sunday when they attend church.
Good Friday is a work day." In the same letter, she explained what had
happened in her room.

⸎ Saturday I came home and found my room in a total
mess. China broken in a thousand pieces on the floor. What
had happened, I wondered. Opposite to my window was a hotel

window only about a yard's distance. When I looked up at the window I saw a man standing naked. I was shocked. I ran to the manager at the nurses' home. She called the police and they arrived after a while. When they went to see the man he had his robe on. He had walked on a board from his room to mine and unhooked the screen. Police questioned him and found out that he had been in my room during the past days and watched me.

I don't recall hearing Ingrid talk about this event, but I am sure she would have mentioned it to my mother.

On May 6, 1949, Ingrid wrote to her pregnant sister, Ann-Marie, that she is now working a maternity rotation at Baylor Hospital, which is particularly significant to my family because my brother, James Dillon Bussard, was born in Baylor Hospital on June 4, 1949. Ingrid was present at the delivery.

   I've started to work in the delivery section and I have a lot to do. One morning we had 6 deliveries in two hours. Here are 3 delivery rooms. I can tell you that to bear a child in America is almost like pulling a tooth. Complete anesthetic for all, the babies are delivered with a half tong [thong, perhaps she means a sling] and that saves the mother and child. I'm very impressed by American obstetrics, they are ahead of Europe.

An important thing that I want to mention to you that during pregnancy eat (as little as possible of fat foods) lentils, corn, yellow or green vegetables. You should control your weight every week and not gain more than 7–9 KG during the whole pregnancy.

Sue Bussard is expecting soon, so I hope she will come in to my department where I am working. I go to her every day and help her with Susibet[h]. Sue has a hard time sleeping because it is so hot.

The 15th of June I'll go to Colorado Springs. Time passes so quickly and I have been here 8 months today.

Ingrid wrote again to Ann-Marie while Mother was in labor!

   It's 12 midnight. I'm sitting next to Sue and give her a helping hand now and then. She's now in the delivery room and is expecting to deliver tonight.

   I was out at the Dillon's yesterday evening. Here it is very warm but the Dillon's have A/C. In the morning Mrs. Dillon and I drove out to see Sue and she was pretty OK. We then went to town and during that time Sue had been taken to the delivery ward.

There is more to the story. Though mentioned earlier that Ingrid was present in the delivery room for the birth of my brother, here is the full context. Ingrid told me that my grandmother, Mrs. Dillon, had told her, "It must be a boy. Sue and Jimmy need a son to join the family business, Dillon Scale & Equipment Company." Ingrid added that she

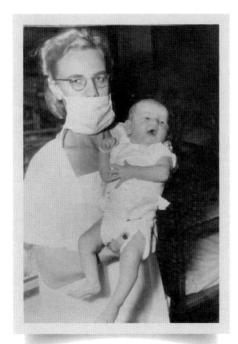

Ingrid holding Dillon, June 4, 1949

was, in fact, in the delivery room with my mother. When my brother was born, Ingrid left the delivery room and telephoned my grandmother. When she answered, Ingrid said, "It's a boy!" and hung up. I have been told that Mother's labor was very difficult and even life-threatening. She went into shock. I do have a photo of Ingrid wearing a surgical mask and holding my infant brother. Ingrid wrote, "Sue got a son on June 4 on our mother's birthday."

* * *

My brother was not the only baby Ingrid helped deliver at Baylor Hospital. There were about half a dozen infants, all born the summer and fall of 1949. The mothers all knew one another, and they often gathered together with the babies for a party. "Ingrid's babies" thrived. After she returned to Sweden in 1950, the mothers stayed in touch with one another. One of the mothers named her daughter Docka, which means "doll" in Swedish. As the children grew up and families moved, we lost touch with each other.

Later that summer, Ingrid traveled to Colorado and through the western United States, visiting cousins along the way. Shortly after Dillon was born, she wrote to Ann-Marie from Colorado Springs:

> Now I'm in Colorado Springs, but the heat is following me. We drove here Friday, started from Dallas at 7:00, drove all night and arrived at 1 pm Saturday, more than 800 English miles. Edgar Dillon stayed at the Broadmoor [a five-star hotel] and I got to stay at the YWCA hotel and went to the Broadmoor during the days. [We] have not decided how long we will stay.

This is one of many trips Edgar took to Colorado Springs and other places in the American West to see if the dry air would help him recover from the lung damage from TB that had plagued him for many years. It didn't. He was ill all of his adult life. He also smoked, which I am sure did not help. He died in 1967; ironically he outlived all his immediate family, including Mother. Ingrid did not travel with Edgar to be his nurse. She came as a friend and a tourist. The letter to Ann-Marie continues:

ᏴᏃᎦ Today I was up on Pikes Peak, 14,000 ft., went by cog
rail up the world's highest railroad and then by car down.
Wonderfully beautiful up there and cold with lots of snow. At
that height I got dizzy and weak kneed. Tomorrow I will hike
up to Seven Falls. Last Sunday we drove up to a restaurant on
the mountain.

Years later, when I was grown and Ingrid and I were adult friends
on our own terms, I wished out loud that she could come to Colorado
Springs to visit me. In October 2009, when she made her final trip to
the US and to Texas to celebrate her ninety-fifth birthday, I gave her
a book of photos from Colorado Springs and Manitou Springs. She
looked me in the eye and declared, "There I have been!" She continues
the narrative of her travels in a letter to Ann-Marie, dated July 19, 1949.

ᏴᏃᎦ From Colorado Springs I went to Denver. Here I met a
lady I had met in a hotel in New Orleans and I had promised
to see her when I came to Denver. They drove me around in
this beautiful town and mountains. They were very hospitable.
Then I traveled on to Wyoming and later to the Black Hills.
Here I met my cousin Raymond and his wife Agnes. They live
in a little mining town where one of America's biggest gold
mines is. I also met Uncle Frank and Winnie. They drove me
around the Black Hills, maybe one of the most beautiful places
I've seen in the heart of the wild west. Raymond is a historian
and he told me about different places. Frank and Winnie live in
Bison. Then I'm going to S. Dakota and see my cousin Dorothy.
Then to see our cousin Helen in Vermillion. Planning to go
Rochester and then to Minneapolis where I am going to see
Aunt Ellen.

Ingrid wrote to Ann-Marie from Sioux Falls, South Dakota. She
traveled extensively in the Midwest, looping back to Dallas in late
summer 1949. She writes on July 23, 1949:

〰 I feel good and I've had nice days in South Dakota. Tomorrow I travel to Rochester, MN and hope to meet people at the Mayo Clinic. If I can get some work here I stay 2-3 weeks. Then I go to St. Louis, into Oklahoma and then back to Dallas. I like it so well in Texas. Sue Bussard is so sweet to me as well as her mother also.

On August 4, 1949, Ingrid wrote to Ann-Marie from Minneapolis.

〰 Now it's not too far off until you'll have a baby. Hope it will be a girl. I've been here a week now and I'm staying with Aunt Ellen. I spent the weekend with the Gordon family. I began working at the Swedish hospital for 3 weeks. I have met nice doctors here all with Swedish relations. I'll stay this whole month with Aunt Ellen. September 1, I will go to Dallas. I had a beautiful time in the Mayo Clinic.

On August 16, 1949, Ingrid received word that Ann-Marie had given birth to a daughter, Susanne, on August 9, 1949. She writes to Ann-Marie:

〰 I was so happy that I couldn't sleep. Your faithful older sister thinks about you every day. Now I'm going to buy some cute dresses for Susanne [Ann-Marie's daughter]. In Colorado I bought 3 dresses for a 1-year old that I sent back with Edgar to Dallas. All American mothers feed their newborns with bottle food. The doctors suggest that [after the baby is nursed for] approximately 2 weeks. Bottle food contains same nutritional value as mother's milk.

Ingrid told me in 2009 that Dillon had been wet-nursed by a black woman when he was a newborn. She was appalled. "This [engaging the services of a wet nurse] would never happen in Sweden!"

By fall 1949 Ingrid had returned to Dallas, where she had become very much a part of our family. She stayed with us in the San Fernando

Way house or with my grandmother, "Mrs. Dillon." On November 1, 1949, Ingrid writes to Ann-Marie:

> ᏮᎡ Would you send an arrangement for candles that I can use for Lucia this year? When you send a letter to a married woman you never write the woman's first name, but the husband's initials, like: Mrs. J. L. Bussard here in America.

Santa Lucia Day is celebrated on December 13. Ingrid wrote to her parents on December 19, 1949.

> ᏮᎡ A Christmas greeting to you all. I am now working in a plastic surgery department with many thrilling facial surgeries. Tomorrow we have a Christmas party with all the doctors. I have baked ginger bread cookies. I have met many nice people. My Lucia party was a great success. I have this year decorated Sue's house in Swedish style, which was really appreciated. Baked lots of cookies. All of them eaten. Sue and

Ingrid wearing Lucia crown December 13, 1949

Jimmy are away for a big party tonight and I'm watching the
children. They are sleeping now. Susibeth really likes the
Advent calendar. She gets up every morning and opens a new
window on the calendar. Merry Christmas from Ingrid far away
in a foreign country.

The Lucia party to which Ingrid refers took place at our San Fernando
Way house. The guests were friends of Mother and Daddy. It was so warm
that the candles dripped wax into her blonde hair. It took her several
days to get it out. In addition to Lucia Day, Ingrid also introduced us
to "Tompte," the elf in a red cap who brings presents to children on
Christmas Eve. I knew Tompte before I knew Santa Claus.

Ingrid stayed in Dallas until fall 1950. Mother's friends had become
Ingrid's friends. Mother hosted a farewell party in honor of Ingrid
on October 8, 1950. Ingrid made all the cookies. She was given an
autograph book in which the guests signed their names and offered
fond farewells and standing invitations to return to Dallas. One of the
most treasured autographs in the book is that of Willie Mae Johnson, the
black maid and cook who had worked for my mother and grandmother
since the 1930s. Willie Mae taught Ingrid how to prepare southern fried
chicken. I have a treasured photo of Willie Mae and Ingrid standing
over a skillet of fried chicken in my grandmother's kitchen. In the
autograph book, Willie Mae wrote, "From a colored friend words can't
express how I will miss you and what a grand person you are. Please
come back to Texas again." Ingrid did return to Texas in the spring of
1957. More of that story later.

Edgar was in love with Ingrid. They had a brief affair while she was
in Dallas. They met at a local hotel. Her last evening in Dallas, there
was a family party at my grandmother's house on Tokalon Drive in east
Dallas, the Lakewood neighborhood. Sometime in early October 1950,
but after October 8, we marked Ingrid's last day with us. My uncle had
an RCA console phonograph that was equipped to record conversation
onto a vinyl disc. We recorded Ingrid's last evening. It begins with her
voice: "My last evening in Dallas." [She is crying.] I am there also, age

*Ingrid, Sue, Eloise at
farewell party for Ingrid
October 8, 1950*

*Ingrid learning to
prepare southern fried
chicken from Willie
Mae, summer 1949.*

three. Ingrid asked me, "Susibeth, what do you want from Sweden?" I answered, "I want a Swedish doll!" Ingrid replied, "You want a Swedish doll? I will send you a Swedish doll." Of course, she did. The recording is lost.

Ingrid's departure on HMS *Queen Elizabeth II* from New York in October 1950 began a long correspondence (1950–1967) with my mother, my grandmother, my uncle Ed, and my father. Ingrid saved many of the letters that members of my family wrote to her.

Ingrid told me Edgar came to Sweden in 1956 to propose to her and persuade her to come back to the US with him as his wife. She turned him down. Ingrid told me in 2004, "I could not marry him. He was sick, you see. But he was a good lover." The rest of the story is chronicled in the letters written to Ingrid by my mother, Sue; my grandmother Ruth; and my uncle Ed from 1950 until early 1960. After Mother's death in 1960, the story moves forward in letters written by my father to Ingrid. Years later letters between Ingrid and me complete the story until her death in 2012.

EPISTOLARY RELATIONSHIP BETWEEN INGRID AND MY FAMILY (Grandmother Mrs. Ruth Dillon, Mother Sue Bussard, Uncle Edgar Dillon): 1950–1952

The early letters between Ingrid and members of my family—Mother, Grandmother Ruth, Uncle Edgar—began in the fall of 1950. Ingrid saved the letters my family wrote to her, but the letters she wrote back have not survived. Judging from the fawning tone of the letters from my family, Ingrid must have been grateful for the physical distance that separated her from us and which allowed her to keep an emotional distance as well. After I was grown, Ingrid shared with me many details of the family dynamic she observed in Texas.

A letter from my grandmother, posted sometime in November 1950 and dated "Friday," furnishes a detailed account of my uncle Edgar's serious health problems. He had suffered from tuberculosis during the late 1930s and into the 1940s, which left adhesions and scar tissue in his lungs. Uncle Ed was also a smoker. In November 1950 he was treated for a pneumothorax (collapsed lung).

⚭ Dear Ingrid,

Edgar appreciated your card that he received from you today from France and I enjoyed your letter very much that you wrote on the boat [*Queen Elizabeth II*].

Edgar came home from the hospital today. They have been trying pneumothorax on him and it hasn't worked, so Dr. Chapman told him to come home and stay ten days or two weeks until his air all get out, then they will do something else. It seems he has so many adhesions. They may have to operate and remove a rib then give it to him again. If they do that Dr. Shaw will do it. If they remove the rib, they will cut the adhesions so they can force the lung down with air. Oh me, he doesn't know whether he will consent to that or not and I don't blame him. However I am not saying anything. I am going to let him make up his own mind. He told Sue he believed he would go to Arizona instead, so it remains to be seen what he will do.

In late October 1950, just days after Ingrid had departed for Sweden, my family moved from the house on San Fernando Way, which had a huge yard, a screened sleeping porch, floor furnaces, and only one bathroom, to a new house on 7124 Westlake Drive, which had a yard large enough to play in, a screened back porch, central heat, two bedrooms, and two bathrooms. Dillon and I shared a bedroom. He was three; I was five. The living room had a fireplace. The house was located just about three blocks from Grandmother's house on Tokalon. Within weeks of moving into the Westlake house, Mother and Daddy oversaw the first of two remodels to the property: converting the screened back porch into large den with a fireplace. The Christmas tree was placed in the new den in 1950.

One of the features of the new house was that the ductwork required to support central air conditioning had been installed when the house was built. We used the central heat in the winter of 1950–51, then suffered through the heat of the summer 1951. That was the summer both Dillon and I contracted the mumps. There was an attic fan in the house that helped some, but I will never forget how miserable I felt in the summer heat of 1951.

In January 1952, Mother and Daddy contracted for a second remodel of the Westlake house. The kitchen in the front became a bedroom for Dillon. The den became the kitchen, with a fireplace conversation pit at the opposite end. A short hall perpendicular to the dining/TV room and a longer hall that ran between the living room and two bedrooms was walled off to become two walk-in closets. Before the summer of 1952, Daddy had central air conditioning installed. An eight-foot wooden cooling tower constructed on a concrete slab in the back yard gave off misty spray whenever the unit was in service. The aromatic mint and flowers planted in the bed next to the cooling tower thrived. By spring of 1952, our house emerged cozy perfect for our family of four! I remember well the pecan tree under which Daddy built a sandbox for Dillon and me, and the fruit (peach) trees across the back fence. The strawberries were tiny.

Ruth wrote to Ingrid in November 1950.

   Sue has moved at last but is not straight yet by any means. They are going crazy about the central heat. It is so nice for the children and aren't you and I glad? Now the babies will stay warm. Each room in the house is the same temperature day and night. They have a pecan tree and some fruit trees in their backyard as well as a bed of strawberries. They are also glad to have an extra bath. Robbie helped me so much to pack your Xmas box. She put in two packages and in addition to that she sent the marsh mallows, the instant coffee, the prunes, the Kleenex and the chocolate syrup, and chili tomatoes. Please write to her and she'll be so glad to hear from you.

The following letter to Ingrid is from "Robbie" Lora Robertson, a colleague who worked with Ingrid at Baylor, and is dated December 10, 1950. Robbie was also a good friend to Mother. Only Two pages survive.

   Poor Mrs. Dillon is so worried about Edgar for as you

know he is not doing any good. Since you left he has been in
Baylor, Dr Chapman tried to start him on the pneumothorax
treatment but he could only take several of the treatments as
he had too many adhesions in the cavity so now Mrs. D. tell me
the Dr. recommends they go in and sever the adhesions which
would mean to cut one or two ribs besides, so that they are
undecided what they really are going to do. Edgar left Tuesday
afternoon for Tucson, Arizona, said he was going to have one
more fling at a good time before he got where he could not do
such. When he left he was to be gone six weeks but Mrs. D told
me the other night she thought she would try to get Edgar to
stay until spring then come back when the weather is better
and maybe by that time he could do what Dr. C wants to do yet
she really doesn't want any surgery done. Of course I feel that
if Edgar doesn't start to try and cooperate with the Dr. he is
really done for, you know as well as I he is not going to do this.

On top of all this Sue moved. Mrs. D looks so bad that she
cannot sleep at night, Mrs. Potter [Grandmother's friend,
nicknamed "Byrd"] has been staying over there with her. Says
she would rather stay at home instead of Sue's as she can be
quiet. I talked with Sue when I received your letter and said
she was only partly straightened up guess she would not get it
all done before Xmas. Seemingly likes the new place yet don't
care for the outside of the house the plans are they are going
to paint it in the spring. I will go over to see them some time
during the holidays.

They all have really missed you more ways than you can
imagine. Sue said Susibeth was getting such a thrill out of the
cards you sent them to put in the window [Advent calendars
from Sweden]. You should have seen her on Hallowe'en night
they had a funny nose and a mask on her and she went around
in the neighborhood playing "Trick or treat." She was so cute
and seemed to enjoy it so much of course this was the first
year she could take part in such [I was three]. Think Sue will
really enjoy the new neighborhood as the people who live in

it are so social and friendly. I know several of them and it is so convenient to her mother's just two streets north of us so about three blocks to walk.

Sue wrote to Ingrid on December 20, 1950, on a manual Royal typewriter that she loved to use rather than writing in longhand. She typed single-spaced letters on onionskin paper to save on overseas postage. It took seven to ten days for letters to make the postal journey between the US and Sweden.

ᏀᏌ My dearest Ingrid:

Your wonderful letter of the 12th arrived yesterday, and how good it was to hear from you! I have wanted so many times to sit down and write you one just as long, but I have never been so busy in all my life. I really think the reason I have been so "snowed under" is that I had just become too

Dillon, age one, and Susibeth, age three, Christmas 1950

used to having you around. I see a thousand things every week that you always did for me, and I am still appreciating you more and more and more. Even when it came time to decorate for Christmas, it was so hard to do it without your wonderful enthusiasm to urge me on. You would be shocked to see how little I have done, Ingrid, but I have really had my hands full. The mantle is real pretty, though, with the little Swedish dolls standing in the middle, the lovely glockenspiel, or whatever you call that beautiful thing on one end, and the lovely red angel on the other. We shall try to take some pictures if we are all well. Right now Dillon and I are a little puny with virus and slight colds. I haven't seen Susibeth in three days, as Grandmother took her over there to try to keep her well.

I had my Christmas Cantata at the White Rock Methodist Church Sunday night, and I am so glad that is over. It was very good, if I do say so. Everybody said it was the best program they had ever had. However, I am resigning as of Jan. 1st, as Jimmy is so much busier with his new responsibilities as General Manager [of Dillon Scale & Equipment Co.] that I just can't do anything right now but run the household. He still continues to bring in the big orders, and I am so proud of him. Our new sales manager is wonderful, too, so if the war in Korea doesn't ruin us all, we should do all right. It certainly looks bad, don't it!

Ingrid, we are really worried about you since you wrote us about your friend coming to Paris to meet you, etc. Now why in the world haven't I heard about this guy! You just write and give me all the low-down! You remember you said you would never marry a man who would not travel with you, so if you do marry, have it put in the ceremony that he must agree to come to Dallas to live, or else it is all off!!! And don't forget you promised me that you would come back. [Mother refers to the Swedish man to whom Ingrid was engaged for a short time.]

I called Sara Everett and told her what you said about her Paris relatives, and of course she was pleased. She said,

however, that she had never heard about what you did with her
New York relatives, so tell me that in your next letter so that I
may tell her. She and her husband have invited Jimmy and me
to the New Year's Eve party at the Lakewood Country Club, but
I don't know whether we will go or not. We sat at the table with
them the other night at the Kiwanis dinner. Remember a year
ago when you took our pictures at 2:00 a.m. after Jimmy's
beard had become a little heavy! I wore my new "wedding
dress" as Susie calls it, as it was very warm that night, and
I felt real dressed up. We surely thought of you on Lucia too,
Ingrid, and I had hoped we could be straight enough to have
some friends over, but I just couldn't do it. I am having some
Dutch curtains in white organdy made for the bay window,
and they are supposed to be here by Christmas. Hope so. I still
don't have my dishwasher, nor do I have my Bendix connected
yet due to faulty concrete in the garage. I also have ordered
a Connsonata organ similar to the one I had at your party,
but two manuals instead of one. Isn't that wonderful! I am
supposed to get it in February.

I am certainly not ready for Christmas. Haven't bought
Mother or Edgar a thing, and don't know what to get. We got
Susie a darling doll bed just like a real baby bed, a baby buggy,
big inexpensive baby doll—but beautiful—and we got Dillon a
black lamb that plays Baa-baa Black Sheep when you wind it
up, a little tiny tricycle, and both of them together a nice red
wagon that they can pull each other in. I hope you received
our Christmas packages, I mailed them on Nov. 15. Tell Ann-
Marie she is just too sweet to do what she is doing for Susibeth,
and that I hope she will forgive my not getting a box off for the
children by Christmas, but I am going to send a box. I shall be
glad to send some of Susibeth's puzzles too.

I know the Nobel celebration must have been marvelous.
I don't know whether Edgar saw any of the pictures or not.
He went to Phoenix about two weeks ago, but stayed only one
week, as he couldn't rest or eat. He has received the pills to

ease him, and he is so grateful to you all for them. He went to
the doctor this morning, and they are supposed to run some
sort of sedimentation test on him, as he is in pain from his
head to his foot, and they don't seem to know why. Bless his
heart. I haven't even seen him since last Friday night when he
came in.

I know Ockie and Susanne are adorable. They are just like
beautiful dolls in their pictures. Thanks so much for sending
them. Tell Ockie that Susibeth is really enjoying opening the
"lee windows" [on the Advent calendar from Sweden] every
morning. She gets to open Dillon's too, but I told her next year
she would have to let Dillon open them himself. Bless his heart,
he still has only 4 teeth! When do you suppose he will ever get
any more? He is saying a lot of words now and says "Iny" every
day. The other day Mother and I were talking about you, and he
looked up from his play and said your name with his sweetest
smile. He is so pretty. I weighed them both the other day at the
office. He weighs 28 and Susibeth 31.

Ingrid, I must tell you about my big thrill the other day. You
remember my prettiest dishes with all the roses on them? You
may remember that they were Japanese copies of a Bavarian
pattern that I had bought 13 years ago [in 1937] at Kress. Of
course I had given up ever being able to finish the set. Well,
I was down town Saturday morning and when I got to Kress'
window, there was a window full of them. My heart nearly
pounded out of me; I was so thrilled. I went in and bought
enough to complete a set of 12 of everything. Isn't it exciting!
Anna has the same pattern, so I called her and she did the
same. I don't know when I shall ever be as excited again until
you come back, Ingrid!

I hear Dillon waking up, so must quit for now, Ingrid.
Remember we all love you so much over here, miss you terribly
and are expecting you back real soon. Better not wait too long!
Worlds of hugs and kisses.

    Sue

I remember Dillon's baby talk: orange juice was "or-nah-noo," the electric streetcars were "geet-geet cars," a train was "doo-doo-dah," the dinner party paddleboat on White Rock Lake, named the *Bonnie Barge*, he called "bah-wah-bee-wee."

Mother died in 1960; we moved from Westlake in 1964. The Bavarian china dishes were packed for storage carelessly. When I unpacked the dishes some thirty years later, most of them were broken.

All Mother's letters to Ingrid plead for her to come back to Dallas. I wonder if Mother had a premonition how much she would need her best friend in the years to come.

Ingrid and my uncle Edgar corresponded regularly in 1951. He was undergoing treatment for tuberculosis, which he had contracted in 1935 when he was in his twenties. He faced life-threatening surgery. He traveled frequently to Colorado Springs and Arizona to see if the dry air of the mountains and desert would help him feel better, i.e. breathe easier. It didn't.

Ingrid returned to Sweden in the fall of 1950, but my family's connection to her was never to be severed. My father and my uncle sponsored other Swedes who wanted to come to the US for schooling and job opportunities. The first among them was the oldest son of Bishop Bo Giertz, Lars Giertz. We called him Lasse. He emigrated to the US in 1951, attended Southern Methodist University in Dallas, served in the Army of the United States in Korea, became an American citizen, married a Texas girl, and raised a family.

Uncle Edgar continued treatment at Penrose Saint Francis Hospital in Colorado Springs after undergoing unsuccessful surgery to remove tubercular lesions and to restore a collapsed lung. He made contacts with Southern Methodist University (SMU) on behalf of Lars "Lasse" Giertz.

March 10, 1951

〜 Dear Ingrid—

I received the letter from Lasse Giertz and wrote him today. I am having information sent to him from SMU here in Dallas. I talked to the dean there and he says that their engineering school is very good and they offer plenty of courses he might want for at least two years. If you think he would like Dallas, I'll go ahead and may even be able to get him a scholarship. SMU has 18 scholarships available each year for foreign students but about 4 or 5 times as many requests for them. If these are all taken up, it may be possible because of his father's position. They offer a few scholarships for ministers' sons.

As you have heard, I had my operation but it did not turn out as they had planned. Instead of an air space above the left lung, I have fluid which has the lung compressed about 50% from the top.

I am going back to Colorado Springs next Monday and stay in the hospital till around June. The doctor says I can get up then and stay somewhere else.

You must be busy because we don't hear from you very often. Take a day off and write to me (on the typewriter if you can) the address is on this letter (Penrose St. Francis). I am glad you had Lasse write me and I'll do all I can for him. If there's anyone else that might come with him, he might not get so homesick in America.

As ever, Edgar

Letter from Ed Dillon to Ingrid, from Penrose Saint Francis Hospital, Colorado Springs:

April 20, 1951
❧ Dear Ingrid—
I know you enjoyed the trip home and I wish I could have been with you in Paris. Maybe I can get there someday if I ever get well enough.

My real problem now is the fact that I still have a cavity on my right side but can't do anything about it except rest. I will be a long time getting over the operation I had in January. I plan on staying in the hospital here until July anyway and maybe longer if the doctor thinks best. On top of everything else, I took the intestinal flu more than two weeks ago and have had no appetite. I have lost seven pounds since I got the flu and that is too much.

I had a letter from Mother today and she said that Sue had just received a letter from you. They read between the lines that you might come back this winter. If Dallas and Sweden were closer together maybe you wouldn't have such a decision to make. You know that you're always welcome in Dallas and everyone is really looking forward to your return.

You might assure Lasse's father that we certainly will see that Lasse is well taken care of if he comes to Dallas. I'm sorry I can't do more for him right now but I believe the dean at SMU will advise him properly about his mathematics, etc. I had a letter from Lasse a few days ago and will write him again soon. I get behind on my correspondence since the flu. Just haven't felt like doing anything, I've been so weak.

Johnnie Johnson got a new car [a Nash] just before I left Dallas and he was thrilled to death. He always said that the two things he wanted after coming to this country was one trip back home to Sweden and a new car—so now he has both.

I will look forward to some pictures of Gothenburg this spring. I know it must be pretty there.

I showed Lasse's letters to a young girl patient who is just down the hall from me and she said she would like to write to him. I gave her his address and she promised to write him soon. She's only 21 and has been in bed five years now with T.B. She's from Waco, Tx about 100 miles south of Dallas. One of the patients I knew last summer died shortly after surgery the first of this year.

If there's anything I can send you from the U.S. that you can't get there, please don't hesitate to ask. Food is very high here also since the Korean situation. The quality of the food served here at the hospital is not as good as it was last summer, particularly the meats. There is an acute shortage of nurses everywhere, even worse than when you were here as so many are going into the service. We have no students on our division—just old women. You should get some of your nurse friends there interested in coming here to help the situation. I wouldn't recommend Baylor though.

Don't wait so long to write next time and hurry back! Love. Edgar

This letter speaks to Edgar's own understanding of the seriousness of his condition. Ingrid must have felt pressured from him and especially my mother to return to the US. However, even though Ingrid felt a strong bond to my mother and her family, her life and career were in Sweden. She chose not to respond to my family's pitiful pleas. Uncle Ed did make a trip to Europe and Sweden in 1956, Ingrid did return to the US for a visit to Dallas in 1957, and Mother and I made a trip to Sweden in 1959. More about all that later.

Mother wrote/typed a letter to Ingrid, dated February 13, 1952, about the TV show *Playbill*, mutual friends, her first party in the new house, and family news. *Playbill* was produced for twelve weeks in the summer and fall of 1951 with Elizabeth Peabody. Mother played her Connsonata organ, and Elizabeth told the story and sang the songs of Broadway musicals. Mother and Elizabeth would attend the dress rehearsals of the Dallas Summer Musical season at the State Fair Music Hall in Dallas. Before opening night, Mother and Elizabeth performed an eleven-minute review on live TV of the musical that was in town for its ten-day run. From early 1951 through late 1959, Mother and Elizabeth performed for ladies clubs throughout the Dallas–Fort Worth area. Mother also played for fashion shows. Elizabeth was the emcee/commentator. As a child, I modeled in several shows and was paid five dollars a show.

   My dearest Ingrid—

It is early, and I shall try to at least begin a letter to you before the children wake up and want their breakfast. I have wanted to write you for so long, but I have been so busy, and get busier all the time, it seems. I am playing so many fashion

shows, and I just love it. My television programs are over, and
I am glad to have had the experience. There is too much work
involved for the little money you get.

I am sending you a new picture of the children. The man
who did it advertises on TV and wants to show their picture on
a day when I can take them both down so they can appear with
the picture. Susibeth is so thrilled over it. [That photo hangs
in my bedroom: a professional photo of me, age five, and my
brother Dillon, age three. It faces a photo of our mother, Sue,
age five, and her brother, Edgar, age three.]

Ingrid, Dr. Morris [Mother's OB-GYN doctor, whom Ingrid
worked with at Baylor] has had some pretty tough luck. He
had a spinal fusion operation and is still unable to go to his
office more than an hour or so a day. While he was the sickest
his son's wife had a baby and it died. Of all the babies to lose, it
would have to be that one.

Eloise Pavey and her family plan to move to South America
for about a year and a half. They will go sometime this fall. Her
husband is gone so much, and I just don't blame her. She is
expecting her third one in June. Mildred Watson lost her baby
right after Christmas, Robbie told us that it was twins, a boy
and a girl. I don't know whether Mildred knows that or not. I
felt so sorry for them, as they particularly wanted a girl. We
haven't seen their new home yet, but I think it is real nice.

Little Docka Stubblefield is a real Swedish doll. She is
beautiful. When I was by the other day she was ill with the flu.
My children had it too, as did most everybody except Jimmy
and me. Stubby lost his father the first part of this month.
[Docka Stubblefield, one of Ingrid's babies when she worked a
maternity rotation at Baylor in 1949, and I played together as
children.]

Took Jimmy to the airport the other day and had a few
minutes before I was to meet Mrs. Roberts at the Neiman-
Marcus tea room [The Zodiac] for lunch, so went to see the
Wharton's. They were just driving out the driveway, so I went

with her to take him to work, and we had a nice visit. They, too, have just finished remodeling. They made the living room a lot longer, added a new porch (made out of the terrace) and another bedroom upstairs. It is really nice. They seemed so glad to see me and of course wanted to know all about you. Everyone is so eager for you to come back, Ingrid.

The New Year's Eve party at Stubblefields was wonderful, and Austin showed a lot of pictures; included in them were beautiful color slides of you. Stubby played that crazy recording we made of you and Jimmy and Margaret Blocker. Remember it?

Ingrid, I gave my first party on Sunday since you left Dallas. I hosted an open house for my neighbors, about 35, and how I missed you. I made 5 dozen cookies, but I bought the rest. Ingrid, you would just love my neighbors, much friendlier than the ones in Forest Hills.

Ingrid, Ed had asked us not to tell anyone that he was to be operated on so don't mention it in a letter to him or Mother. He may not mind your knowing it, but I just don't know. You know how peculiar he is. He is so depressed and worried about himself. Dr. Shaw said he might have to take out part of the lower lobe of the right lung too. I just don't see how we can go through it with him again. Bill and Nina Dickinson [Bill was pastor of Highland Park Methodist Church, spoke at Mother's funeral, friend and counselor to Daddy] are going to Alaska in the middle of March on a missionary trip. They will be gone about sixteen days and her sister will stay with the children. They are so thrilled. She is the cutest thing. Said she ordered long handled underwear from Montgomery-Ward yesterday. The church presented them with a new Chrysler last week; they are really thrilled about that, too. And they could keep their old car too.

I think this is about all the news, except that Anna Wortham was operated on last Monday for gall bladder and a lot of stones. She is doing fine but can't go home until Jess gets over the flu. Betty is going with a man who is divorced and has two children the ages of mine. Anna and Jess are both so worried about it but know it will do no good to interfere. He is her first real boyfriend and is really rushing her off her feet.

Wish you could see the children. They are so big and pretty and sweet. Please write real soon. Love to you and all your family. Sue

I attended Betty's wedding to Earl James with Mother and Daddy and Dillon at Cliff Temple Baptist Church in Dallas, Texas. Mother played the organ. I remember the children, Steve and Beverly..

On March 10, 1955, Betty wrote to Ingrid at Mother and Grandmother's request, as they were both ill: "My children, Steve 7 and Beverly, 6 are precious, you would really fall in love with them. They are my pride and joy. I am kept very busy. My husband is wonderful. So sweet

Susibeth, age 5, and Sue, age 38, in Mother's Day dresses, 1952

and precious. I am very anxious for you to know him." I remember we
dropped in on the James family shortly after they had moved to surprise
them with a housewarming. Betty looked terrible. Earl turned out to
be abusive. He and Betty divorced shortly thereafter.

A long letter from Mother to Ingrid on November 11, 1952:

   ᘊ Dearest Ingrid:

Be sure you have an hour or so to give this, as both Ruth
and Sue are going to be talking to you for quite some time. We
had just decided that you had forgotten your old Texas friends,
when along came your wonderful letter. We have read it and
re-read it and are so very happy to know that you still feel like
you might even like to come back over here sometime. We just
couldn't bear to think that maybe you would not be coming.
Of course, we would love to come to Sweden, but unless our
financial condition improves a lot more than we anticipate, I'm
afraid you will have to do the visiting. [There was an economic
recession in the 1950s. Business was slow, and Uncle Ed was a
drag on the productivity of the business.]

First, the young lady you mentioned who wants to come to
the U.S., please send us her name immediately, and we shall be
glad to send the necessary statement. We would be so thrilled
to have her and would be more than glad to send the letter
for her. [My father and uncle wrote letters of sponsorship for
several Swedes who found us through Ingrid. This one was
Barbro Weber from Växjö. She and Ingrid's sister, Ann-Marie,
were school friends. When Barbro became depressed after
being jilted at the altar in Sweden, Ingrid persuaded her to
come to the US to recover.]

When does she want to come? We hope it is soon. We sent
such a statement for Tott Petterson, Lasse's girlfriend. Did
you know that she came over here this summer? She was a
perfectly adorable girl, Ingrid, and we were so sorry that she
stayed only two months. She said she was going to look you
up and give you all the latest from the Dillon's and Bussard's

if she ever came to Malmö. I know you would just love her,
Ingrid, and we would be so happy to know you two had met.
[Gerd "Tott" Petterson was from Göteborg. She and Lasse
broke up before she returned to Sweden. Mother and I saw her
briefly in 1959 and then we lost touch.]

Susibeth is so thrilled to hear about little Susanne's naming
her doll for her. When I told her she just smiled and said, "Now
wasn't that sweet!" Which reminds me that when Mother
[my grandmother Ruth] gave her a beautiful big doll for her
birthday, as soon as she took her out of the box, she gave her a
big hug and kiss and said, "I'm going to name you Ingrid!" So
you see, Susibeth has not forgotten you. She and Dillon both
pray for Ockie, Susanne, and all the nice people in Sweden, and
of course Ingrid and Tott every night.

Lasse is doing just fine. Mother read every word of your
letter to him last night on the phone, and he was so thrilled
to hear from you. He received his scholarship again this fall
and is studying very hard. He doesn't come over as much as
he did last year because of course he is better acquainted, and
his car is not running right now. He is a very sweet boy. [Lasse
(Lars) eventually dropped out of college and was drafted into
the Arm, where he became a communications officer. After
he came back to the US, married, and moved to Houston, I
saw him briefly in 1972. He died in a crash of his own plane in
1990. His widow and grown children live in Texas.]

Louise Boynton is pregnant with her third one. [Her first
was one of Ingrid's babies.] She wants a girl so very badly,
and I hope she makes it this time. All the rest of the gang are
fine. I haven't talked to Eloise in a long time, but every time I
do talk to her or any of the others they always ask about you.
Mr. Everett's business had a big explosion and fire a couple of
Sundays ago, but it was very well covered by insurance, the
papers said. [Monkey Grip, Everett's tire company, was one of
Dillon Scale's clients.]

You can't imagine how happy we are about Eisenhower's

winning the election. The women of America are largely
responsible for it, Ingrid, and I for one worked pretty hard for
Ike. We mothers just would like to think of our boys growing up
for something besides fighting soldiers, for one thing. Of course,
there was more than that at stake. We are so proud of Texas,
as it went Republican for the first time in my lifetime. [Mother
had her photo taken with Richard Nixon during the campaign
in 1952, and she campaigned for Republican congressman
Bruce Alger in 1954.]

And we are so proud of you, Ingrid! We know how hard you
have worked and are so happy that you have reached your
goal in your profession. The shortage of nurses continues over
here. I shall try to get some literature from the new Baylor
to send you, as you might like to see it. Incidentally, while I
think of it, Ingrid, I remember you saying that you couldn't
use our typewriters over here. Well, Lasse can write like
lightning on them, and he says there are only about two keys
different from yours. [Ingrid completed her degree in 1951 at
Lund University, *Lunds universitet* in Swedish, called *Hälso
och sjukvårdsadministration*, in English, health, and medical
administration. She never mastered the typewriter to compose
in English. Her handwriting was always a challenge to read.]

I went to see Dr. Morris the other day for my yearly check-
up. He is doing a lot better. He had a hard time for a while. He
asked about you, too. He put me on half a grain of thyroid, as
he said my skin was too dry. Other than that, I believe I am
O.K. You wouldn't know me. Everybody who hasn't seen me for
a year or so remarks about how much weight I have lost. I wear
a size 12 now.

Ingrid, I have found the most marvelous hair lightener that
you might like to have. I have lightened my hair to the same
pretty color it was when I was in college. It is just a clear lotion
that you apply to your hair any time you want to. You don't
even have to wash it first—just apply it and let it dry. With
putting it on only twice I have my hair as light as I want it.

It is put up by Richard Hunt and is called "Light and Bright." If you would like for me to send you some, I will be glad to. It doesn't do anything at all to your hair except to make it softer and easier to manage. You don't even have to be careful about getting it on your clothes, as it is perfectly clear. It is truly marvelous. It will lighten anyone's hair at least four shades.

We are so sorry that Ockie has been sick. I know he and Susanne must be perfectly adorable. I wish I had a lot of money, Ingrid, I would certainly send them loads of gifts from America. If you think Ann-Marie would like, I will send her some of the things Susibeth has outgrown. She has a winter coat that she has outgrown that is still good, and Susanne might wear it for second best. I also have some dresses. I doubt that I have anything Ockie would want but shall send him something from America in the box. The little coat is bright green—about the shade of your green coat you bought over here, maybe a little lighter, trimmed in dark green velvet.

Jimmy [Daddy] and I were at the Fair [the State Fair of Texas] one night and met Mrs. Roberts [not Robbie of earlier letters] and the Swedish Consul from Houston. He was so very nice and most gallant. Mrs. Roberts has been pretty sick with a virus too, but I talked to her just last week and she was all right. She says she is going to call me to play for her sometime at some of her clubs. I am really busy, Ingrid, I played for a style show at the Woman's Forum on Thursday. I just wish I had not been so tied down when you were here, Ingrid, as we could have had so much fun together. You must come back, Ingrid, and give me a chance to really be a hostess to you. It makes me shudder every time I think of how hard you worked at my house for me and mine!

Mother is doing pretty well, though she has quite a bit of discomfort from her heart [angina]. Her doctor says she just must not ever hurry again. She was hurrying the other Sunday to go to Fort Worth with us and had a pretty hard "spell" [heart attack]. The children had never been on a train, so Jimmy took us to the depot and put us on the streamliner train, then met us an hour later in Fort Worth. Dillon had his little nose flat against the window all the way looking at everything. Susibeth enjoyed it in an entirely different way. She had taken Martha, one of her smaller dolls with her, and she held her on her lap all the way, and wouldn't raise up to look out at anything, as she was afraid she might disturb her baby. She is a really good little mother. She gets more like Mother every day.

We are looking forward to meeting Lasse's father this Spring. He told Mother that his mother wasn't doing too well. We are so sorry to hear it. Ingrid, please try not to wait so long to write us ever again, as we mention you every day and just hope and pray for the day when you will come back. I had the most wonderful airplane dreams the other night and they went from there to your home. I thought it all looked just like I had thought it would, and we were eating a lot of your wonderful goodies. Ingrid, do you suppose you could send me your "peppacocka" [sic] recipe? Susibeth just begs me to make it for her. Please excuse all the errors, but the children and Mother are all three standing around telling me what to do, and Dillon and Susibeth asking me all about the typewriter, etc. Hope you can understand it, at least, and know that we all love you, and we do want you to come back as soon as you possibly can!

Worlds of love and kisses from us all, Sue

Grandmother and I wrote a note on the letter in longhand. The first part is from me at age five: "Dear Ingrid, This is Susibeth writing. I am over at grandmother's this afternoon. I am looking forward to coming to see you dear Ingrid. I also would love to see Ockie and Susanne too. I have not forgotten you. Love always. SUSIBETH" [My *S*'s are backward.] Grandmother continues: "Ingrid, I loved your letter. It was so newsy. Please do not wait so long to write again. This letter is from me too."

In the year 1952, Grandmother suffered at least one heart attack— but she was not being treated effectively. There was not much the doctors could do for heart patients in the 1950s, except to prescribe nitroglycerin for angina. As Mother wrote, "She must not hurry." I can't help but wish to read Ingrid's "newsy" letter to which Uncle Ed and Mother responded in November 1952.

In January 1953, before I was to start school in September, our family embarked on a road trip west to visit Daddy's parents, Mama Grace and Papa Bill, in Tucson, Arizona. I was five; Dillon was three. We spent a few days in Grand Canyon National Park. We stayed in Bright Angel Lodge in the park. Mother remarked, "What a heavenly place!" After visiting Grand Canyon and the grandparents, we stopped at a resort in Phoenix, where Uncle Ed was "taking the cure" on the company's dime. I remember that the Arizona desert country was warm in January. The next year, 1954, perhaps at Daddy's urging, Mama Grace and Papa Bill Bussard moved from the desert landscape of Tucson, Arizona, to the humidity and tree-lined streets of Dallas, Texas. Then, after only a year in Dallas, they moved back to Tucson. Papa Bill complained that he couldn't see the sky. Both of them were in declining health.

The years 1953 and 1954 were rife with challenging developments. Uncle Ed's unending search for a cure of his lung disease put a strain on the finances of Dillon Scale, Grandmother's heart disease advanced, and Mother received her first breast cancer diagnosis.

LIVING WITH BREAST CANCER
AND HEART DISEASE
IN THE 1950s

I started school in September 1953. Mother and Daddy had moved from Forest Hills to Lakewood because Dallas ISD was building a new elementary school about a mile from where our new house was located on Westlake Drive. As public kindergarten was not offered by Dallas ISD in 1953, Grandmother taught both Dillon and me the alphabet, how to count to one hundred, and how to print our names. I was enrolled in Mrs. Allen's first grade class at Lakewood Elementary School in September 1953; Dillon followed in 1955. I remember the self-contained classroom with an attached bathroom for the students. I remember the tiny desks for twenty students in rows. I remember the blackboard on which Mrs. Allen printed the story we were to copy and illustrate. I remember that there were funny marks (punctuation) interspersed within the text. I chose to ignore those marks and just copy the letters. Whether or not a first grader noticed the punctuation and copied it accurately seemed to determine the difference between "satisfactory" and "outstanding" progress on the report card. I remember reading groups. The class worked on the "story" lesson for the day while

groups of five students sat in a reading circle with Mrs. Allen to read
Dick and Jane stories out loud. If we completed class work before our
reading group was called up, we were allowed to visit one of the "play"
stations in the classroom. My favorite was the rather large dollhouse,
populated by miniature figures that reflected the 1950s white middle-
class culture in which we all lived. There was even a black maid figure
dressed in her gray uniform with a white apron. The year 1953 was good
for me and Dillon, not so much for my parents. I remember that Daddy
worked very hard. Uncle Ed was back in Dallas, drawing a salary from
the company but not doing any work. Mother and Elizabeth played lots
of gigs for the Woman's Forum and various ladies clubs in Dallas. No
letters between Ingrid and my family have survived for the year 1953.
During that year, Mother was seeing her doctor about a lump in her
right breast and a mass in her left breast. Shortly before Mother's first
cancer surgery in 1954, Daddy sat me and Dillon down and told us,
"Mother has a lump in her right breast, so the doctor will take it out to
see what it means. She will be home in a few days." Up to that time,
Dillon and I had enjoyed a care-free childhood. Our family life changed
profoundly after Mother's diagnosis.

Mother wrote to Ingrid on Saturday, April 24, 1954. I was six years
old; Dillon was four.

൏ Dearest Ingrid:

In February I asked my cousin Betty James to write to you
about all our bad luck in the Dillon family, and since I have not
heard from you, I am assuming you did not get the letter (she
said she sent it Air Mail) or else you or some of your family
have been ill. I hope the latter is not true!

So forgive me if I am repeating anything but thought you
might like to know a little more than she told you anyway.
On Monday Feb. 22, 1954 I had a tumor removed from my
right breast at Gaston Hospital, and the surgeon, Dr. John
Goode, was very surprised to find that it was malignant. So
the next morning I returned to the operating room for three
and a half hours and had my right breast removed plus the

two big muscles below and the fifteen glands under my arm. When Mother learned that I was going to have that done she had a very severe heart attack, and they brought her in to the hospital while I was in the operating room. Luckily she and I were too sick to worry about each other, but poor Ed and Jimmy really had a rough time of it for a while. I got along fine after the first couple of days, however, and was able to come home after ten days.

Mother [Ruth] stayed in hospital three weeks. I am just now beginning to feel like myself again, and I am not having to have the usual follow-up X-ray, as all the glands removed from under my arm were clear. I am sure you understand all about that.

Then to complicate things Ed sold the house on Tokalon while we were in the hospital, so as soon as I was able to get my clothes on and ride in the car I had to help Ed find a house for Mother to buy. She did not want to rent an apartment, as Ed did. But I think he is going to enjoy the new home as much as she. She is 1¼ miles north of me at 6730 Blue Valley Lane. It is a darling little 3-bedroom, 2-bath, air conditioning, dishwasher, etc. only two years old. It was built by a couple for a home and it is really a wonderful little house with lots of storage, and a small but pretty yard. It is an Early American type, and Mother's furniture looks lovely in it. I only wish Mother could get well enough to enjoy it, but she isn't yet. She hasn't driven her car in two years. Imagine it!

Ingrid, tell Ockie and Susanne that Susibeth and Dillon surely enjoyed the darling little calendars, and they are so happy about their little new baby brother. [Thomas Lundqvist, Ann-Marie's third child, was born in 1954.] We shall certainly see that he gets a stocking like theirs.

We have a little new puppy. Jimmy and I have fought it for a long time, but we finally had to come to it this past week. He is a darling little toy terrier and he doesn't cry at night, so we are thankful for that. He is not going to be a house dog. [Dillon

named our dog "Inky." He lived in our backyard for a time.
Daddy even built a doghouse. However, the rule that Inky could
NOT be a house dog severely impacted his quality of life. We
ended up giving Inky to Wiley, a warehouse worker at Dillon
Scale.]

I hope you are feeling all right, Ingrid. We are sorry that you
haven't been well, either, and trust that Ann-Marie's family as
well as your parents are all fine.

I know you are terribly busy, Ingrid, but do try to drop
us just a little note, as we are so lonesome for you. Harold
Johnson [Ingrid's cousin who worked for Dillon Scale] was
out the other day and Mother told him that we surely wish
you would come back. If you can't right now, do you know
somebody who might come? They would never be as nice
as you, but they might do until you could get here! [I am
embarrassed at my mother's presumption that Ingrid should
come to Dallas or send "somebody" to take care of our family.]

Eloise Pavey has built a beautiful great big mansion of a
house over close to me on this side of the lake [a rancher near
White Rock Lake, two blocks from our home on Westlake].
They are really wealthy people now. They have three boys and
a girl. They even have a swimming pool, and she has asked
me to bring the kids over a lot this summer, which I certainly
intend to do, as I do not like for them to go in the public pools.
[During the polio epidemic of the summer of 1954, it was
thought that the virus was spread among children in public
swimming pools.] You should see her house! She came by one
day and asked me to go by to see it, as it was almost complete.
She said, "Sue, you look tired", and when I told her that I was
just out of the hospital she nearly fainted. I thought Dr. Morris
would tell her about me, but he hadn't, and she felt so bad that
she had not known. But you can't imagine how wonderful my
neighbors were, Ingrid. They just took charge of all the meals
here for my family and Ed every evening and ten evenings
after I returned from the hospital. I never knew I had so many

wonderful friends!

We will get together with the quartet bunch [the families of Ingrid's babies, all born in the summer of 1949 when she worked the maternity rotation at Baylor]. There is no particular news from them except that Dottie Stubblefield's father passed away last week.

I'm getting a little weary, as this is the first time I have typed [since surgery in February], but I just can't use a pen or pencil at all. It has not hampered my playing the organ, though, for which I am thankful.

Please write to us. All my love, Sue

Mother was discharged from the hospital the first week of March 1954. I remember coming home from school that day to find her in bed ,resting. It was very warm, as early spring can be in Dallas. I remember begging her to let me put on shorts to play outside. I was in first grade, six years old. Obviously, cancer treatment was primitive to nonexistent in the 1950s. These days a tumor like she had would be treated very aggressively, with chemo and radiation. The fact that she was diagnosed at age forty-one made her risk of not surviving even higher. From this time until Mother died on May 23, 1960, I remember her as sick in body, but she was always healthy in spirit and kept her head until the end. Grandmother, too, never fully recovered. But she never went into cardiac rehab either. Did they have such a thing in the 1950s? She died in 1958. More about that later.

Mother's next letter is dated December 12, 1954. Eight months have passed. She has recovered from the surgery enough to resume her role as wife and mother, but she is still not her former self. Also, she is looking after Grandmother, who is still not well at all.

Dearest Ingrid:

At long last I will sit myself down to write you a letter, and I am so ashamed that I have been so long. Ingrid, I have really been busy this Fall with Mother being so sick. Since we last wrote she has had another two and a half weeks in the

hospital, but she is doing better now. She is over here at my
house for a few days as Ed had to make a trip to Cleveland,
Ohio. She is in bed most of the time, but I think it has been good
for her to come up here and see something besides her own
little room.

Ingrid, I do wish you could see my home now. It is
everything I used to want. We have three bedrooms now, a
large living room, television room and huge dining-kitchen
with fireplace. We have just bought carpet for the living room,
TV room and hall in a soft shade of green to match the walls
and woodwork. About the shade of green that we had in our
den on San Fernando—remember? We miss you so much at
the Christmas season particularly, Ingrid—no pretty cookies,
decorations, etc.

Please forgive me if this letter sorta rambles around in
subject matter, as Susibeth is on one side and Dillon on the
other. They both say to thank you and Ockie and Susanne for
the lovely Advent Calendars. They still get a real thrill out of
opening the little windows. Susie says to tell Ockie that she
will write him a letter real soon. Ingrid, I haven't been able to
get any packages off to Sweden, but I will send something even
though you get it after Christmas. I am sick myself right now
with a sort of virus which I can't seem to get rid of.

Ingrid, don't you think you can possibly get back to see us
any time soon so that we will have something to look forward
to. We miss you so much and shall never get over wanting you
to come back. We are so sorry to hear of Elisabeth Giertz's
serious rheumatoid arthritis. I shall try to write the Bishop
too. I haven't even done my Christmas shopping for the family
yet, as I have been feeling so bad.

During the Fair in October I played for a big fashion show
every day, and I really do enjoy playing for that sort of thing. I
have been real busy playing my organ all this fall. I have a man
to haul it for me. I don't believe I know any news of the people
you know, except that Landon Neal's father passed away last

week. Oh yes, Sara Everett just returned from South America. She called me the other day and said that her cousins from Washington were here and she would like for me to come by to meet them, but it was the day before Thanksgiving and I was so busy. She said they had adopted a precious baby, and they knew you would be glad to hear it. I believe they were the ones who saw Paris with you. Jack Everett [Sara's brother] is still unmarried and pining his heart out for you in that great big beautiful house of his! [Jack had proposed to Ingrid before she returned to Sweden in 1950. I don't think he ever married.]

Tuesday night I am supposed to go to the Lakewood Country Club with Jimmy again to the big Kiwanis dinner-dance. Remember when you took our pictures at two o'clock in the morning. Though I am five years older, Ingrid, I am not so matronly looking as I was then, because I am not so fat!

I have forgotten when you said your sister was expecting, but I surely am thinking of her, and know how tired she gets during the last days, as you used to say. [Thomas was born in April 1954.] Hope you can see Barbro soon, as I know you two could have fun comparing notes on your Texas experiences. I surely love you and Barbro and Tott and would give anything if we could see you again. Believe me, if my ship ever comes in, the first thing I will do is get the first boat to Sweden.

Merry Christmas and the happiest of New Years! SUE

P.S. Last Christmas I gave Ed a little parakeet, and you should hear him talk. He is saying "Merry Christmas" now. He even says, "Isn't it preposterous that a little bird can talk!" I think Jimmy is going to get the Christmas tree this afternoon, and I surely wish you were here to decorate it for us.

* * *

On the back flap of the air letter, Dillon penciled, "Dear Ingrid. I love you. Want you to come see me. DiLLOn." My printing is neater: "Dear Ingrid: I love you. I wish you had time to write more often. Merry Christmas. Love. Susibeth"

* * *

Ed Pickett was the man who hauled Mother's Connsonata organ and the free-standing amplifier/speaker all over the state of Texas until her last performance sometime in early 1960. When Daddy sold the organ and speaker after Mother's funeral, Ed came to our house to collect them for delivery to the new owner. Daddy said Ed sat down on our front porch and wept over Mother's death.

Barbro had spent six weeks in Dallas the summer of 1953. She and Mother became great friends. Barbro came to my sixth birthday party. She helped Ingrid shepherd Mother and me during our trip to Sweden in 1959, and I saw her again when I visited in 1975, and in 2002 she attended my fifty-fifth birthday, celebrated with Ingrid at Hagavik! Barbro and I last met in April 2012 when I traveled to Växjö for Ingrid's memorial service at Växjö Cathedral. Barbro died in 2014, age ninety-four. I am still friends with her nieces, Ninna and Teta.

As 1954 ended and 1955 began, Mother continued to be uncomfortable and unwell. She and Elizabeth grew their business as performers of musical reviews, and Mother played for as many fashion shows as she could. I think she probably turned down several jobs due to fatigue. I can't help but think that the aggressive cancer was sapping her strength.

Mother wrote another letter to Ingrid, dated November 16, 1955; eleven months had passed since her last letter.

    ◦∾◦ Dearest Ingrid:

While Jimmy and the kids are looking at Davy Crockett on the TV, I will take a little time to write to one of my very most precious friends. Ingrid, I will never forget you, and I had so hoped that you might be coming back to see us at least by this Christmas. Mother and I are always dreaming of going to Sweden, and also that you have surprised us with a visit. Surely wish one of these things would come true.

In your last letter you mentioned one of your friends was thinking of coming to Texas. We certainly could get her on at Baylor. You will recall that Boone Powell, the administrator, lives across the street from us and is a very good friend. We certainly miss having a Swedish friend around, you know. Tell her to let us know if we can help her any way.

Barbro wrote the other day that she still hadn't seen you but had talked to you on the phone. Be sure to have her show you the pictures of our new kitchen when you see her. Ingrid, we gave the spoon to Robbie, and Robbie says she wrote you about it the same time she wrote you about Mother and me being in the hospital last Feb. Maybe you just did not get her letter. Barbro also mentioned that Lasse was back in school but not married yet. Is he in S.M.U? Of course, we could call and find out. Is he still engaged to that same girl? [This might be Lars's first wife, Penny.]

We are so sorry for the Bishop and his precious wife. I am sure they must get terribly discouraged. [Bo's wife, Elisabeth, suffered from severe rheumatoid arthritis.] Mother is much better, but still can't do much. She had a little girl from Italy for three months, but she has to go back, and has already gone to Philadelphia to stay with her sister a while before returning. [This Italian girl was Rita Tonderock, a lovely lady in her twenties. Evidently, she hired herself out to care for old people. I think she lived with my grandmother for three months. We lost touch with her.]

I called Titche's [now Dillard's] today to try to order the stocking for little Thomas, but they do not have them yet. Think I will try to get one from Sangers [now Macy's], as we want to be sure he has it by Christmas. I also have a box of clothes ready to send, and I will do that soon—just some things that Ann-Marie's kiddos might like to have.

Dillon and Susibeth are both so thrilled over school. Susibeth is in the third grade, and Dillon is in the first. Dillon is very definitely one of the brightest in his class. He is really a darling little boy. Susie is much prettier now that she is getting her permanent teeth. I talk about Dillon more to you, I guess, because I feel that he is half yours! His teacher is crazy about him. Both of the children love people and are completely extrovert.

I am doing just fine, Ingrid. I have pretty good use of my

arm. Just can't reach straight up or behind me too well. There is practically no swelling, except in my shoulder, and I understand I will always have that. I go to my doctor for check-ups every three months.

I talk to Sara Everett pretty often. Her husband continues to have heart attacks and is put back to bed periodically. Dear Jack is the same as ever. Still waiting in his big house for a gal!

I think I wrote you about my twelve-week TV show this summer. We enjoyed it very much, but it really was a lot of work. We have twelve musicals in our repertoire now, though, that we can review. We are reviewing "Fanny," which is currently on Broadway, this Friday.

Ingrid don't ever forget us, please. We love you so very much and can't help but pray that you will come to see us again someday!

Lots of hugs and kisses from all of us. Lovingly, SUE

P.S. Barbro also wrote that your mother had an operation. I do hope that she has recovered nicely, and that it was not too serious! Please remember me to Ann-Marie, and also to your parents.

MEMORIES OF LIFE ON WESTLAKE IN THE 1950s

Stepping back in time brings up memories from the sublime to the ridiculous. What follows are memories from Dillon's and my lives as children in Dallas, Texas, in the 1950s. We grew up in a three-block radius of single-family homes with about twenty children ranging in age from five to eighteen. The older children often babysat the younger children. Every home was open to all children, and we were all subject to the disciplinary authority of each other's parents. Dillon, my brother, was a resourceful, clever child. He loved to play in the alley behind our house. John, one of his best friends, lived across the alley. We think of those childhood years as idyllic, even when real life brought pain.

In 1957, Mother organized a neighborhood Christmas choir. She played Christmas carols on the organ while we children stood on the steps of our house and sang carols. One of the other mothers, Doris T., sewed "choir robes" from white sheet material. Each of us sported a red velvet bow at the neck.

This performance event coincided with the annual neighborhood Christmas party, where we all exchanged gifts, each child having drawn the name of another child just after Thanksgiving. One neighbor couple, Charles and Helen W., who had no children of their own, bought gifts

Westlake Christmas Choir 1957

for all the children in the neighborhood. After Christmas, but before we returned to school, the Christmas trees were put on the curb to be collected for trash disposal. We would ride around the neighborhood, tie the discarded trees to our bikes, and drag them to a backyard. We built two forts, then staged a "war." The goal of the game was to capture the other team's fort. If there had been a snowfall, we had snowballs for ammunition. If snow came heavy enough to close school for the day, we went sledding on Delrose Hill at the end of the block.

Other activities included roller-skating in the Frasiers' smooth driveway. We had roller skates that were adjustable to the foot size of the individual child. The skates were secured with straps and tightened with a skate key. On hot summer afternoons, we girls gathered in each other's homes. We played "house" with our dolls, bought and sold property in Monopoly land, dealt cards for canasta and casino, and played jacks on the kitchen floor. Daddy built a soap box car in the shop at Dillon Scale. All the children in the neighborhood enjoyed driving it down the sloped driveways. We played with that car until the wheels fell off.

The cultural ethos of the mid-fifties in Dallas, Texas, was informed by the vicious discriminatory "Jim Crow" laws, most of which were enacted during the 1930s. Blacks lived in a segregated neighborhood south of downtown, across the Trinity River; sat in the back of the bus; and never crossed the line if they wanted to live peacefully. Black public school teachers were paid less than white teachers, and of course the schools were segregated, never mind *Brown v. Board of Education,* which desegregated public schools in 1954. Dallas ISD was not desegregated until 1967 after many lawsuits, and then, starting with first grade, only one grade each year. The whole district was not desegregated until the mid-seventies.

Both boys and girls played softball in the street and hide-and-seek among the shrubbery. We pretended that the mailbox on the corner was a horse. We took turns sitting astride our "horse" and told stories, counted the stars, and followed the fireflies. Two of the older girls on our block, Pam T. and Kathy K., organized a summer play school for one week in June or July for several summers. We played games, went on nature walks, read stories, had juice and cookies—all outside under the shade trees of the Townsend backyard. We spent summer evenings outside catching fireflies and watching moonrises. Labor Day weekend, before school started, two or three families would take breakfast fixin's to the park on White Rock Lake, just two blocks from Westlake. At the picnic area one of the fathers would build a fire and prepare breakfast as we watched the sunrise.

Most of us attended Lakewood Elementary School, located about a mile from our block. We walked or rode our bicycles in good weather. The mothers took turns driving carpool in winter or on rainy days. When we ran out of things to do, we gathered in backyards, where we played in a sandbox, tried to dig to China, or flew to the clouds on swing sets. Such was the life of childhood on Westlake Drive 1950s Dallas. All this time, Mother was ill with cancer, Grandmother had heart disease, Uncle Ed suffered from the lingering effects of TB, and the correspondence with Ingrid continued.

A CHILDHOOD REMINISCENCE FROM 1954

By Susan Bussard (1993)

I was born in a wing of Baylor Hospital called Florence Nightingale, now called Hoblitzelle because that family gave several million dollars to have the old maternity wing of Baylor torn down and rebuilt. My parents told me that the summer of 1947 in Dallas was one of the hottest on record, but I can imagine that being nine months pregnant in July before the days of air conditioning would make any summer feel like the hottest on record. Mother was experiencing labor pains on the gurney in the hallway, waiting for a delivery room to open up, as there were more babies arriving that day than there were delivery rooms to accommodate them. The mothers were wheeled into delivery rooms according to how dilated they were. Well, it was, after all, the post–World War II baby boom! I don't remember being born.

My earliest memories date from when I was two or three years old. I was playing in the corner of the room I shared with my baby brother. He was just learning to stand, about to take his first steps. I had that sibling jealousy response to keep him out of my way by pushing him down whenever I had the chance. That alone would have resulted in punishment, and probably did. What I do remember about that time is sitting on the shiny hardwood floor, painting the polished pine boards with white shoe polish. I don't remember being caught, but I do remember being put to bed while the sun was still shining. Another strong memory is that of a little girl sitting in a tiny rocking chair, singing nursery rhymes while cradling her favorite doll. Mother sang to me and Dillon from infancy. She was a fine musician who played both the piano and the organ.

My next vivid memory is falling on the gravel playground of Lakewood Elementary School in the second grade. I had been playing "Red Rover, Red Rover, Let ____ Come Over!" My feet slipped on the gravel while running to "come over," causing me to land hard, scraping my right elbow and left knee. I did not go to the teacher or school nurse because I had heard they used methylate on skinned knees and elbows. I was more afraid of the sting than I was of the infection I could contract from unclean wounds. I endured the pain of the injury and the humiliation of a dirty dress until I got home. Mother cleaned the wounds with peroxide and dressed them with a kiss and a Band-Aid.

My fear of first aid, though, did not deter me from conquering every tree in our neighborhood that was climbable. We had two mimosa trees in our front yard. One had several sturdy limbs that could support the weight of a four-foot seven-year-old. I liked climbing the mimosas because the smooth bark did not scratch the skin, as that of most other trees did. Mimosas also give off the most deliciously sweet fragrance when they bloom in June. Perching in a mimosa tree was like sitting in a perfume shop.

The tree that became another world for me grew in Lisa's, my best friend's, backyard. It was a huge (or so it appeared to us) pecan tree that stood at least forty feet high. To climb it, we had had to grab the lowest limb with both hands, then swing up both legs and wrap around the limb as if we were mounting monkey bars or a jungle gym. We straddled the bottom limb, then stood up to reach the next limb, and climbed up what we imagined to be a winding staircase. We constantly dared each other to go one limb higher. Often we sat in the top of that tree on limbs no larger than three or four inches in diameter. We perched above the concrete alley below. A fall would have meant serious injury, if not death. But our parents never said anything more than, "Be careful!" and "Hold tight!" Daddy used to say that if I climbed up, I would have to climb down. He would not come get me.

From the top of that tree, Lisa and I could see what seemed to be the whole world. Birds nested above our heads. We could see rooftops for several blocks. Once when it was foggy, we climbed to the top and could not see the ground. We pretended we had climbed to heaven through the clouds. We watched birds dart in and out of the mist. We listened to cars passing on the neighborhood street and to the doors of neighbors' houses opening and closing. We delighted in the realization that we were eavesdropping on the world beneath us without those who dwelt below knowing we were anywhere around. We imagined we had transcended time and space.

Sometimes we became princesses imprisoned in a tower, like the maid in Tennyson's "The Lady of Shalott." We waited for Lancelot of the neighborhood to ride by on his Schwinn bike with chrome fenders to rescue us. Beneath the tree, we played house with miniature furniture and doll dishes. We hosted many tea parties under that tree, serving mud pie cuisine and sand-colored tea. Lisa and I planned our whole lives in the cool shade of the thick canopy of that massive pecan tree.

I don't remember the last time we climbed the tree. It was probably when we were eleven or twelve. I remember becoming aware of the danger of climbing too high as I grew taller and weighed more than I had as a child of seven or ten. I remember feeling afraid when my foot slipped on a weakened limb. I didn't fall, but my stomach jumped up into my throat and stayed there as I gingerly climbed down. I remember feeling weak in the knees when I reached solid ground.

Lisa and I had a brief reunion and visit the spring of 1979 when she came home for her father's funeral. We were both grown, with families and professional lives of our own. I went to her house, and the conversation turned to our childhood. We recalled sleepovers and hours spent playing jacks, canasta, casino, checkers, and Monopoly in her den. We walked out back to see the tree. It had shrunk! No longer was it forty feet tall, more like thirty feet! Such is a consequence of growing up. Perspectives change. We gazed at the tree. The lower limb that had been our castle gate was gone! Lisa said her father had sawed it off years ago to save the tree when bores had infested the limb and threatened to kill the tree. I had wanted to climb to the top again, but I knew this adult body would never have made it. Perhaps it is appropriate and right that the gateway limb is gone. It's as if the tree said to us, "Climb me in memory and you'll reach the sky. Climb me in actuality and you'll break something." I'll take the memory.

THE SANDBOX 1956

By Susan Bussard (1992)

When I was a little girl, Daddy built a sandbox in the summer of 1956 for my brother and me. Little did we know that he was building a sandbox for the whole neighborhood. It's funny how I remember that backyard and sandbox as huge. The yard was big enough for baseball if the players were less than four feet tall. We had a red swing set that had two swings, a monkey bar, and a contraption suspended from the top but attached to a pole with a seat on each end, handlebars, and pedals. Two riders pushed with their feet and pulled with their hands to swing back and forth. My brother's favorite game was to pretend he was Superman. He pinned a bath towel to his shoulders, pushed the swing as high as it would go, then jumped out to fly into the yard. He managed to play that game successfully until he broke his arm. That was when our daddy decided we needed somewhere else to play in the backyard that kept us on solid ground. Hence the sandbox.

Daddy spent a whole Saturday assembling it because he took great pains to sand each board so we would not get splinters when we sat on the edges. The box was large—probably eight by eight, made of plywood and two-by-fours. He placed it under a large pecan tree in the backyard on a stretch of ground where grass refused to grow because the canopy of the pecan tree constantly shaded it. When he had placed the sanded boards on edge under the tree, he finished off the sandbox with plywood strips nailed on top of each side to serve as a bench all around. The sandbox sat empty for a week until the truck came.

Early next Saturday morning, a dump truck loaded with enough fumigated, insect-free sand to fill the eight by eight box to a depth of three feet crept up our one-lane alley. Two burly giants (at least they appeared so to me when I was nine) with mammoth shovels climbed out of the truck and began pitching sand into the box like firemen stoking an engine with coal. As sand flew in the air, we children had to step back to keep the sand from stinging our eyes. After the truck left, Daddy took the garden hose, set the nozzle on mist, and sprayed the sand to moisten it just enough to pack down. By noon, the whole neighborhood knew we had a sandbox ready for transformation.

Children came from all over: Lisa, my best friend, whose pigtails bounced when she walked; Wanda, whose brown eyes resembled saucers; Jan, the neighborhood tomboy whose athletic dexterity I envied. She rode her bicycle the first time she tried without training wheels. Then there were Ricky and Ronnie, two curly-headed boys with fair skin who lived next door. Ricky was diagnosed with juvenile diabetes when he was ten and ate a whole head of lettuce for a snack every afternoon at three. The family was from Chicago and spoke with a strange accent that did not sound Texan. Their father chewed tobacco and took his sons to the drive-in every Saturday night in the maroon Kaiser to see the latest western or Godzilla movie. Mother never let us go with them. Finally, there was Livonia. She had three brothers and a sister. Her front yard sported the best climbing tree on the block, a large mimosa that had grown above the roofline of her house. Eight altogether, we gathered under the pecan tree and surveyed the mound of damp sand.

Since the sandbox was located in our backyard under our pecan tree, my brother and I took charge. And since the girls outnumbered the boys, the group decided to construct a mountain village with roads for a family vacation route rather than wage a war. Pack down the big mound and make a pass by slicing off the top with an extended arm. Tunnel through the peaks by digging with fingers working like a bulldozer scooping out the handfuls of sand and setting it aside for future landscaping. As soon as fingers met, the tunnel road was patted firm so toy cars could traverse the switchback roads we carved out of the sides of the mounds of sand. On hands and knees, we played for hours—the boys providing engine sounds for cars and all of us creating dialogue of family on vacation in the car:

"Now, honey, don't drive too fast!"

"Molly, don't jump in the backseat."

"Mommy, I'm hungry!"

"Daddy, are we there yet?"

It didn't take us long to learn family secrets. Our parents would have been amused and at worst appalled at what we revealed. Mercifully those secrets bury themselves in the subconscious not long after utterance. Such is the dialogue of children at play.

When the families in the toy cars on the imaginary vacations arrived home, the members gathered for tea and cakes. Sand cakes, made by packing moist sand into assorted plastic or tin cups and turning them out on a board to dry in the summer heat. and brown water tea comprised the main fare. A prized "delicacy" for sandbox tea parties was the accidental sand cookie that could be shaped by gently scraping away sand that had dried hard naturally. These "delicacies" took the shape of triangles, trapezoids, and parallelograms. We decorated the sand cakes and cookies with bits of green grass, small pecans, and flower petals. Lisa was able to dribble water off her little finger gently on each "cake" to form what looked like icing. Her cakes reminded me of petit fours. Of course, Mother made sure we had some real cookies—chocolate chip and peanut butter were our favorites—and cold lemonade on hot summer afternoons.

Time passed lazily from May to September those summers we spent in the sandbox. Mother didn't seem to mind our coming in for tuna fish sandwich lunches tracking sand, even though we had hosed off outside. As children, we didn't mind the heat of July and August or the insects of summer. The sandbox village was safe and peaceful and totally subject to the will of our collective imaginations. The eight of us learned to get along as citizens of a world beyond ourselves, though we didn't realize it at the time.

The sandbox lasted three years until the spring of 1959. We must have noticed subconsciously that the time spent in sandbox play had diminished. As we grew older, the girls in the group became more interested in playing with dolls and staying clean. The sand didn't have the attraction it had when we were younger. Sometimes weeks would go by without our even venturing to the sandbox. Mountain villages constructed from sand lost their charm. Ricky and Ronnie moved away, Lisa got a horse of her own, Wanda and her sisters went to Disneyland, Livonia traveled with her parents, and Jan got a trampoline. In the spring of 1959, Daddy asked us if we wanted new sand for the summer. After thinking about it for a minute, my brother and I looked at each other and shook our heads. "No thanks, Daddy. We'd rather play on Jan's trampoline."

In the fall of 1959, Daddy dismantled the sandbox he had so carefully built for us and stored the boards in the garage. And once again, he struggled with trying to grow grass under the canopy of the pecan tree.

BOYS ARE US: AN EVENT FROM THE SUMMER OF 1957
By Dillon Bussard (2018)

I was eight. The neighbors behind us had a son named John. He was a year younger than I, and we spent lots of time catching bugs and snakes, playing with electronic things, and other activities. We were fortunate because the TV was about ten inches across, so no distraction there. One day we were exploring the alley behind our house and noticed a porcelain lid in the middle of it. It was removable so we did the obvious: we removed it. We realized we could not see the bottom of the hole we had uncovered, and no flashlight. But there were some bricks around, so we dropped one in the hole, hoping to determine the depth from calculating how long it took to hear a noise. After the first drop we heard a splash. Interesting. Water? Oil? Lava? Our imaginations ran wild. We were so distracted by the unexpected discovery that we forgot to time the descent of the first brick, so we had to do it again. Another splash. Wow. Fun. One more? Why not. Splash. Neat. Time to go home.

That night I was in my room, and I heard a commotion

from my parents' end of the house. Raw sewage had started to fill the tub in their bathroom. It kept coming and then started coming up in the shower in the bathroom I used. Keep in mind this was a long time ago, but I do remember seeing raw sewage flowing out of the bathroom, over the recently installed green carpet, and cascading over the little step that led into the den, somewhat like a little obscene, filthy Niagara Falls. My dad didn't yell or anything, I just remember him moving very quickly. After some time I heard someone say, "I think it's under control." Whew. I have no idea what he did. Call to the neighbors upstream, "DON'T FLUSH"? We'll never know.

The next morning the backhoe guys showed up in the alley and started digging. My dad and I stood and watched. We were both very interested to see what could have caused this horrible disaster. Eventually they hit bottom, and one of them held a brick over his head. We all said "Wow." Then two more came up. These hardworking city employees had successfully solved the mystery. Obviously, the bricks had clogged the sewer line just downstream from our house. John wasn't there, by the way. I'm sure at some point I discerned that we had caused this, but surprisingly I don't remember having that realization during the deluge. At that point I guess I was okay: no fingerprints on the bricks, not possible to be incriminated.

I did tell my dad shortly before he passed that John and I were responsible for that historic event. He laughed.

A little more information about the "sewer incident": Daddy was calm. He got on the phone to the city and said something like, "We have an emergency. Raw sewage is backing up into our house. Send a crew immediately!" Of course, nothing happened until the next day. Thank goodness it wasn't a Friday or Saturday night! Daddy stuffed bedspreads in the toilets, which caused the backup to move upstream to the neighbors. I don't remember how far up the neighborhood the backup went. It was determined that the house was unfit for human habitation, so wearing our pajamas and carrying our toothbrushes Dillon and I were sent knocking on the doors of the neighbors across the street, asking to be taken in like refugees. They were on a different sewer line, so they were not affected by the backup. Who was the couple who lived in the red brick house next door to the Powells? I think Dillon slept there. I might have gone to Lisa's. Does anyone remember?

No letters to Ingrid have survived from early 1956. However, it is worth noting that Mother, Daddy, Dillon (age seven), and I (age nine) drove from Dallas to Tallahassee, Florida, to spend two weeks in a cottage on Saint Teresa Beach, located fifty miles due south of Tallahassee, on the Gulf of Mexico. We were visiting Daddy's twin, Uncle Bob, and his wife, Katheryn, and their two daughters, Karol Kay (age twenty) and Kathey (age nine). Karol Kay had married her high school sweetheart, Donald Lee, the year before and was pregnant with her first child. Daddy and Dillon fished in the bay from Uncle Bob's boat, *Kathey B.* I tried to water-ski; Kathey could slalom. She introduced me to her friends. We took long walks on the beach and collected scallops at low tide, which Katheryn cleaned and boiled. Dillon, fascinated with the Seminole names of the rivers that flowed through the South, made up names for the freshwater streams that drained into Saint Teresa Bay. Of course, Mother was not feeling well, as she never fully recovered from the cancer surgery of 1954. We loved the beach; Mother hated it. We did not go back to Saint Teresa Beach until the summer of 1961.

I remember that my uncle Edgar continued to struggle with his health. He never put on weight and he smoked! In the summer of 1956, he was told he needed to have surgery to clean plaque buildup from his carotid arteries. It would be a delicate surgery without guarantee of success. Rather than face the surgery, he decided to take a trip to Europe and, of course, Sweden. He set sail on Cunard Line's RMS *Queen Elizabeth II* in late September 1956. My grandmother wrote to Ingrid to give her a heads-up on his arrival.

      ᐳ My dear Ingrid:

      Thank you so very much for the lovely candles that you sent to us by Ingrid Giertz and the pressed flowers too. [Ingrid Giertz was the nineteen-year-old daughter of Bishop Bo Giertz. A debutante in Sweden, she had been presented at the court of the Swedish king and queen. She came to Dallas to visit her brother, Lars, and to meet my family. She stayed with Grandmother for a short time.]

Ingrid is a very sweet girl, so much like her father. [Bishop Bo Giertz had already visited Dallas.] We are getting along so well. Thank you for all the Swedish people that we have known through you.

Sue is a little better now, but still gets very tired. The doctor finally made a metabolism test last week and now has her on 1/2 gr. of thyroid per day.

Now sit down, Ingrid for here is the big surprise. Ed is on the way to Europe. He is on the RMS *Queen Elizabeth II* and will arrive in London Oct. 1. He will be at Hotel Westbury there through Oct. 4. He then will fly to Paris at Hotel George V. From there he plans to go to Germany for a while then return to Malmö to see you between Oct. 15 and 18. He said to tell you that he will contact you later as to when he will arrive in Malmö.

Now about your friend who is coming to Dallas. I could not read all of it, so will you please type me all of the details about him and we will meet him at the plane and do all we can to help him get located.

I do hope Ed can go on to Växjö and see your parents, Mr. Johnson's sister and Barbro, but I do not know whether he will or not. He plans to go to Göteborg see Bishop Giertz and Gerd Petterson. He will probably start home from Sweden, either by plane or boat.

He is travelling with Ann and Jean Smith, two of his best friends [from his Bridge Club]. They are on the way to Africa to hunt. Ed will leave them in Paris and come to Sweden.

Please know we all love you and wish you would come back to see us.

Love always. Ruth Dillon

Uncle Ed wrote to Ingrid from the RMS *Queen Elizabeth* on September 29, 1956.

Dear Ingrid:

I will be in Malmö around the 14th of October. I will write you later when I know my exact schedule. I will be at the King George V hotel in Paris from Oct. 6-11. Drop me a note there. In case you might not be in Malmö around the 14th. The trip has been wonderful so far. We arrive Southampton Monday evening Oct. 2. Will be at Hotel Westbury in London for about 4 days. Love. Ed

Between Mother, Grandmother, Uncle Ed, and me, Ingrid was slammed with letters. This was my first letter, dated October 1, 1956, when I was nine and home from school, sick:

Dear Ingrid,

I love you. I am watching TV. I have a bad cold. How are all you [sic] little Swedish friends? I wanted to write to you sooner but I haven't had the time. Now you will really be shocked. Uncle Ed has docked in England. He will be on his way to Sweden soon. He came on the Queen Elizabeth. How is Ockie and Susanne? Grandmother is fine and Mother feels better. I hope to write to Ockie and Susanne.

Love you lots. Susibeth

A few days later, Mother wrote a note on the back of my letter. She had hoped to send a money order to Ingrid for the purchase of Swedish items, but instead she sent cash.

October 3, 1956

My dearest Ingrid,

I have taken Susibeth and Dillon to school and am at the Lakewood Post Office. Remember it? I am sending a money order and would like to ask a big favor of you. Before Ed gets there or while he is there will you please get me some Swedish things. One thing I particularly want is 18 little dancing Swedish dolls on strings. Remember them—like you gave us—

the little girl and boy. I want them for my neighbors at Xmas. With the rest I would like something sort of in the antique line from Sweden for mine or Mother's house. Of course, I don't know how far this will go, so will leave it up to you. I am trying to get a lot done for Xmas while the weather is still warm, as I dread cold weather. I am so weak most of the time, particularly in my chest and take cold so easily.

Have fun with Ed! Dillon wants him to bring you back with him. This is a post office pen, so hope you can read it. Love you! Sue

P.S. Couldn't send a money order, so here's the money. Just anything will be fine: for kids or grownups.

I am struck by Mother's comment on her own health. It has been more than two years since her mastectomy. If she had been cancer-free, she would have been feeling well. I was aware that my friends' mothers were not sick like mine. However, Mother continued to live her life, be a wife and mother, and partner with Elizabeth P. in the performance of musical reviews.

Uncle Ed had a wonderful time in Paris and Sweden. He purchased Christmas presents for the family in Paris, but the only one that stayed wrapped until Christmas was the French doll he bought for me. While in Sweden, he stayed with Ingrid, they rekindled the love affair begun in 1950, and he proposed to her. He borrowed about $ 3,500 from Ingrid's father to buy a Mercedes, which he had shipped to Dallas after driving it in Sweden. Daddy was furious about that, as Uncle Ed charged the cost of his trip *and* the Mercedes to Dillon Scale. I don't think the family knew about the affair. Ingrid told me about it in 2004 as we ate morel mushrooms on toast and drank martinis in her Malmö apartment. All the participating players are long dead. Uncle Ed wrote to Ingrid upon returning to the States.

November 13, 1956

Dear Ingrid:

I had a wonderful trip home. Arrived in N.Y. Nov. 7 and got

into Dallas on Sunday Nov. 11. I want to thank you again for being so nice to me and I enjoyed every minute of it.

I don't know how much money you are talking about that I gave you too much, but I would suggest you just keep it and maybe I will want you to buy something for me there later. I will go to the bank and get my finances straightened out tomorrow or the next day. I have to get my car title etc. cleared with the state before I can do the banking but it will only take a day or two. I will write just as soon as this is done so you can deposit the check for the $ 3500.00 to your account.

Everyone here is well and sends their love to you. Please give my best regards to all of my friends there. Please let me know how you are feeling. I do hope you are well and I wish I could have stayed a while longer with you. Love, Ed

Shortly after Uncle Ed returned home from his European trip, he did have successful surgery on his carotid arteries. Mother wrote a thank-you letter to Ingrid on December 9, 1956.

൙ My dearest Ingrid:

Thank you a thousand times for each and everything you sent us by Uncle Ed. I know too how much of your valuable time it took to get all those things together. I shall certainly welcome all the paper things which you wrote about sending from Stockholm.

I also want to thank you for the beautiful beads [china beads with matching earrings embossed with pink and purple flowers]. I get so many compliments on them. Right after you sent them Neiman-Marcus ran a big ad in the paper on similar ones. And the lovely mirror. I shall put it in Susibeth's room. We shall certainly treasure it as a wonderful token of your family.

The children will never cease to get a kick out of the Advent calendars; in fact, I think they enjoy them more with each year. Stores have them here now, but they are not nearly so pretty.

We shall certainly enjoy the little wooden dolls and all the pretty candles too. We would try to have a Lucia this year, but Jimmy's Kiwanis dinner-dance at the Lakewood Country Club falls on that night.

We haven't seen the Eliasson's [a doctor from Sweden and his family] since they moved, though Dillon and I went by one day and they were not there. Some of us have had colds ever since they moved, even Dr. Eliasson, so we have had to stay apart. Dillon has had a stomach virus the past three days and is just beginning to eat solid food again. Susibeth is making her professional appearance with me Thursday at the Dallas Athletic Country Club. I'm giving her $5.00 to do it with me. [I was nine and had a sweet voice. I sang mostly on pitch, as Mother would set the key in my range. I sang songs like "Be Kind to Your Parents," from the musical *Fanny*. This was a Christmas program, but I do wish Mother had been more specific!]

I manage to keep going, Ingrid, by taking various drugs to get me going, but I surely do not feel good at all. I just keep on; anyway, I think I shall change doctors after the first of the year if I do not feel better.

But enough of that, as this is a Christmas greeting to my most wonderful friend, and I hope you and all your family will have a perfectly wonderful Christmas. Please remember me to all of them and thank you again for all your kindness to my little brother! [Uncle Ed, of course.]

Love always, Sue

The mirror, with a wooden frame painted in gold leaf about twenty by twenty-six inches, hung over an antique dresser in my room. I kept it until 2014, when I sent it to a consignment auction house. I did not remember that it had come from Sweden (there was no writing on the back); otherwise I would have kept it. I do still have the antique dresser.

In 1959 when we traveled to Sweden, Mother was under the care of Dr. Don Brown. I remember two drugs she took: Miltown (an antianxiety drug) and Cytomel (for her thyroid), neither of which could treat metastatic breast cancer.

Grandmother penned the following on December 14, 1956.

> ᏜᎤ My dear, dear Ingrid,
>
> Thank you so much for the nice things you did for Ed while he was in Sweden. He surely did enjoy it. Also please let me thank you for the lovely candles and the knife you sent me. I really did need it. All the things Ed brought us were wonderful.
>
> I hated so much to see Ingrid Giertz leave, but she was anxious to get on with her education. She was truly a ray of sunshine and I love her very much; we all do.
>
> Dillon has been quite ill for about two weeks with a virus infection and he is still in bed, so I am staying with him today.
>
> Sue and Susibeth have gone to the Dallas Athletic Club to put on a Christmas program. They will sing and do some original dialogue that Sue wrote. Susibeth has on a Christmas red velveteen dress and looks real sweet. I wish you could see the children before they are grown. Please know that we love you very much, and we wish for you and your family a very Merry Xmas and a Happy New Year!!
>
> Love. Ruth D.

Uncle Ed continued to correspond with Ingrid after his visit to Sweden in 1956. It took several weeks after he returned home to sort out the currency exchange to pay for the purchase of the Mercedes. An interesting letter, dated January 26, 1957, surfaced.

> ᏜᎤ Dear Ingrid:
>
> I hope you are well and not working too hard. I have been very busy since I got back, but I am glad that business is good.
>
> I had dinner with Mr. and Mrs. Jack Kemp a week ago and they are looking forward to Viola's coming. [Viola Fröler, another friend of Ingrid and Barbro, came to Dallas to work at Baylor Hospital.] They are now building a swimming pool so I

hope Viola likes to swim.

I am enclosing $25.00. Is this enough? I am sorry that I didn't understand the proper exchange rate.

Jimmy had to leave yesterday for Tucson, AZ as both of his parents are very ill. His dad is in the hospital and his mother had a stroke and has a nurse with her 24 hours a day. Everyone else is doing very well. I am supposed to go to Chicago day after tomorrow on business but may not if Jim doesn't get back. I hate to go north in the winter time anyway. It is cold here today with freezing rain. We have had mostly warm weather however since I got back. Give my love to everyone. I miss you all.

I received one copy of the Industrial Magazine and I certainly do appreciate it. Is there anything in particular that you would like for me to send you? I think that Mother or Sue is getting your cards printed that you wanted. Let us hear from you soon.

Love, Ed

The next letter I have is from Grandmother Ruth, written to Ingrid in February 1957. Mother and Elizabeth were playing a lot of gigs across the state of Texas. Mother pushed herself to work/play, but I know she found it difficult. Grandmother wrote:

ᠭᠥᠥ My dear Ingrid,

I am so sorry to hear that you have been ill. It seems like those virus infections are everywhere. Jimmy, Sue and Ed all had it last week, but are better now, and I sincerely hope that you are entirely well by now.

Ingrid, I am enclosing a sample of my note paper and I would like to know whether this is what you would like for yourself. Would you like Miss Ingrid Jaensson or just Ingrid Jaensson on it? Please let us know as Ed said you would like some. I am enclosing a clipping of Dillon, so that you may know what your little friend is interested in. [Dillon got his photo taken by the *Dallas Morning News* while he was kissing his classmate on Valentine's Day in 1957.] I am sorry to hear that Elisabeth Giertz is going to have surgery. Please let us know how she gets along. She really has a struggle, doesn't she? Ed liked her very much.

Ed is still enjoying his Mercedes, and now I have his Buick. I like it very much as it is air conditioned and that is quite an asset in the summer.

Mildred's mother is not at all well. She had a heart attack about two months ago and her mind is not good either. I feel so sorry for them.

Sue is still very busy with her music, though it is still a struggle at times. She loves it, though and I really believe it is good for her.

I took Susibeth to the school last Friday night to be in a square dance party. She really had a wonderful time. You know how she loves music; she has started her ballet lessons again and she likes it very much.

Please make up your mind to come back to Dallas soon. "Tott" has talked of coming to Dallas this summer, but I don't know whether she will or not.

Love always, Ruth D.

Dillon and I both had sickly childhoods. We caught every cold or stomach virus that came around. I suffered walking pneumonia or bronchitis most of the sixth grade. Our pediatrician, Dr. Roach, who was six feet tall and very handsome, made house calls. He often brought the dreaded penicillin shot with him. Medical science had not yet made the connection between stress and illness. Mother was sick all the time. I am certain the stress of her illness took its toll on the health of me and Dillon, not to mention Daddy. We also suffered all the childhood diseases that today are prevented by vaccines. I always caught it first; then Dillon would have his turn. We survived countless strep throats, three kinds of measles, mumps, and chicken pox. I remember that Mother received a call from Leona A., the mother of my best friend,

Lisa, who said that Lisa had measles. Sure enough, Mother looked at my tummy and I had it too. Our immune systems were strengthened by the experience.

Miracle of miracles! Ingrid wrote to tell us that she and her best friend, Britta, were coming to the US in the spring/summer of 1957 for about two months. There was great exultation in our house. Mother joyfully spread the word to all the Dallas friends who had met Ingrid in 1949 and 1950. Several ladies' luncheons and teas organized by Mother's friends welcomed Ingrid back to Dallas.

Ingrid and Britta came to Dallas for about three weeks. They stayed with Grandmother for two weeks; then Britta left to spend a few days with Harriet and Jay Armstrong in Grapevine, Texas. Then Britta flew to New York to visit friends and wait for Ingrid to join her for the return trip to Sweden. Thankfully, we had Ingrid all to ourselves for a whole week. She joined us on a family trip to a dude ranch in the Texas hill country west of Austin. Mother, Daddy, Dillon, and I—along with Ingrid—drove to Bandera, Texas, in June to Peaceful Valley Ranch, located on the Medina River. We stayed in our own three-bedroom cabin with a kitchen. That summer Ingrid taught me to swim the breaststroke.

Sue and Ingrid, summer 1957

We rode horses and fished in the river. I am sure Mother and Ingrid had intimate conversations about Mother's health. I was ten; Dillon was eight. We just enjoyed being together at a time when Mother did not seem sick.

Mother wrote to Ingrid after her visit to us in June 1957.

June 29, 1957 [Saturday]

☙ My dearest, darling Ingrid:

Well, you are still in the U.S., but not for long! Golly, how we all still miss you! We have all been thinking about you every step of the way and loving you more and more. It all just seems like a wonderful dream that you were ever here! I am enclosing the four pictures that turned out, as I know you will want them. The man said four seemed to have been on time exposure, and therefore were no good. I think these four are real good, though, don't you! I know Bo would like one of Lars, so we will send another to you for him. We are taking slides today and shall airmail and insure the slides when we return them to you. Be assured that we will send them very soon, as we know how eager you are to get them.

I came home yesterday morning [Ingrid must have flown from Dallas Love Field on Friday morning, June 28] and put on my shorts and took a sunbath for an hour so that I could at the same time watch the sky where you were! I am back out this morning, as I really got quite a tan from yesterday morning and want to get back like I was when I returned from Bandera. Susibeth stayed all night with Grandmother, and Dillon and Doxie (dog#2) are talking to me and pestering me between thoughts, so please forgive any incongruous statements.

We watched your plane until it was just a small speck in the sky, then Dillon [age eight] gave a big sigh, turned slowly around, and said "Well—that's that!" Golly we all felt so let down but so grateful to God at the same time that we have had these glorious days with you. You are still the very most wonderful person any of us has ever known! I am sending you this clipping out of this morning's News which sort of explains why you are so glamorous, Ingrid! [The clipping is missing.]

We went to Mother's and fixed breakfast yesterday and when we asked Susibeth to say the blessing she said yours! I am so glad that Dillon knows you now, too, Ingrid! You have enriched our lives so very much. I know this sounds like a love letter, and that is precisely what it is!

Sara Everett came over to Mother's about nine yesterday morning and got your packages and took them to Jack to mail, so you should be getting them soon. She stayed and visited with Mother about an hour, and I am sure your ears must have been burning then, too. We had watermelon last night again, and it was just like the one we had in the picture.

Elizabeth Peabody called yesterday and said we had another engagement in Tyler, a direct result of the Rotary programs. She said she was sorry she wasn't home the night before to talk to you, but to tell you that she certainly enjoyed meeting you, too. If we keep on with so many programs, I might get to Sweden yet.

Ingrid, it was still wonderfully cool last night and the moon was so gorgeous. There is a nice breeze this morning, and I am really drinking in the sun. Louise [our maid] is defrosting the refrigerator, a job I am glad to turn over to her, and I really must come down off of Cloud 9 now and get down to mundane things like cooking, etc.

I hope you and Britta had no difficulty meeting in New York, and that you had a pleasant stay with your friend last night. Over a week ago we ordered corsages for you girls to be sent to your plane when you leave New York. Remember a world of love was with them. If you did not receive them, just tell us, please.

Tell Britta and Viola I shall write them both real soon, and of course Ann-Marie and Barbro. Their gifts were so lovely, and I shall certainly thank them, but please thank them for me in the meantime.

I must turn on my tummy now, and I am afraid that will be a little difficult to swing with the typewriter! Dillon is terribly disappointed that the other picture of Lars didn't turn out, for that ruins his newspaper you have, you know. Anyway show it to Bo and Elizabeth and give them all our very warmest greetings. I shall write them too. I find this is a pretty good place to write as there is not phone or doorbell to disturb me, and Dillon and Doxie finally gave up trying to get my attention!

I love you very much, Ingrid, and shall think of you every, every day. So write when you can, and I promise to do better now! Hugs and kisses. SUE

Mother wrote to Ingrid again one week later.

Friday, July 5, 1957

᪇ Dearest Ingrid:

Well, it is just one week this morning since I was writing to you as you sailed off over the old U.S.A. This time I am not outside getting a sunbath, as there are yard men mowing next door and I just hate to give them such a treat of pulchritude! I just told Jimmy that I would write you while HE fixed breakfast! After all, this is my holiday too! Of course it remains to be seen whether he does it or not! He worked real hard in the yard yesterday, and I cooked a lot, as we had Mother and Ed and the Whitcombs over for dinner last night. Dillon has been sick this week with a sore throat, so I didn't think it wise to have anyone with children over, as he would play too hard and then might expose them to it. He is better now. He helped me with the decorations which I thought I had none of!

Of course, I wanted an American flag to display somewhere in the dining room, so sure enough, tucked away on Dillon's closet shelf was an American flag, and neatly by it the Swedish flag you had given him. Believe me we are going to keep it where we know where it is from now on. I had the red and white candles which we had used in the Swedish holder while you were here, so I used my blue table cloth. Then Dillon thought of some plastic letters about an inch high that Dad Bussard had given him, so he spelled out GOD BLESS AMERICA on the mirror reflector on both sides of the candles so that both sides of the table could see them. I thought it was real clever. We lacked one "E" to match all the rest of the letters, so we painted a yellow one with red nail polish. Of course, I had them help themselves, so on the kitchen table which I pulled up to the doorway between the kitchen and dining room he spelled out "HELP YOURSELF" in multi-colored letters. Isn't he a sight! He and Susibeth were both a big help in setting and clearing the table too. I made the prettiest and best salad ring I have ever made with 2 cans of tuna, finely chopped celery, apple, onion, 3 eggs and sweet pickle relish, all molded in two packages of lemon jello with an extra package of gelatin to be sure it didn't tear up like it did when I made that ring for you. [Jello rings were a popular home dish in the 1950s and 1960s, but this one sounds AWFUL!]

Sunday we got back into the swing of things by going back to teaching our class [Mother and Daddy taught children's Sunday school at Highland Park Methodist Church], then we took Mother out to eat with us at Luby's [a local cafeteria], and later went over to see my former roommate visiting here with her four children from New London, Conn. Monday morning the kids and I met her over at Llano Park and let the kids go swimming and had a picnic lunch under the trees; believe it or not, there was still a cool breeze. Anyway, I was really bushed, so I came home and went to bed for three hours. I just can't understand why it tires me so to visit with a big group when I enjoy them so much.

I guess nothing particularly interesting happened Tuesday July 9, then Wednesday July 10, 1957, Mother had Anna and her sister [Aunt Eula "Eudie"] and two nieces [Patsy and Linda] and their three babies [Vicki, Karla, and Kerri] over for lunch. The babies were so cute, but of course into everything, so I took Susibeth along to help watch them [I was ten]. Well, after about three hours of that, Mother and I went to bed for another 3 hours. I had to leave Dillon home, as he had 103 fever.

Gee, I do believe Jimmy is fixing breakfast—bless him!

Let's see, where was I. Thursday I took Mother to the Lab and they just had an awful time finding a vein from which to draw blood. They had to try three different times and probed around so long and hurt her so bad that she just got real sick. Since then she has had quite a bit of pain and is really feeling very bad. I really believe she meant it when she told them she would rather die than have to hurt like that. I just can't understand why there isn't some way to locally anesthetize her arm to keep it [a blood draw] from being so painful.

Sara Everett called day before yesterday and I told her about your three cards enroute, which we enjoyed very much. She has really been busy. She had a party on Saturday for some friend who was moving out of town, then her Polish friends came and stayed three days and she had to drive her all over town looking for a house. She said they had left, but that this woman had left Sara's number with all the real estate people in town, as her phone is ringing so much that she can't even call her [Christian Science] practitioner! Poor Sara!

Oh yes, I want you to know that Lars called Tuesday noon and asked if Dillon was all ready to go to the TV station with him, and I told him Dillon was sick. He was so sorry and said to tell Dillon to call him just as soon as he got well, and he would take him. We surely appreciated it.

Incidentally while I think about it, if you will pick out the black and white prints you have made there that you think we might like to have, we will send you the money to pay for them. And please include some of you!

Yesterday at 1:20 we had just finished our noon meal and our devotion when all of a sudden, I said, "Ingrid is thinking of us right now, " and Jimmy said he was thinking about you too. Try to remember if you were. We are missing you more and more, Ingrid, and how I hope and pray that we can come to Sweden before too long.

Elizabeth continues to call every day with one or two more jobs for us, including the Women of Rotary. We are going to Colorado City, TX and Abilene, TX [250 miles west of Dallas] on Sept. 25 and 26. Franklin [Elizabeth's husband] will plan a trip to El Paso so he can drive us out and pick us up on the way back.

Ingrid, I ripped out the hand stitching on the straps of the costume, and I can wear it exactly without even taking it out in the waist! It really makes a beautiful dress, and even that placket in front doesn't show, as it just hangs as a fold. I think I shall wear it some this winter. I thought I might talk to Inge Johnson [a Swede working at Neiman-Marcus] about the idea of making something similar in a good quality of cotton and getting Neiman's to run an ad on them. I know the gals would go for them as patio clothes, etc. I'll get Mrs. Roberts advice on how to present the idea to them so that Inge would get something out of the idea besides just actual sales. Of course, Inge may not go along with it at all, but I thought it might be an idea that might help her financially. What do you think about it?

Ingrid, we know you are terribly busy writing to so many people, visiting with all your family, but we shall certainly look forward to hearing from you when you can write. You are at Ann-Marie's this week-end, and how we are thinking of you! It's about 4:30 in the afternoon there, so I imagine you will soon be eating a wonderful Swedish meal with the family. Will you please send this note I am enclosing on to Ann-Marie, as I do not know her address? Tell Viola and Britta that I will write to them real soon. In the meantime, they can read your letters. Be sweet, and never forget that I love you. Last night at dinner after Jimmy said the blessing, Susie said yours!

Hugs and kisses, SUE

When Ingrid came to visit in 1957, she brought a Swedish costume to mother. I still have it and have worn it, though I had to have it let out in the waist. It is a hand-woven dress with a red wool skirt and a brocade lace-up bodice. A wool apron covers the skirt. It's all worn over a white puffed-sleeve blouse and a brocade cap that matches the bodice. I wore it to World Communion Sunday service when I was twenty pounds lighter than I am now. I sent a photo of me wearing it to friends in Skåne and Småland to see which province it represented, but no one recognized it!

Grandmother's heart issues continued, but she had been stabilized on blood thinner medicine for about three years. Then in early December 1957, Grandmother suffered a hard fall at the home of her friend, Mrs. Potter. Mother's next letter to Ingrid was handwritten from Grandmother's hospital room on December 18, 1957.

     My dearest Ingrid,

Thank you so very much for your sweet cards to Mother and to us. My how we miss you, too, particularly at this time! Viola and Mr. and Mrs. Anderson brought us Lucia early Friday morning and it was so beautiful. Then that night the Eliasson's [Louise and Sven] had a Lucia party to which the whole family was invited. You should have seen Mrs. Dillon drinking GLÜG! We just love Lennart and Siv and their precious boys! [Dr. Lennart Anderson and his wife, Siv, and their toddler sons, Anders and Martin, arrived in Dallas the summer of 1957. Dr. Anderson worked as an internist at Baylor. They were friends of Ingrid. They stayed in Dallas only a year or two. I remember Siv invited me to her home to make pepparkakor for Christmas. I was ten.]

Then, after that beautiful day, Mother had a fall on Saturday afternoon over at Mrs. Potter's. [Grandmother called her "Byrd." Did she have a pointed nose?] She didn't think it was too bad and she drove home but suffered terribly all night. Saturday at 6:30 a.m. Ed called me to come over and go to

Baylor with Mother in the ambulance. They X-rayed the hip, and fortunately there was no fracture, but she was in terrible pain, so they kept her there.

She is having all sorts of complications, though she is not in such pain. You know she has been on Hedulin to thin her blood for 3 years and the doctor has always said that she would always have to have it. However, he has been forced to take her off the Hedulin as she has been and still is bleeding internally. Her red count is only about 1/3 of what it should be and they may have to give her a transfusion. They have her legs wrapped to prevent clotting and she wears a girdle night and day. This evening the orthopedist said he still may have to operate on her hip. She is in very good spirits and is so thankful the hip wasn't broken that she can't get too worried. I helped her walk up and down the hall today. I shall let you know of any changes. They are really watching her closely. Taking electrocardiograms every day. I doubt that she will be home for Christmas.

Her sister, Aunt Eudie had a slight stroke today too, so I don't know what kind of Christmas we will have.

Just the past two months, I have been feeling better. I still get very tired but am not as weak as I was. Just writing this much makes my whole side hurt. I hope you can read this.

Sara Everett and I have a mutual friend marrying on the 28th and I am playing for the wedding. We were at a luncheon Saturday together and Sara tells me she and Jack [her brother] are leaving March 5 for Europe and Sweden! They will go to Spain first and drive up the continent making it to Sweden about May or June. She said one time you mentioned you might meet her in Paris, so you might write her. She definitely wants to see you and Barbro both. I shall try to write Barbro this week if I possibly can. I have been very busy with Mother, and Dillon has been at home with a bad throat. He is all right now, however.

Ingrid, do try to come over for a visit soon. We could have

such a good time and we all love you so much. Viola says she
has 4 days off for Christmas and will spend two with Eliasson's
and two with us. She is a darling!

Love you lots and lots. Don't worry about the little windows
[Advent calendars]. They [Susibeth and Dillon] can use them
next year. They really enjoy them still! If you see Bo tell him
about Mother. I will try to write to them too.

Your devoted friend. SUE

Mother has developed an obsessive emotional attachment to all things
Swedish and to Ingrid in particular. Her fixation, while endearing, was
probably tiresome to her friends on the receiving end of her passionate
devotion, but they loved her anyway. How I wish letters from Sweden
had been preserved!

January 14, 1958

◌ My dearest Ingrid:

I cannot remember exactly where I left off in my last letter
to you, but I believe Mother was in Baylor. We brought her
home on 21 December, but she was miserable the whole time,
and as the doctor suspected, began having very severe angina
pains every night. Then Christmas night she had a slight
coronary occlusion, we had to take her back to the hospital
in the ambulance at midnight. This time we were fortunate to
get in Gaston. She is still there but is doing very nicely, and as
soon as Dillon gets over a little cold, we will bring her here to
my house for two or three weeks before taking her home, as
she needs someone with her all the time. People like that are
very hard to find. On January 2, her older sister, Aunt Eudie,
passed away, and of course we had to tell her that. I told the
doctor beforehand, though, so he gave her a hypo, and we
watched her very closely for a day or so. The doctor said that
it did not set her back as much as he had thought it might.
I really think she is going to be all right now, though, as the
damage to her heart was not as severe as it has been before.

Ingrid, on the night of January 4, I dreamed so very plainly about you. I thought you were right with me with your arms around me, and I was so happy to see you that I couldn't do a thing but cry. I could feel your cheek against mine. I told Viola and Mother, I just know you had to be thinking about me at the moment, as it was so vivid. I still hope and pray that you can come back for a visit before much longer. We have enjoyed Viola so very much, too, and she is so much like you in your talking and mannerisms that we call her Ingrid half the time. We do not see her as often as we would like, though, as she works at Parkland, and that is so far from us, and she must live near there.

Ingrid, I know I have never even thanked you for the lovely little gifts you sent us by Viola, much less your sweet Christmas remembrances. Please forgive me, I simply don't know where all my time goes, but I have felt so bad for so long that it just seems to take all the energy I can muster just to do the everyday things for my family. I think a rest like a trip to Sweden would be just the thing for Mother and me, don't you?

If it had not been for our precious Swedish friends I am afraid Christmas would not have been very merry for us. But on the 13th, Viola and the Andersons brought us Lucia in our beds. Then that night the Eliasson's had a big glüg party, which of course we thoroughly enjoyed. Every time we go to the Eliasson's we feel like we are really in Sweden. They are so precious. We even took the children, and they got such a kick out of everything. Sven played the little singing games with them. Even Ed joined in! Believe me, we were really thinking of you good people all day that particular day, but every day is full of thoughts and prayers for all of you. Then of course Mother had her fall the next day, so we were glad she could enjoy that much. Yes, Ingrid, Mrs. Dillon even drank glüg, and not out of a spoon! Remember how we laughed at her with her wine!

I spent Christmas Day in bed with a virus so didn't eat any

Christmas dinner. I am feeling some better, however, but get so
very weak and tired if I do the least bit of extra activity.

Ingrid, I hope you have a wonderful new year, and that
included in that year will be a trip to see us! Each one of us
sends love to your sweet family. The children are keeping their
Advent calendars until next year. Thank you again very much.

Love. SUE

P.S. Eloise is having her fifth child in about another month.
Have you heard from Sara? She was going to write about the
same time I wrote you last. Dillon got tired of waiting for me
to get coffee beans to show him how the coffee mill worked, so
I came home one day and found he had been grinding pecans
in it!

Grandmother's cardiologist had recommended that she drink a glass
of wine with dinner to settle her heart and perhaps lower her blood
pressure. Being a die-hard Baptist teetotaler all her life, Grandmother
balked at the very idea of consuming alcohol! Ingrid convinced her to
give it a try. Grandmother agreed to take the wine by the tablespoon,
as medicine, rather than from a glass!

Once again, Mother comments on the state of her health, which
manifests itself as profound fatigue. The metastatic breast cancer is
consuming her, as cancer "feeds" off the protein in the body. I remember
Mother's spending many hours in bed and generally being unwell, so
unlike the mothers of my friends.

Viola returned to Sweden shortly after Thanksgiving 1958. Mother
and I saw her in 1959. Mother wrote to Viola after Christmas.

January 31, 1958

 My dearest Viola:

Please forgive my being so slow to thank you for the lovely
Christmas gifts and letter. You are so sweet to think of us, and
we are all so proud of your gifts. Thanks a million! Christmas
for us this year was of course pretty difficult without Mother,
as she was always at the center of everything.

I didn't even get to town to shop. What little I did was on the telephone or in the neighborhood. I haven't been to town since July, as I just haven't felt like it. I have about two or three hours in the morning when I feel like doing a little, but the rest of the day I must rest. The past month, I have developed a new ailment—lots of pain all through my body from the middle of my back down to my legs. I thought it might be in my back, particularly in my bones, so I cannot sit very long without very severe pain. I had three X-rays of my back last week, though, and nothing showed up, so we are still trying to figure it out.

Please show this letter to Ingrid, Viola, as I am such a poor correspondent. I know you understand, though. The Anderson's little girl and the Eliasson's little boy are both such beautiful babies. They are all fine, and the Eliasson's have moved this week to a lovely big house at 3525 Princeton Ave. in Highland Park. It is just a block and a half from school, too. [The wealthiest neighborhood in all of Dallas. Mother and Daddy had many friends from that neighborhood through Highland Park Methodist Church.] Louise is so happy about it, and I really think she is going to be just fine now. [Louise had suffered postpartum depression after the birth of her son.] She has full time help now, as do I.

If any of you girls know of someone who would be interested, I certainly would love to have someone to come live with us. I am paying $32.00 a week for a colored girl, but I would so much rather have someone that I could talk to more. I am sure you know what I mean, as colored people are not the most interesting conversationalists! Of course there are times when I need to be quiet, but I was just thinking that if you knew someone who would be interested in a home and that much income, it would mean so much to me.

Please excuse the errors, as I am using my little portable and if I get any speed up at all, strange things appear on the paper. Oh, yes, you might let Britta read this too as you know we love her too. I had so hoped to be able to come to Sweden this summer, but maybe next!

Ingrid, we have had quite a time with Uncle Jim Gilliam.
[Grandmother's bachelor brother who lived in San Marcos,
Texas; he had heart trouble like she did.] Ed and Jo had to go
down last week and move him to a private home where the
woman could look after him. He of course could not understand
why, but the doctor said he must not be alone anymore. He
has had several bad falls. He spent six weeks in the Veterans
Hospital, but got tired of that, so we had to do something. He
is so senile that one cannot reason with him. He just can't
understand why he can't live alone, but we just can't let him.
I'm sure you know how it is with people with hardening of the
arteries.

I am resting up hoping to be able to fly to San Antonio next
Sunday and do two benefit reviews on Monday with Elizabeth.
We will do "The King and I" in the morning and "My Fair Lady"
that night. I have rested this whole month of January, so I do
hope nothing happens to keep me from going. Viola, I do hope
this winter finds you feeling much better than last winter.
Ingrid, hope you have found a nice apartment by now. Britta, I
know this past Christmas was hard for you without your dear
father. In other words, girls, we love you all, and are hoping
you each have a very good new year! Jimmy and the kids join
me in sending our best love. SUE

In February or March 1958 on a Saturday, Uncle Ed drove his black
Mercedes with Mother, Grandmother, and me (age ten) to San Marcos
to visit Uncle Jim. I developed a raging fever and sore throat on the
way that necessitated a call to the local pediatrician. He came to our
motel and prescribed an antibiotic. We drove back to Dallas on Sunday.
I probably missed a few days of school.

The 1950s have been romanticized by Hollywood and in the white
Southern press. I did not even know a Negro press existed until I was
in college! However, no matter how idyllic life seemed on the surface,
we only need peel back one layer to see the reality. In junior high

school, I met girls and boys who regularly skipped school, smoked in the restrooms, and talked back to teachers. I knew girls who disappeared for six months, only to return as the subject of gossip. I learned later that there was a "home" in Dallas for teenage mothers who signed over their babies for adoption. And they were the lucky ones. I became aware of classmates who resided in a group foster home in east Dallas for abused and neglected children, mostly teens. They had a hard time making and keeping friends, much less maintaining a decent GPA. I mention this to emphasize how fortunate my brother and I, and most of our friends, were to live in a safe home with two loving parents, Mother's illness notwithstanding.

In the 1950s and 1960s all major department stores were located in downtown Dallas, mostly on Main Street, Elm Street, and Pacific Avenue. As children, we often rode the bus downtown to go shopping or to go to the movies—whites in the front, Blacks in the back of the bus. Now shopping centers are located all over the city and suburbs.

Oh my dear mother, a woman of the racist "Jim Crow" South! How could she even have imagined a live-in maid! The footprint of our house was about 1,200 square feet, with three bedrooms, two baths. Mother and Daddy shared the master; Dillon and I each had our own room. In 1958, $32 had the buying power of $277 in 2018. No one came from Sweden to live with us. When Mother told our maid, Louise, about Ingrid, her friend from Sweden, Louise asked, "Is that near Chicago?"

Willie Mae Johnson, Grandmother's maid, worked over thirty years for my family on occasion. Like most maids in Dallas, Willie Mae traveled to work from Oak Cliff to our neighborhood on a city bus. Grandmother included "car fare" in her wages. Willie Mae was raising her niece, Georgette. She and I were the same age. In the summer of 1957, Willie Mae sometimes brought Georgette with her to work. We girls played with dolls and worked board games in my room. If we wanted to play outside, Willie Mae cautioned that we were not to play in the front yard, but we could play on the swing set in the backyard. I asked why we couldn't play in front, and Willie Mae said, "You are nice to Georgette, but I am not be sure the other children would be." I didn't quite understand. All my friends were "nice." I later realized that Willie Mae was being protective of Georgette—a black child in a white neighborhood was vulnerable. Willie Mae was loved by our family, but I did not realize as a child what that "love" meant. Like so many black women who worked for white families, she "raised" children who would grow up to become her employer. She had raised Sue and Edgar when she worked for their parents, Ruth and Marvin. Daddy met Willie Mae in 1936 after he and Mother married. He always called Willie Mae his "brown sugar." I am sure he never thought of himself as a racist. Willie Mae retired shortly after Uncle Ed married Josephine in February 1959.

There were several women who worked in our home when Mother was ill and after she died. Daddy realized we needed someone to clean house and to prepare supper for the three of us each evening. We also needed an adult in the house when we arrived home from school at four o'clock. I never will forget the day in the fall of 1960 when I learned that my father did not know our maid's name after she had been working for us at least a year before mother died. Her name was Jerlene; Daddy had called her Geraldine! I was thirteen.

By the middle of June 1958, it was clear that Mother had advanced-stage cancer and that Grandmother was near death. The cancer had metastasized to tissues surrounding her bones.

Mother wrote in longhand to Ingrid, Britta, and Viola while sitting in Grandmother's hospital room.

June 12, 1958

⟋ Dearest Ingrid, Britta, and Viola:

I had intended to write separate letters to each of you this time, but I know you will forgive me. Firstly, it is very different for me to write in pen, but it is too early in the morning to get the typewriter out.

I took Mother to Dr. Scurry's office yesterday and while she was getting a cardiogram she had a bad heart attack, so I took her straight to Gaston Hospital and as soon as we got to the room and before we could get her undressed she had another very bad one, so she is there for an indefinite period again.

After a shot of Demerol and oxygen she was easy when we left her last night, and I am sure she had a restful night as I have heard nothing to the contrary. I am going down soon. She and I both have felt pretty bad this past week.

I went to Dr. Brown Monday and he found a lump in my left breast and sent me to my surgeon. He confirmed it but said we would wait and examine me on the 23rd, so keep your fingers crossed for me. I am not worrying as I just have too much else to think about right now.

We know you will be remembering us in your prayers, and that means so much to me. I must get dressed now and go down there. I want to be there when the doctor comes.

We're mailing the slides insured, Ingrid. Air Mail! Were Britta's insured? If so, we would like to trace them for you.

Be sweet girls, all of you, and remember we love you very much. I shall keep you informed. Worlds of love, SUE

In June 1958, Mother paid another visit to Uncle Jim (Grandmother's brother) who was living in San Marcos, Texas, to tell him that his sister Ruth was gravely ill. We must have gone as a family (Daddy, Mother, Susibeth, Dillon); perhaps we spent a few days at Peaceful Valley Ranch, because she sent Uncle Jim a postcard from Kerrville, Texas, on Monday morning, June 9, 1958, to let him know we would arrive Saturday afternoon. She wrote, "Uncle Jim, I am sending this in care of Elizabeth as I thought you might not get to the post office. We will see you around noon or later Saturday afternoon. This is a beautiful country around here. Love. Sue."

Mother wrote again to Ingrid on July 21, 1958. She seems to be venting and relieving stress by writing these letters to Sweden. How gracious of our Swedish friends to receive her feelings. Of course, Ingrid and Britta had just visited in June 1957. There was no way Ingrid could have returned to Dallas to be with Mother at this time. Mother's typewriter was her "laptop." She composed her letters on the typewriter whenever possible.

July 21, 1958

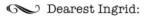 Dearest Ingrid:

I do hope you are not ill, as we have not received any news
from you since your return to Sweden. I have written you three
times, the last time to you and Brita and Viola together telling
about Mother's illness. Did you get it? I hate to repeat if you
have received it now, but she has been terribly ill. We took her
to the hospital on the 9th and she usually improves greatly, but
this time she is no better than she was. She is still in terrific
pain. Ed and I were down there five hours last night waiting for
her to get easy. The nurse called us Saturday morning that she
was very bad and that we had better get on down there. When
she feels better, she feels better, but the pain is just almost
unbearable when it comes. Dr. Scurry says he does not know
why she must have so much pain. He put her on a liquid diet
today to see if that might help.

Susibeth had a nice birthday. [I turned eleven on July 17,
1958.] She had eight little girls over. Marjorie H. and Leona
A. took them to play miniature golf before lunch while Louise
[the maid] and I prepared lunch for them. They were a darling
bunch of girls, and they seemed to have a good time. I couldn't
have done it without Marjorie and Leona.

I am going this afternoon to get this lump checked in my left
breast, and they will tell me whether I must have it out. I am
not so concerned except for what it will do to Mother, as I know
how frightened she might become. I will add a note to this
letter after I see the doctor. I don't mind just having the tumor
out, but I just hope and pray it is not malignant.

Tell Britta I enjoyed and appreciated her sweet letter so
very much, as did Mother, and Susibeth received a nice card
from her today. If you will forgive us we will try to write to the
two of you together for a while. I am ashamed that I have not
written to Viola and Barbro yet either, but please tell them for
me that we have been in a heap of trouble around here, and we
will write when we get straightened out a little better.

Ed had a letter from Birgitta on Saturday which he is answering today, and she wrote as though she had no idea who to write to at S.M.U. He has written her again today telling her to just write to Dr. R. G. Storey, Dean of the Law School, sending his [husband Carl] scholastic record. As for jobs for any of them, they would just have to be here to apply personally, and I am sure they would have no trouble finding something.

I must stop here and get ready to go to the doctor and will finish this later. Please write if you can, as we have not heard anything since your return, and we love you and miss you so very much!

Well, I went to my surgeon, and he said the lump they were speaking of was nothing more than a fatty tumor and said I could forget that. I was relieved, then he went on to say that there was a mass farther down that he was more concerned about as a potential hazard, and he would advise surgery on it and while he was in there he would remove the little tumor. I know that Dr. Morris had mentioned this mass many times over the past twelve years I have been going to him, and said it was nothing at all to worry about, so I just called him, and he advised me strictly against surgery. Dr. Morris said while he respected Dr. Goode very much, as he had sent me to him before, he definitely did not agree that I should have this done. I feel that Dr. Morris knows me and my history so well that I can put complete confidence in him. He said he would keep a close watch on me, and just not to worry about it. Both he and Dr. Scurry agree that it would be very bad for Mother right now, so I told her yesterday that we had nothing to worry about, and of course she was relieved.

Mother's night nurse called me this morning and said she had a much better night and had to have only one hypo [Demerol] for pain about 1:30 a.m. Dr. Scurry told me not to be too optimistic about Mother, though, as so far she has made no progress.

Ingrid, please write us a note when you can. I do hope you
are not ill. Give my love to all our dear friends over there. Did
you get the slides? SUE

Oh, how I do remember that birthday! Of course, it was hot, but
the miniature golf course was shaded. We played from 10:00 a.m.
until lunchtime, then food and birthday cake. Since Mother was a
consummate Southern belle cook, the menu was probably chicken
salad and a jello fruit salad, and always ice cream and chocolate cake.
The girls: Lisa, Livonia, Wanda, perhaps Alicia and Alanna, Jan, Docka,
and Marjorie H's daughter, whose name I don't remember. I am struck
by Mother's statement: "Please write if you can, as we have not heard
anything since your return, and we love you and miss you so very much!"
It has been more than a year since Ingrid had written to Mother!

Mother, always feeling poorly by this time, worried constantly about
Grandmother. TWELVE YEARS this mass had been on Mother's left
breast and it's NOTHING? Her doctor has known about this mass since
1946, before I was born. Could it be that the cancer that took her life
began in the left breast and metastasized to the right breast only to be
discovered as a lump in 1954? She never had a chance!

RUTH'S DEATH

Grandmother, Ruth Collier Gilliam Dillon, died at Gaston Hospital
in Dallas, Texas, on July 25, 1958. She was sixty-eight. The obituary in
the *Dallas Morning News* that ran on August 2, the day of her funeral,
did not give her Christian name. As was the custom, she is referred to
as Mrs. Marvin D. Dillon. Women were named only in the context of
their husbands. Both Mother and Uncle Ed suffered profoundly the
grief of losing their mother. As a child of eleven, I was allowed to visit
Grandmother early in this last hospitalization, but not in the last days
of her life. Mother did tell me about her last hours. Grandmother was
heavily sedated; her breathing was shallow, and her blood pressure was
dropping. The nurse in charge of her care recommended that Mother
and Daddy wait down the hall in the family sitting room. This was late

in the evening. I don't know if Mother wanted to remain in the room as Grandmother passed. Anyway, the nurse came into the waiting room and said, "It's almost over. When I come back, she will be gone." That is how it was done in those days. Dillon and I spent the night with neighbors and did not get the word until the following morning. After Grandmother passed, Daddy drove Mother home, both very tired. She took a shower and washed her hair. Then she and Daddy took a late drive around White Rock Lake, something we did as a family almost every Sunday afternoon. I learned to drive on those White Rock Lake Sundays, sitting on Daddy's lap. There is no record of their conversation, but it must have included discussion of the state of Mother's health.

Grandmother's funeral was held on August 2, 1958. Mother's and Ingrid's dear friend Sara Everett stayed at our home on Westlake. Sara did not attend funerals, as she was a practicing Christian Scientist. Willie Mae, Grandmother's and Mother's beloved maid, waited at the house with Sara also. Sara wrote this letter to Ingrid on the day of Grandmother's funeral:

August 2, 1958

☙ Dear Ingrid,

While the service is being held for our beloved Mrs. Dillon and I am staying in Sue's home, I think they both would be pleased for me to talk to you. Willie Mae is in the kitchen and sends her love to you. She told me that Mrs. Dillon said she was so glad that she had the good times with you. She and I had a good visit when I accompanied Willie [black employee of Dillon Scale] to pick up your packages. He put them in my car, then Jack [Sara's brother] took them out to Monkey Grip, so you see, it was easy all the way around. I'm glad they arrived safely.

We are looking forward to receiving your package, although you were too busy, I'm sure, for it to be right for you to take the time. We thank you from the bottom of our hearts. The pictures you sent are treasures, especially the family group. Thanks again.

Sue and Ed are holding up beautifully. I trust they will
realize The Source of their strength as the days follow. They
feel that they would not want their mother to have more of the
suffering of these last days. There is always a helpful thought
to replace the sad one, I have found.

I wish you could know how very much you mean to all of us
here. You thought you were describing me in your letter, but
that is a picture of your own dear self. Much, much love to you.
Pass along my thoughts and good wishes also to your family
and friends as you see them.

As ever. SARA

Sara Everett, one of Mother's best friends, watched over our home
the day of Mother's funeral in 1960 as well. I wish I had a letter written
on that day from her to Ingrid.

Mother wrote to a family friend, Alma Edwards, Uncle Jim Gilliam's
caregiver in San Marcos, Texas, thanking her for looking after him
during the time of his sister's death.

August 24, 1958

 My dear Alma:

Please excuse the typewriter but writing with pen is my big
handicap. It is very painful for me, and you could not read it
either. Since returning home you can imagine how busy I have
been, and the fact that I have had so much to do with such a
heavy heart has made it even more tiring. I have had so many
acknowledgment to send out to all our wonderful friends, and I
am still not through.

Alma, you will never know how much we appreciated what
you did for us the other night, and we appreciate all the other
wonderful things you have done for us in the past. I will not
take the time today to write Uncle Jim, but will you please call
him and tell him I am going into the hospital on Wednesday
to be operated on Thursday. They will not know until the lab

work is done while I am still under the anesthetic whether
it will have to be a radical like the last one. I just hope and
pray that it will not, as it is no pink tea. [Uncle Jim Gilliam,
Grandmother's senile brother, lived in a nursing home in San
Marcos. He did not attend Grandmother's funeral.]

Ed has done none of the things we discussed while we were
there [in San Marcos in February 1958], as we have had so
very many things to attend to. We still do not know what we
are going to do about the home [the Blue Valley Lane house],
etc. I have, however, gone through Mother's things and taken
care of all of them. I am enclosing a copy of the story from the
newspaper here. Tell Uncle Jim when you give it to him that
we did not leave his and Aunt Kate's names out of the list of
survivors, both newspapers [the *Dallas Morning News* and
Dallas Times Herald] did. It seems that they do not list any
survivors outside the immediate family; not even brothers and
sisters unless they live in or near Dallas. Aunt Kate wrote a
very ugly note to us wanting to know why she was left out. I
know Uncle Jim will understand, though. I wrote her and told
her she should know that we would not have done it ourselves,
but that Dallas is a big city, and the newspapers have so much
to print that they cut everything they can.

Fay said you would be up here next week, so let us hear
from you. You are the only one in San Marcos I am writing, so
if you see any of them, please tell them we do appreciate all
they are doing for Uncle Jim, and I would write, if I just weren't
really sick. I remember I had the same reaction of nerves after
Dad's passing in 1943. Fondly, SUE

I remember this time very well. At age eleven, I had learned to write
in cursive, so I assisted in the signing of the acknowledgments. I wrote
the phrase "The family of Mrs. Ruth C. Dillon" on the cards until writer's
cramp forced me to stop. Dillon, age nine, may have helped also, stuffing
envelopes and licking stamps. Mother was grateful for our help.

The year of Grandmother's death was difficult. Mother had her second surgery, and she continued to "feel bad." Here is a letter she wrote to Ingrid, dated August 26, 1958.

ᏟᏬ My dearest Ingrid,

Just a quick note while I am at the beauty parlor to tell you that I am going to have surgery on Thursday, the 28th, and of course do not know how long I will be there, but they will make an incision under the general anesthetic between the lump and the mass and determine whether to go on with a radical. I do so hope it will not be a radical. I am not too worried about myself, Ingrid, because I have had so much bigger problems all summer. If I had not had that happy month with you [in June 1957] I don't see how I could have stood the past two months.

My biggest problem though I am trying not to let it be, is Ed. He did real well during Mother's illness, but since her death he has really given me a great deal of concern. I have talked until I am blue in the face, but he will not go to a good psychiatrist for help. I will not go into detail, for I know you understand. My cousin [don't know which one] is with him but Ed has asked him to leave. I did ask him to wait until after my operation, as I am so afraid Ed will set himself on fire. I have gone through Mother's room and disposed of her clothes, which was very hard of course, but I am glad to get it over. I brought her bedroom suite to my house, as I want to keep it in the family. [I still have that bedroom suite. It came to Texas with the Dillon family after the Civil War in 1892 on a covered wagon from Kentucky.] I took the twin beds from Susibeth's room over in its place, as I do not want the house to look bare.

I don't know what Ed plans to do, but we are still planning for Birgitta and Carl to come. I will just have to explain the problem to her when she comes. You know how hard Ed is to pin down, but I don't think he plans to sell the house any time soon. [Uncle Ed kept the house. When he married Josephine in January 1959, she moved into Grandmother's house after their wedding. She redecorated it mostly in white. They sold it in late 1960.]

Lars called and asked to take Dillon to the weather program, which he did. He said he and Penny were moving to a 3 bedroom apartment so they would have room for his sisters, and I told them we had invited them, so I am sure they will have a place. If they don't mind, I think Ed would love to have them. I just wish he would take care of his problem before they come. [Uncle Ed's "problem" was clinical depression. He never sought treatment.]

I have told some of his close friends about it, Ingrid, in the hope they might help him, as I have not accomplished one thing in 7 years. I feel like I just cannot shield him like Mother did, as I have bigger problems of my own plus Jimmy and the children to consider first. Poor Jimmy really has a load too and has to cover for him at the office.

Sara came by and brought me the lovely color prints she took of us. She is leaving for Georgia this week and will sail for Hawaii on Sept. 24. I did not tell her about my going to the hospital for obvious reasons.

I am playing at noon tomorrow for a Father & Daughter program at the Rotary Club then checking in at the hospital at 2:00! Susibeth will be Ed's "daughter" and we are using Susibeth and Elizabeth's daughter, Beth in the last number, which will be "Be Kind to Your Parents." Ed doesn't know that Susibeth will be in it yet. We're going to surprise him.

Bill, Jimmy's younger brother, has moved to Dallas for at least a month. They live just a mile back of us in some lovely apartments with a swimming pool, so you know how good this is going to be for Jimmy and the kids. Their children are so sweet. Ralph is 13, John 7 and Virginia 5. Susibeth and Dillon are so thrilled to have some little cousins nearby.

Ingrid, you are the only one I am writing, as you can imagine how busy I have been, so you might send this to Bo to read as I don't mind his knowing all this. Just don't tell the others the news in it. It gives me such strength to feel the love of my precious Swedish friends, and if I am physically up to it next summer, I hope I can come to Sweden.

I love you very much Ingrid. Please give my love to each one of my precious friends. I will tell Ed to drop you a line Thursday eve as to the extent of my operation. Affectionately, SUE

P.S. We gave "Pretty Pinkie" [the parakeet] to the Eliasson's today, as he was just beginning to talk when we brought him to our house. Now he sounds like a canary!

Birgitta Giertz Helmstrom, husband Carl, Ingrid Giertz, and Bishop Bo Giertz sailed to US on the HS *Kungsholm* in late August, arriving in New York City in early September 1958. Carl was applying to SMU Law School. They came to Dallas to visit Lars, their brother and son of the bishop. All of us were happy to see them.

The months of July, August, and September 1958 weighed on the family, but Dillon and I found refuge in being children. Mother's battle with cancer took a toll every day. She received strength and encouragement through the correspondence with our dear Swedish friends. Uncle Bill and the family stayed in Dallas for two years. They moved to Austin shortly after Mother died in May 1960. I truly believe their coming to Dallas at this particular time was a God thing. Daddy leaned on his brother, and Aunt Ruth "mothered" Dillon and me during Mother's last illness.

From Gaston Hospital, Mother wrote to Bo and Elisabeth.

September 4, 1958

Dear Bo and Elisabeth,

I hope you can read this, as it is very difficult for me to write, but I feel that I must write to you. I asked Louise Eliasson to write Ingrid Jaensson for me.

What a year this has been! If it had not started off with such a happy June 1957 [Ingrid's visit and the time at Peaceful Valley], I know I never could have endured the rest.

Perhaps you know from Ingrid that there was some malignancy on my left side, so they did a simple mastectomy and recommended 21 X-ray treatments which I started this last Tuesday. They have already begun to make me feel pretty bad, so I shudder to think of how I will feel after 21 of them. That is why I must write you now before I get more "down in the dumps" than I am. I know you have not been well, either of you, but if you can write I would so enjoy a note from you!

I had so hoped that maybe I could come to Sweden next summer, but with all this I doubt that I will be fit either physically or financially!

I do not know how long I will be here, but the doctor just told me not to plan on going home any time soon, so if you can write real soon you can send it here.

I must admit that I have not been the usual good patient this time, as I have always said that I would never let them use X-ray. However, I suppose I must do as they say. I have little faith in X-ray.

I do hope and pray that you are both feeling better by now, and please know that my thoughts and prayers are with you always.

Ed is alone now, and I just hope that Birgitta and Carl can work out some arrangement with him, as he is so lonely.

Dillon is at home with a cold today, otherwise Jimmy and the children have been fine. You know how many wonderful friends and neighbors we have! My room looks like a flower shop!

You might send this on to Ingrid at Malmö, though there is little of interest in it. I am looking forward to seeing your sweet girls and Carl.

Your Texas friend. SUE

Radiation treatments for cancer were in their infancy in 1958. Of course, today the patient would receive them as an outpatient rather than as an in-patient resident in the hospital. I am struck by Mother's presumption that Birgitta and Carl are somehow expected to cheer up Uncle Ed! Mother remained hospitalized for most of September 1958. The next correspondence to Ingrid was written by Sara Everett.

September 5, 1958

〰 Dearest Ingrid,

Your gift of love arrived in good time—the lovely linens and treasured book of Malmö—and I have sat down several time to write my thanks only to be interrupted. This last time, I let the thought of Sue's operation deter me until I could make sure that the family was telling it. It was not the extreme one of last time [her surgery in 1954], and Sue is doing well.

I saw her day before yesterday. She was her pretty self, sitting propped up a bit and dialing Elizabeth's number, as I went in to talk of the "keys" in which she accompanies her. I know of no one else who could possibly match Elizabeth as Sue does.

Sue is not letting outside things bother too much, I'm glad to see; she is relaxing, and will soon be active, I'm sure. With the children in school, Jim assures me that he has things under control at home. Love. Sara

Sara is ever the consummate optimist. I know Daddy was under tremendous pressure. It's a wonder he didn't have serious health issues. As children, Dillon and I pressed on with school and growing up. Mother's illness was the defining feature of our lives. About this time, it became apparent that Elizabeth Peabody could not rely on Mother's being able to keep the performance schedule they had together. The Lord provided Elizabeth with another accompanist, Elizabeth Soderstrom, a neighbor and friend of Mother's. I think the two Elizabeths performed together about a year.

Ingrid also received correspondence from Willie Mae Johnson, Grandmother's maid for some thirty years. She is "heart broken and sad" over the passing of Grandmother and Mother's current illness.

September 9, 1958

⟳ Dear Miss Ingrid.

I am very sorry indeed to be as long writing. But dear, I have been heart broken and sad. I haven't had the heart to do anything. I like the gift so much, you were so sweet to think of me. Please thank Miss Gerta [Giertz] for the picture, it is so good. All are as well as could be expected. I talked to Sue today she is still in the hospital feel fair. Ed is OK, worked for him Sat. You are a nice person. I sure hope to see you again loads of love to you and your family. Willie Mae Johnson

Bishop Bo Giertz, Ingrid Giertz, and sister and husband Birgitta and Carl Helmstrom arrived in Dallas in September 1958 to visit son and brother Lars. Lars was now an American citizen working for a local ABC affiliate TV station WFAA. Bo returned to Sweden in a few weeks. Birgitta and Carl stayed until April 1959. Ingrid Giertz stayed until we (Sue, Susibeth, Ingrid G.) boarded a plane in Dallas bound for New York City to board the MS *Gripsholm* to sail to *Göteborg* in early June 1959.

Mother endured the twenty-one X-ray treatments and came home from the hospital in late September or early October 1958. I remember for Christmas 1958, both Dillon and I asked for new bicycles, but Santa could not afford them. I doubt Mother cooked Christmas dinner; we probably spent Thanksgiving and Christmas with Uncle Bill, Aunt Ruth, and cousins Ralph, John, and Ginny or perhaps with friends. Mother's health was not improving, but she possessed an incredible will to live.

In early winter 1959, Uncle Ed married Josephine Hunley. The wedding took place in the Hunley family home in Lancaster, Texas, south of Dallas (where Grandmother Ruth had taught school before her marriage to Marvin in 1912). The whole Dillon family attended. I remember wearing a blue taffeta dress and shiny black patent leather shoes. Mother played the "Wedding March." I remember Mother's being so happy for Uncle Ed. Now he had a wife who could look after him.

Mother resumed playing the organ and performing with Elizabeth Peabody, in spite of having another round of radiation, this time on her back. I can only imagine the conversations that must have taken place between Elizabeth Peabody, Elizabeth Soderstrom, and Sue Bussard, as Elizabeth S. graciously waited in the wings to step in for Mother as necessary.

TRIP TO SWEDEN IN 1959:
A DREAM COME TRUE

*J*n the spring of 1959, serious plans for Mother to travel to Sweden
in the summer were in the works. I was to accompany her. A flurry
of surviving letters written by Mother to Ingrid between April 12 and
May 29 chronicle the events leading up to our departure. I am certain
that the doctors had told Mother that the twenty-one X-ray treatments
had only kept the cancer at bay, not cured it. Mother knew she did not
have long to live, but the power of the Holy Spirit, a strong desire to
see Ingrid and Sweden, and a growing realization that the bond with
her daughter needed to be strengthened energized her to make the
journey.

These letters begin Sunday, April 12, 1959. Mother wrote to Ingrid
in longhand.

> My dearest Ingrid,
>
> You have been on my mind so very much lately—more than
> usual—and I do hope all is well with you and yours. Please tell
> Britta I enjoyed and appreciated her sweet letter so very much.
>
> I am just finishing up another series of deep therapy X-ray
> treatments—this time on my back. You know I said I would

never have more X-ray but was suffering so much with my
back and left leg that I had to do something. [The cancer is
deep in her bones.] My leg is about half-numb in the thigh, and
yet very painful. I never knew I could suffer so much as I have
these past months, Ingrid. They say they think it is arthritis,
but they aren't kidding me. I manage to keep going and playing
for reviews but have had to cut out all long trips by car. I also
have a friend [Elizabeth Soderstrom, mentioned previously]
who plays for me when I don't feel up to it. We have been doing
"Song of Norway" and "The Music Man." The latter is a load of
fun, and of course "Song of Norway" has Grieg's music. [Mother
taught me the songs from this musical. I performed "I Can't
Dance, You Can't Dance" in the school talent show dressed as a
Norwegian peasant!]

Ingrid, if I can possibly feel up to it physically and can
arrange something about my children, maybe I can come to
Sweden. I have asked Harriet Armstrong from Grapevine to
consider flying over with me and maybe Barbro or someone
else could come back on the boat with me. I will probably buy
Ed a Volvo while there. (I wrote Barbro recently about coming
back.)

I take my last X-ray treatment tomorrow, so it is too early to
know if it will help me. I am not an invalid, but I cannot take a
long trip alone.

Ed and Jo are fine, but they too have had their troubles.
Her mother fell halfway down their stairs and crushed both
wrists and a neck bone, so she has really suffered. Her cancer
problem is also returning, as it is in her liver. Ed and Jo moved
down to Lancaster when it happened but brought her up here
Thursday. She is still almost entirely helpless.

Ingrid, you know how I have always dreamed of coming to
Sweden before I die [she has long known], and please pray with
me I can work it out. The children are my biggest problem,
of course. [Evidently, it has not yet been decided that I am to
accompany Mother to Sweden.] Did I tell you Jimmy lost his

mother [Mama Grace] on Feb. 10, 1959? I can't remember what I have told you.

If Harriet comes, we will fly to Paris as she has a friend there who has been wanting her to come. She is the only one of my friends besides Sara who has both the time and the money to consider it. Keep your fingers crossed!

Ingrid G. went with us this afternoon to see "Gigi." It was so lovely. It was at the Wilshire where you and I saw "Sayonara" and I thought about you! We wanted Ingrid to come home with us but she said she must get home and cook for Lars. Penny will be coming home in about a week or so, and I know Lars will be happy.

I must stop now, Ingrid, as I am very tired! How many times I have wished for you! I really believe if anything can help me live longer and healthier it will be seeing you and my other precious friends in Sweden!

Tell Ockie Susibeth was just over-joyed with his letter and is waiting for another one from him.

Give my love to Viola, Britta, Ann-Marie and all the others you might see. Also please write me what you think of my dreams!

Barbro hasn't answered me yet as to whether she might come back with me. You know she might come as an exchange teacher. Please write to me, Ingrid.

I love you. SUE

I just discovered I was out of matching envelopes, so please excuse it. We thought about all of you so much at Easter [March 29, 1959]!

The logistics of getting Mother ready to travel to Sweden required much correspondence. I would love to know the substance of the conversations across Sweden about how to manage it. I believe that the hand of God touched her in those days, giving her energy she didn't have and granting her a reprieve from suffering. When we returned home in August 1959, Mother crashed, as the cancer spread relentlessly through her body.

Mother wrote to Bishop and Elisabeth Giertz on April 20, 1959.

   ◠◡ Dear Bo and Elisabeth:

You might have heard from one of our Ingrids that I am thinking of coming to Sweden if my health permits. I have been having so much pain in my back and leg that I have just undergone a series of X-ray treatments again and of course feel those too. It is too soon to know whether they will relieve the pain, but my doctors are urging me to make the trip if I can get some relief. The doctors see no tumors in my spine, but they do see something abnormal and we are hoping and praying that it does not mean more cancer.

I am sure you know how very much I have always wanted to come to Sweden, and I know Mother would want me to. I have considered bringing Susibeth but have made no plans whatever, and I know I must. Your Ingrid said something about Ingrid Jaensson's friend who is a travel agent in Malmö being able to obtain tickets at a discount. Susibeth will not be twelve until July 17, so I am supposing that she could come over half fare. Please send this note on to Ingrid, as I would like for her to answer if it is possible to get passage on the Kungsholm on May 27. I would prefer to come in June, but I am sure that is impossible. I shall start to work on my passport this week. I go to the doctor for a check-up on Thursday, so say a prayer with us!

Your little Ingrid G. is so precious to me, and I just can't tell you how much she has meant to me. We talk almost every day on the telephone and manage to see each other about once a week. I haven't seen your precious little grandson [Lars and Penny's son, Riley Bo] yet but intend to very soon. We are so happy for all of you. She called me Saturday and said she was keeping him and that he was such a good baby! She keeps urging me to plan to come to Sweden, and Ed and Jimmy want me to also, so MAYBE it will work out. I just must be a little more comfortable, though, before I try to go anywhere.

We surely hated to see Birgitta leave, but also are happy for her to be with her husband again! We thought of all of you so very much at Easter [March 29]. Did you receive the TOGETHER magazine subscription, Bo? Our family enjoys it very much. Please excuse the bad typewriting, but it is so difficult for me to write in longhand, and this little portable will not allow any speed without "stacking" the letters.

I hope this finds you all feeling well and happy, and we would love to hear from you when you have the letter. Devotedly yours, SUE

Communication between Mother, Ingrid J., and the bishop continued furiously, and they finally arrived at a firm plan and itinerary by the middle of May 1959. Although there is some repetition in the letters, I include all as Mother's enthusiasm for the trip grows. Also, she seems to complain less as our departure date nears.

April 27, 1959

◟◞ My dearest Ingrid:

I have a letter from Bo today and he tells me what a state of indecision you are in with your apartment, etc., and believe me, I do understand. I have been so sorry all the time about your having to give up your apartment and had so hoped that you would not have so much difficulty. Please do not worry about my coming before you are settled, Ingrid, as I will put my reservations up not earlier than June 5 or 6 and if I don't get anything then I shall try up to June 15. Just don't you bother from that end, as I know you are snowed under with work. I have asked the Arthur Strain Agency here in Dallas to see what they can do, so please do not bother yourself one minute about trying to get anything over there.

IF I do come, I will not arrive in Göteborg before the 13th of June at the earliest, and of course I can visit Öland or go to Växjö and see Barbro first, or even Birgitta. In other words

I could wait until July to come to see you. If I come by boat, which I would rather do, I would plan to be there about a month, so there would be plenty of time to see you, Ingrid. And PLEASE believe me when I say I understand that it is much trouble for you to even think of our coming when you are unsettled, and we certainly do not want to be any trouble to you. I am still planning to bring Susibeth with me, and I do hope I will not have to disappoint her. [Of course, I was excited about the prospect of going to Sweden with Mother, but I do remember trying not to think about it too much. Mother often canceled plans at the last minute.]

Also, please do not think that you will have to take me around a lot, as I just cannot ride in a car for any length of time and can do very little walking. The main thing for me would be to see you and all my wonderful friends in Sweden. I thought maybe after I got there and could possibly feel like it I might like to fly over to Paris for a day or so, but if I would never be disappointed if I just got to Sweden.

Remember how I was when you were here in summer 1957? I didn't have any excess energy to do anything "extra" for you, and I still feel that way only more so. The damp cool weather doesn't seem to make any difference in how I feel, as we have had a very cool damp spring. I can feel just as punk on pretty warm sunshiny days. My only thought in coming early was that Susibeth could come on half fare until July 17. Mrs. Strain will hear something from Chicago this week, and I definitely will not plan to leave earlier than the 5th of June, and preferably will make it as late as July 1st, so please do not fret. I may not be able to come at all, but my doctor says he will not let me if he has any idea that I might get sick over there. But just remember that you will be having a very slow old grandma that will not need entertaining or taken around. It will be enough to realize a wonderful dream I have had a very long time to visit a country very, very dear to me and all my family! I love you lots. Just take it one day at a time, Ingrid, and do not

worry. It will all work out if it is supposed to!
Worlds of love. SUE.

The ticket that cost about $2,500 for Mother's and my trip to Sweden was booked in early May 1959. Mother was experiencing a Holy Spirit blessing, a surge of adrenaline and profound joy. The new drugs she was on were merely analgesics and antianxiety drugs. Nothing to treat the cancer. I came home from school on May 7,1959, and Mother told me we were really going to Sweden! I was incredulous at first, then overjoyed!

Ingrid was a single woman, working on the nursing staff at the main hospital in Malmö. I am not familiar with Swedish housing laws, but I do know that Ingrid was allowed to rent only a one-bedroom flat in government-controlled housing. She told me when I visited in 2004 that Mother and I arrived in Göteborg on the same day she was moving into her new apartment on Lorensborgsgatan 13A in Malmö. Her sister, Ann-Marie, supervised the move. Ingrid moved into the building that had been built in 1958. At that time she entered a time warp, living in that apartment until her death in 2012. When I visited in 2004 and stayed with her, I was struck by the fact that her apartment had not been updated.

May 15, 1959

⟨⟩ My dearest precious Ingrid:

I received your wonderful letter today, and please excuse me for not telling you sooner our definite arrangements to date. I am trying so hard to keep my composure and not get too tired, while I am so excited over getting to see all my wonderful friends. I did write Bo about a week ago, and you may not know of this by now, as I realize you are not in the same city, and I did not tell him to send you the last letter. At his suggestion, and Ingrid's [Giertz], we have decided to stay in Göteborg a day or two until I get rested and then go straight to Öland for the week that Bo will be there. But to go back to the beginning.

Ingrid Giertz, Susibeth and I are leaving here on June 1, flying to New York, and sailing from New York on the

Gripsholm on June 5, and we are due to arrive in Göteborg
June 13, which is on a Saturday, so I hope you and Britta can
meet us. Ingrid G. says her home will be all closed up then, and
there will be some re-decorating going on, but we are welcome
to stay there until I get my land legs.

Then we will go over to Karlan [Does she mean Kalmar
or Öland?] where Bo will meet us, and we plan to stay there
a week. Then Bo will be leaving, and Ingrid G. said I might
want to go back from there to Växjö and visit Barbro the week
beginning June 21. Since Midsummer Eve is the following
week-end, Ingrid G. thought you might want to come to Växjö
to the festivities, and as you say, we can take it a day at a time
from there. Maybe you could get some time off in July, and that
would be too wonderful to be true!

You may remember Dr. and Mrs. [Don and Betty] McMullen.
They visited with you one night when we went to my thirtieth
high school class reunion. Remember? Well, he is with World
Health Organization in Geneva, or was Christmas, and I have
written her that if I felt like it, I might like to come down
there. I have not had time to hear, but even if they have left,
Switzerland is a country I have always wanted to see even
more than France or England. I thought I might go by train,
and therefore see more country. If possible I would like to do
this while Susibeth is with Ann-Marie. Bless her heart. Please
tell Ann-Marie, Larse, and Ockie that they are so sweet to
invite her on such a wonderful trip. She is just beside herself
with excitement. Of course, her mother isn't a bit excited. I just
can't believe it, and Susibeth says she won't believe it until she
is out of sight of Miss Liberty!

This is the deal about me now, Ingrid. My pain in my back
and leg is nearly all gone but begins to return if I walk too
much at a time or ride in a car too long. I get very tired and
have to turn in pretty early at night, and also rest in the
afternoon, but maybe after my Gripsholm trip I will already be
rested a great deal and will not be such a sissy!

I would also like to see Oslo, if possible. I have reservations on the Kungsholm, departing Göteborg Aug. 1. I do hope you will not find our stay too long, as I know how hard you are working. I am writing Barbro these plans tonight, as she wrote me such a nice note and said she was off from June 10 to August 15. [Mother tried to extend our stay by changing the return booking, but there were no open cabins until well into September!] You gals just toss it around, and we will conform to your schedules. Ingrid, I know Mother would want us to come, and I can't tell you how happy I am. Also, tell Ann-Marie how much we appreciate her offering her house in Malmö before you get your apartment. However, as it looks from here it will be almost July 1 before we get to Malmö.

I forgot to tell you that Harriet Armstrong is flying to New York with us to spend those four days and see us off! We have tickets to "The Music Man" and "Destry Rides Again," both leading musicals! Harriet is having us and Ingrid and some others out for dinner Sunday night of the 24th, so be thinking of us, as we will of you. Mr. Hibbard, her father, speaks of you and Britta so very much, and is sending you some pictures. He has had two hernia operations recently and is doing nicely now. You and Britta really made a hit with him, as with others too!

On second thought, Ingrid, would you mind just to send this to Barbro, and I know she will understand that there would be so much repetition in your two letters and I am so tired. I am playing tomorrow for a style show at the New Sheraton Hotel, and Ingrid and Penny [Lars's wife] are going with me. I have been in the doctors' office all afternoon with my Aunt Lera [Grandfather Dillon's sister] and she will be here all weekend. I have two reviews Monday of "The Music Man" with Elizabeth, a party for my trip on Wednesday at Leona Allman's, play Thursday, and Josephine is having a coke party for Susie and me Saturday. I have so much to do, but I guess it will be done. Just send this on to Barbro, as I am so sleepy, and I know she will understand, and whatever you gals work out will be fine with us. Ingrid G. is an angel to me, and I am so happy that she is going to be with me all the way over.

All of your girl friends over here are so thrilled and envious of me and wish to be remembered to you. I have not been able to reach the Wharton's yet but will keep trying. Sara Everett is a real doll, as you will find out when I see you. All my friends have been so helpful and are trying to keep me from getting too tired. I must sign off now, girls. Remember I love you very much, and just can't wait! Surely wish at least one of you could come home with me! Always, SUE

P. S. Please don't worry about the weather! Just to be with you will be all I need. Jimmy even suggested that I stay over there and teach English next winter! I think he is trying to get rid of me, and I can't blame him. Believe me that would be all I could teach!

Mother had graduated from Sunset High School, class of 1929. The school, located in the Oak Cliff area of Dallas, Texas, opened in 1925 and is still viable. When I attended Woodrow Wilson High School from 1963 to 1965, we played Sunset in football.

Mother had no concept of distances in Europe or Sweden. It is at least a three-hour train ride from Malmö to Göteborg. Ingrid J. told me that the very day we arrived was the day she was to move into her new apartment, but she did meet the boat! As a bishop of the Lutheran Church of Sweden, Bo and his wife, Elisabeth, lived in an eighteenth-century house in the midst of Göteborg Vestra Hammgatan 17. There was a ground floor entry foyer, then a spiral staircase leading up to the living quarters. A lift had been installed in the stairwell for Elisabeth. The drawing and dining rooms were on the first floor, and five bedrooms and one bathroom were on the second floor. I remember the formal dining room, where we took meals. A long table was set with sterling silver, fine china, linen napkins with silver napkin rings, and candelabras. I remember we "dressed" for dinner. The walls of the living and dining rooms were hung with fifteenth- and sixteenth-century tapestries that came from Elisabeth's family castle in Finland. Ingrid G., age twenty, and younger brother Martin, age sixteen, lived in the house. Older brother Lars lived in Dallas, and sister Birgitta was married, living with husband Carl in Göteborg.

Our Westlake neighbors, church friends, and Sara Everett threw bon voyage parties for us the week before we were to depart. Somehow, Sara had arranged for me to "borrow" designer clothes to take on the trip. These included skirts and several matching sweater sets—short-sleeve sweater with matching cardigan. We packed a footlocker with clothes for the eight weeks we were to be gone. Mother's friends put together a money tree that came to about $200. We spent that money in New York and Sweden.

Mother wrote to Viola Fröler the details of the trip plan:

May 19, 1959

♋ My dearest Viola,

Susibeth and I can hardly wait to see you and our other precious friends. If you see a lot of stuff all over the paper it will be because I am in the beauty parlor! I take turns writing to each of you girls, hoping you will share the letters and what news they contain so that I will not have to repeat so much. I know you all understand!

Ingrid Giertz just called that they [Bo and Elisabeth] will stay over in Göteborg and meet us on Saturday, June 13th, then take us to Öland with them on the train on Monday. As I wrote Ingrid J. this past week, anything they plan for us will suit me just fine. I do so want to be as little trouble as possible to each one. I do feel that the week of rest on Öland might be good for me, then perhaps I will feel like a trip to Switzerland while Susibeth is gone with Ann-Marie. Tell Ingrid I heard from my friend in Geneva (she knows her too) and she wants me to come, but we will have to make hotel reservations, as her twins will be there from the States during the summer, and they have only a one-bedroom apt around the corner from the da Rhone Hotel, which is very expensive. Betty says she

has a Volkswagen and will take us all around! I surely hope
you or Ingrid or Barbro or Britta, or all of you can go down
there with me! I think I would like to go by rail so I could see
more. Perhaps if Ann-Marie knows the dates in July when
they will be going, it would be well to make the train and hotel
reservations for a few days' trip—whatever you wish. Ingrid G.
thinks I might want to see Paris on the way down or back. But
Sweden and my precious friends are my main dream! I love
you all so very much.

The paper is spotted with drips of hair color, as Mother had her
hair dyed blond like when she was younger. She didn't sign her name,
as she probably had to stop for the hairdresser to work on her. I am
amused that she is giddy with anticipation of seeing Europe, but still
has no concept of geography and travel distances.

Mother's last letter is written in longhand to Ingrid before our
departure.

May 29, 1959, Friday a.m.

൧ My dear Ingrid,

Guess this will be the last before we leave home at 7:00 a.m.
on Monday. We will fly American to New York arriving at one
twenty-five p.m. Then we will be at Hotel Piccadilly, 43rd at
Broadway. [I went to New York City for a week with my friend
and colleague in June 1980 for the Picasso Centennial Exhibit
at MOMA. We stayed at the Piccadilly Hotel! It is there to this
day!]

I am very tired, as my X-ray bump has come out on my back,
and of course with all the excitement, etc.! Ingrid G. is here
with us now. We shall try to squeeze in the rest of our things to
the 132 lb. limit for the 3 of us! We sent our trunks Tuesday, so
we're beginning to begin!

The friend whom I mentioned lives in Paris will be there
June 25 thru July 3 and if I can she would like for me to come
by there either on the way to or from Switzerland IF I feel like

going there. So many IFS! This is not too important.

All I know is that it looks as though I will really be seeing you, my dear Ingrid, in just a few more days! I would not attempt this at all without Ingrid G. as she is so helpful and precious! Tell Ockie and Susanne the kids really loved their letters. They had to wait 24 hours for the translation! Isn't it going to be fun to see them try to talk to each other! I must get busy! Hope you can meet us in Göteborg, but know you are terribly busy. Love you, SUE

THE NEW YORK ADVENTURE

Mother kept a travel diary of the trip to Sweden that started with the flight to New York on June 1, 1959, and ended on August 15, 1959, when we returned home to Dallas. At Mother's insistence, I kept a diary also, but so far I have not been able to find it. Perhaps it will turn up one day. However, I am grateful to have Mother's detailed record of the trip.

She had a tremendous surge of energy and adrenaline when we arrived in New York. We flew propjet from Dallas Love Field to Idlewild (now Kennedy) Airport. We were scheduled to have breakfast on the flight, which we did, but rather late. We had gotten up very early to check our luggage and board the plane for a 7:00 a.m. takeoff. Breakfast was served about two hours into the flight: scrambled eggs with ham, toast, and orange juice. The dishes were porcelain and served on a tray balanced on a pillow on the lap. I did eat, but when we were making our final approach to New York City, the plane dipped and I lost my breakfast.

Upon arrival, we loaded into a taxi with our luggage, then off to the Piccadilly Hotel in midtown Manhattan. My first cab ride in New York was an adventure in itself. When we got stuck in traffic, the driver laid on the horn and yelled at the driver in front of us—no obscenities, just heavy New York accents. We checked into the hotel with Ingrid G. and Harriet Armstrong. We probably went to lunch, then somehow Mother, having noticed Helen Hayes's name on a Broadway theater marquis, decided we should attend the Helen Hayes Theater production of Eugene O'Neill's *A Touch of a Poet*. The cast included Helen Hayes,

Eric Portman, Betty Field, and Kim Stanley. It was a rather heavy drama for a child, but Mother wanted me to see Helen Hayes, a grand lady of the American theater, perform. She wrote in her diary, "We are so glad for the privilege of seeing this great lady of the theater, a moment I hope Susibeth will long remember." I DO remember the theater and seeing Helen Hayes cry onstage.

The next, our first full day in New York, Mother took me to Riverside Church, where she had served as an assistant organist in 1943. She had enrolled at Columbia Teachers College to work on a master's degree in English and music education while Daddy was overseas during World War II. We went to the office of Dr. Harry Emerson Fosdick, minister and theologian at Riverside Church. Mother introduced herself to his secretary. It had been sixteen years since Mother had been there, but she was remembered. Dr. Fosdick invited us into his office, as his next appointment was running late. I remember him as a white-haired gentleman with a kind face. Mother asked me to step outside so she could talk with Dr. Fosdick privately. I was eleven years old. She records in her diary, "Saw Dr. Fosdick and he autographed his book 'The Power to See It Through.' What a thrill to see him looking so well at 81." Looking back, I am sure Mother told Dr. Fosdick about the state of her health. I imagine he prayed with her there in his office. I hope the book helped her. We went up into the carillon bell tower of the church. We had lunch at T.C. Cafeteria (an automat where you put coins in slots that opened little doors to reveal sandwiches, salads, or slices of cake or pie). We had cafeterias at home, but nothing like the automat! Mother showed me Whittier Hall on the campus of Columbia University, where she had lived during her time in New York City. We visited the United Nations complex in the afternoon (got caught in a downpour) and met friends from Dallas, Eleanor and Frank Chappell, for dinner that evening. After supper, I think Eleanor came back to the hotel with us, then took me out for a walk in the rain down Broadway.

The next day, Wednesday, June 3, we met with Dillon Anderson (Mother's first cousin and author; he was the son of Bessie Dillon Anderson, her father's older sister) at Gene Davies's (art editor of *Good Housekeeping*) penthouse at 44 East Fifty-Seventh Street, next to Suzy

Parker's penthouse, then had lunch at Sea Fare Restaurant in Greenwich Village. We dined on lemon sole filet with asparagus and white sauce, sliced tomatoes with cottage cheese and french fries. The meal cost about three dollars each.

DILLON ANDERSON: A COUSIN AND NOTEWORTHY PERSON

Dillon Anderson was born on July 16, 1906, in McKinney, Texas, the son of Joseph Anderson and Bessie Dillon, sister of Marvin Dillon. After attending Texas Christian University, Anderson received his BS from the University of Oklahoma (1927) and his LLB from Yale Law School (1929). He served in the United States Army during World War II (1942–1945) and earned the Legion of Merit. This is a military award given for exceptionally meritorious conduct in the performance of outstanding services and achievements. The decoration is issued to members of the eight uniformed services of the United States as well as to military and political figures of foreign governments. He worked on lend-lease materiel and military government planning, attaining the rank of colonel.

Anderson was also a partner at the law firm of Baker Botts in Houston, Texas, beginning in 1940. Before becoming National Security Advisor in the Eisenhower administration, Anderson was an official on the National Security Council from 1953 to 1955. He was elected a fellow of the American Academy of Arts and Sciences in 1959.

On another note, Dillon Anderson was also a novelist. His most popular book is *I and Claudie*, published in 1951. He also wrote a sequel, *Claudie's Kinfolks*, and *The Billingsley Papers*. After that day in 1959, I never met my "noteworthy" cousin, Dillon Anderson, again. He died on January 29, 1974, in Houston.

MORE OF THE NEW YORK ADVENTURE

After lunch at Sea Fare, we toured Rockefeller Plaza and Saint Patrick's Cathedral. That evening, we attended *The Music Man*. The production featured the original cast with Robert Preston, Barbara Cook, and Eddie Hodges. Mother and Elizabeth Peabody included *The Music Man* in their repertoire. They had reviewed it for ladies' clubs in Dallas. They rehearsed at our house. I listened and learned ALL the songs. Where did Mother get the energy to do all this? Sometime during our time in New York City, we went shopping at Macy's Department Store. Mother bought me a pink brocade dirndl skirt. I wore it in Sweden and again in Dallas. Loved that skirt!

Thursday, June 4, was a rainy day. Mother writes in her diary, "We took a boat trip around Manhattan to Pier 97 to check on our trunks. The Gripsholm is so beautiful! We can hardly wait to get on board. Jay Armstrong [Harriet's husband] brought us some books we had forgotten and took us to dinner." That evening we saw *Destry Rides Again*, starring Andy Griffith. It was a silly western that enjoyed a short run.

THE ATLANTIC CROSSING ON THE MS *GRIPSHOLM*

On Friday, June 5, 1959, we set sail at 11:00 a.m. from Pier 97 on the MS *Gripsholm*. Mother and I shared a second-class cabin with two elderly ladies from Chicago. The cabin had two sets of bunk beds and a bathroom. I, of course, took the top bunk. I remember sleeping deeply through the night as the ship rocked on the Atlantic Ocean. Mother writes, "Got table 109 at the second seating for meals—very good! Turned in early, as we were so tired!" Ingrid G. had her own stateroom, also in second class. As the daughter of Bishop Bo Giertz of Gothenburg, she had social contacts. She dined at the captain's table and danced with the ship's officers.

Saturday, June 6. Foggy, but not rough. Mother writes, "We are enjoying every minute. We are eating with Mrs. Clementson and her granddaughter, Lynnea, Susie's age." They were from Whittier, California. The grandmother was Swedish, so she was taking Lynnea to Sweden for the first time to meet relatives. Lynnea and I became instant friends and even kept in touch for several years after the trip. As luck would have it, they were booked on the *Kungsholm* to return August 1, same as us. When Lynnea and I met again for the voyage back to the States, she was speaking what seemed to me to be fluent Swedish! Boy, was I ever jealous! As there was a cinema on the ship, we went to the movies often. Among the movies playing was *Auntie Mame*, staring Rosalind Russell. I must have watched it at least five times. Every evening after dinner, there was dancing in the main lounge. Everyone was welcome, including children. Mother says we danced until midnight. "Susie is having a ball!" We also played bingo and watched the ocean. I remember standing in the sheltered walkway of the promenade deck, leaning on the rail, watching the waves. The Atlantic was a deep blue with five- to ten-foot swells and whitecaps. Occasionally, we would see dolphins and other sea creatures swimming within sight of the ship. We might have even seen a whale.

Monday, June 8. Foggy. Mother writes, "Sat on the deck about two hours this a.m. Temperature 60F and just right to sit out." I have a photo of Mother wrapped in a blanket and lying in a deck chair. "Tonight was the welcome dinner with all the fixings. I danced about 3 dances, though I know I shouldn't." Mother was enjoying several days in a row of feeling well. She and Daddy used to dance all the time before she got sick. She was also a beautiful woman, and several handsome men were asking her to dance.

Tuesday, June 9. Foggy. She writes, "Today is the first day I have felt bad since I left home, but I just didn't have anything to do but lay around all day. Hope I snap back." She did.

Wednesday, June 10. Foggy. Mother writes, "This was the night of the Farewell dinner and such an elaborate one I never saw! Dessert was Bombe ala Gripsholm (flaming baked Alaska) processed into the dining room with candles and orchestra." Everyone dressed up—men in tuxedos and ladies in taffeta and lace, the ship's officers in their dress whites. I wore the same blue taffeta dress that I wore to Uncle Ed's wedding earlier in 1959. "Got a written invitation to the Chief Officers cabin with Ingrid and about six of her friends. The officer Karl Eric Otterman is a very charming man."

Thursday, June 11. Foggy. There was a talent show on the ship. I volunteered to sing. Of course, Mother accompanied me. She writes, "Susibeth sang 'Why Can't the English' and 'Wouldn't It Be Loverly' in the talent show tonight. I was real proud of her. All the other numbers were songs, but hers sorta livened things up. Played Bingo before that."

Friday, June 12. Sunshine!! Mother writes, "This morning we woke to the sight of land and sunshine. The Orkney Islands, mountains arise! We are on the North Sea and north of Scotland with its green cliffs and white bright house on the south side. The rest of the day we were out of sight of land and the sea was extremely smooth. Had to get our trunks and bags ready by 6:00 a.m. Sat on deck from 5 to 6:30. Visited with the orchestra leader, Mr. Fox."

SWEDEN: A ZONE OF DAZZLING ENCHANTMENT BETWEEN LIFE AND DEATH

Saturday, June 13. Arrival in Göteborg. Perfect weather. The first view of Sweden, about 10:00 a.m., was beautiful, particularly the island of Vinga. Ingrid J. commented on seeing the island of Vinga as she was leaving Sweden in 1948: "I will never forget how beautiful the archipelago was. We went with a ships pilot out to Vinga Lighthouse." Mother continues, "The harbor is so busy with everything in the way of a boat or ship. When we looked at the pier, it took a while to spot our friends, but there was Ingrid J., Birgitta, Martin, and Bo! I was so overcome with joy that I simply could not hold back the tears! I still can't believe it all. We took about two hours getting off the ship, then came straight to Bo and Elisabeth's house—so very lovely, and a dinner fit

Sue aboard MS Gripsholm, June 13, 1959

for a king. Very tired but very happy. Gothenburg is beautiful." Mother
suffered travel letdown and caught a cold the next day.

Sunday, June 14. Göteborg, the Giertz home. Mother writes, "I have
a pretty bad cold so Ingrid J. has given me medicine and brought my
breakfast to bed. [Ingrid also made Mother a hot toddy with whiskey.]
All but Birgitta and I have gone to the cathedral just down the street.
The bells are so lovely and the quaint red roofs are so beautiful. I may
not feel like going to Öland tomorrow, but Susibeth will go on with
Bo, Elisabeth, and Martin. I may follow in a day or two. No mail from
home yet."

Monday, June 15. Göteborg to Kalmar and Öland. Clear and cold,
probably in the fifties. Mother writes, "At 8:15 a.m. we boarded the
strange Little Swedish train. Feeling better, so decided to come on.
Arrived in Kalmar about 2:20 p.m. then took the ferry to Öland. [Now
there is a bridge across the strait.] This is a most lovely island about
120 miles long and 12 miles across at the widest point. The island is
dotted with old red wooden windmills, and a Viking castle dating back
2000 years is outside the capital city of Borgholm. The Giertz cottage is
very high on a ridge overlooking the Baltic Sea. The view from Martin's
attic room is absolutely priceless: red windmill and a cottage with the
Baltic in the background."

Tuesday, June 16. Öland. Still cold. The Giertz summer home faces
east, so we got the morning sun. Mother writes, "But we had breakfast
out front, as the sun was shining, but I wore about 4 layers clothes and
a robe! Had coffee and Swedish breads with butter and local honey
and cheese about 9:00 a.m. Luncheon about 12:00, tea in the back,
west side, in the sun and protected from the wind, then supper about
7:00. All so delicious. Ingeborg is such a jewel. [Ingeborg, the cook
and housekeeper, had worked for the Giertz family for thirty years. Her
assistant/maid-in-training was named Helga. Helga was still working
for Bo Giertz in 1975 when I made my next trip to Sweden.] My cold is
better but not well! Barbro called me long distance and talked a long
time. It is so wonderful to be here with all my dear friends."

Wednesday, June 17. Öland. Cloudy and cold. Mother writes, "Martin
and Susie are playing checkers. He arrived yesterday noon on his motor

bike. Elisabeth has shown Susibeth how to do cross stitch work on linen. I do hope she will inhale some of Elisabeth's artistic abilities as well as her patience. She suffers so much [Elisabeth had rheumatoid arthritis] but keeps right on to her full capacity. This house is so perfectly decorated, makes me want to go home and start from scratch."

Martin, age sixteen, had persuaded his father to let him ride his new motorcycle from Gothenburg across Sweden all the way to Öland. Sweden is about the size of California. The route across the country is not a straight shot but takes a winding path that traverses a landscape dotted with lakes. Martin left the same day we did, Monday, June 15. We arrived at the summerhouse on Öland by early evening. Martin arrived midday on Tuesday, June 16, tired, hungry, and COLD, as he had not dressed warmly enough for the journey. Father and son had WORDS—in Swedish, of course—about the venture. He was sixteen and bored with the notion of spending his summer on Öland with his parents. I was almost twelve, with no one my age to talk to or play with. He and I became friends over a checkers board. Martin found me a willing conversation companion. He practiced his English and I found a "big brother." Martin took me on his motorcycle to the Baltic side of the island to see the rocky beach where the tide rolled in.

Thursday, June 18. Öland. Cold and sunshine, then warmer. Mother writes, "Had breakfast outside in the sunshine again, then went into the little village of Borgholm and did some shopping. Visited the lovely old antique shop where Bo had bought the little silver shaped heart box for Mother [Ruth] and got Susibeth a little sterling silver chair about 100–150 years old bought at Maxwell's in London. [I still have that little silver chair. Craftsmen made silver miniature models of their furniture designs, which they showed to prospective customers, who would place orders based on the models.] Got two vases for Jo too. Susibeth and Martin took a tour of Kalmar Castle then met us in the market place. Caux, the little girl next door came over for dinner, after devotions went to bed."

I visited Sweden again in 1975 (age twenty-eight), basically retracing the trip Mother and I had taken in 1959. By then, Bo's wife, Elisabeth, had died, but he still spent summers in the Örland cottage. Helga was his housekeeper. While revisiting Borgholm, as we were walking down the main street of the village, I swear I saw, about one hundred yards ahead of me, two women walking with a girl child about twelve between them. I gasped and burst into tears. I had seen a vision of Mother, Ingrid J., and me from 1959!

Friday, June 19. Öland. Beautiful day. Mother writes, "Britta and Ingrid came tonight. Elisabeth and I did our hair today. It is so good to see the girls and we had a wonderful Mid-summer eve dinner with all the fixings. This has been such a beautiful experience on Öland with the Giertz family. Walked down to the ocean with Bo and the kids. Quite a walk for 'Mama' but well worth it."

Saturday, June 20. Öland. Beautiful Midsummer Day. Mother writes, "Went to Mid-summer services at church in Borgholm, then after dinner took a wonderful drive in Britta's car to the east side [the Russian side] of the island for another view of the Baltic. Just like a book comes alive with old, old, old and beautiful churches, farms, etc. Remember the minister's home with all the young people playing where young people had been playing since the 14th century—and all next to the very old and beautifully kept graveyards. These old churches unlike any other old ones I have seen have such a warmth and freshness about them. Remember, Susibeth?" Of course, Mother. You knew I would read your diary one day.

Sunday, June 21. Öland to Växjö. Beautiful day. Mother writes, "We had to say adjö to Elisabeth, Bo, and Martin Giertz after such a heavenly rest. Ingeborg too was so darling. Ingrid and Britta brought us via the Castle at Kalmar [twelfth century] to Hagavik, Ann-Marie's and Ingrid's summer home on the lake [Helgasjön]. I have never seen more beautiful country. Just a veritable fairyland. Met all of Ingrid's family and had a wonderful 'Valkommen' dinner in the cottage full of flowers, good food, and the American flag! Susibeth went swimming and boating with the children then we came back with Barbro to her beautiful apartment in Växjö."

Mother and I stayed with Barbro in Växjö from June 22 through June 30, 1959. During that time I met Kristina, Margaretta, Per, and Gunnar, children of Karen and Torstein, Barbro's sister and brother-in-law. Kristina ("Ninna") and I are the same age, and we have stayed in touch over the years. She and her husband, Vijay Manna, visited me and Ron in Manitou Springs in July 2012. I visited them, with friend Judy, in Lammhult in May 2017. Mother has written several pages about our time in Växjö, not trying to keep up with daily entries. During this interval, Daddy wrote to Ingrid J. about how he and Dillon were getting along without Mother and me. Mother's diary entries reflect the heavenly JOY of our time in Sweden!

MOTHER'S TRAVEL DIARY CONTINUES

Mother writes, "I shall not try to write this by the day, as I have had such a wonderful time with Barbro in her lovely apartment at 23 Backgatan [Back Street]." I visited Barbro again in 1975 and 2012 in the same apartment, a three-story walk-up.

In 1959, the building across the street was a women's prison. One of the inmates hung a red handkerchief on the bar to signal her boyfriend.

Barbro taught home economics to teenage boys. I visited her school, where the students asked me if I knew Elvis Presley!

Mother continues:

⟶ I have not felt too well so Barbro has just done everything to make me happy. Bless her precious soul! She and Ingrid have talked back and forth almost every day about me, my plans, my mail, etc. Ingrid is so busy this week so we are staying here. Barbro's mother is a darling and I only wish I could talk to her more as she is one of those perpetually happy people. We went out to Reppe to see her a couple of times at Karin's [Barbro's sister] house. It is so lovely out there too.

Kristina "Ninna" came in to visit Susibeth, and though she was rather shy about talking at first, she and Susie have had a wonderful time together—language barriers notwithstanding . Kristina and Susibeth have been staying at night in Mrs. Waller's apartment in Växjö, and they feel so big! Since it is daylight nearly the whole night, we feel no fear for their going over there to spend the night alone. One day, Torstein took us for a lovely ride around Växjö in his Mercedes. So many beautiful old houses, fences, churches, flowers, lakes, farms, etc. This land is almost entirely used for lumber, and so many beautiful pine woods! These people are very prosperous from all the lumber.

Another day Thorstan Petterson [friend of Barbro and Ingrid] took us in his Volkswagen to a glass factory, Kosta, about 50 American miles away. Such beautiful work being done by real masters of the trade. They gave Susibeth and Kristina little vases with butterflies etched on them. Saw an old church from the 14th century and the old parsonage with its quaint furniture. Remember the chairs that make tables? And the handwork on the beams, the old kitchen, the hourglass in the pulpit, etc. Ended our trip with Mr. Petterson at his summer house—a gorgeous place, an old house rebuilt, and very old furniture.

June 27, 1959. Susibeth was invited to go to Halmstad with Kristina and her father, but due to a cold we decided against it. We just kept her in bed and had quite a nice restful week-end. Barbro is such a marvelous cook, and we have really eaten and eaten!

June 28, 1959. Another quiet day with good food and rest at Barbro's home. Harold Johnson's sister [Yngve] came over yesterday and brought some lovely rose buds and a package for Harold and Mildred. Of course, she knew no English, but she is a darling little Swedish lady. Went out to Reppe this afternoon and Susibeth learned a little more about the linen handwork. [Alas, I did not master linen cross-stitch.]

June 29, 1959. Went out to Hagavik [to the Jaensson's summer home] this afternoon and Susibeth went to a birthday party for a little cousin of Eva's and Inga's. This is a beautiful spot. I have never seen such huge begonias in

a bright orange color. Ann-Marie and Grunneborg brought
their kids in with us and we all went to see "Daddy Long
Legs" starring Fred Astaire and Leslie Caron. [I remember
going to the movies in Växjö. It was really interesting to
see the Swedish subtitles for American movies.]

June 30-July 1, 1959. We went to town [Växjö] on a lot
of errands today. Bought lace for bedroom curtains with my
"money tree" funds. [I remember Mother's measuring the
lace from the tip of her nose to the end of her outstretched
hand. She measured eight yards, which the shop clerk
converted to meters. Mother had the curtains made for
my room at home. I kept those curtains hanging in my
bedroom wherever I was living until they literally fell
apart.] There are so many things to buy, but I must not. It's
just like at home! Barbro got linen for the napkin holders
and will teach Susibeth how to make them. Have received
4 letters from home today and one from Harriet and Ed
and Jo. Packed for our bus trip to Halmstad and Frösakull,
Karin's [now Ninna's] summer home.

This has been a beautiful trip over to the west coast
with more gorgeous scenery. The wheat fields, rolling hills,
flowers everywhere, the little red farm houses, etc. We got
our room at Hotel Mårtenson [still there], then went out to
Frösakull. Susibeth will stay there. Such a lovely summer
home. The North Sea is beautiful with sandy beach.

I have visited the old churches and glass factories in Småland several
times: 1975, 2002, 2017. Some of the wooden churches have been
restored, and still have frescoes painted on the wood walls and ceilings.
Hand-blown glass is a dying art. There are only two glassworks still open
in Sweden. I no longer have the vase with etched butterflies.

While Mother and I were traveling to New York and Sweden, Daddy
and Dillon (age ten) passed the summer together in Dallas. Daddy
worked at Dillon Scale every day, and Dillon was home with our maid/
housekeeper. She left at 4:00 p.m. Daddy left the office at 5:00 and was

home by 5:30. Dillon would sit on the front steps of our house every afternoon to await Daddy's arrival. The letters that Mother and Daddy exchanged have not survived, but a letter that Daddy wrote to Ingrid has. Daddy wrote in longhand.

June 25, 1959

 Dear Ingrid:

I know you are enjoying the girls and I do appreciate so much your looking after them. This trip will do Sue a lot of good and of course is a wonderful experience for Susibeth.

Monday June 29th will be 4 weeks since they left. How time flies. It hardly seems possible that it has been 2 years since you were over here. Dillon and I talk about Bandera and our vacation last summer—some wonderful memories. If my gals had not gone to Sweden this year, we would have gone back to Bandera for a week or two. But I'm glad they could make the trip to Sweden and are grateful to my wonderful Swedish friends for also helping to make this trip a "dream come true." Thanks again for all you have done and are doing for our family. Love, Jimmy

Mother's travel diary picks up in Halmstad:

 July 2, 1959. Barbro and I were very comfortable in our room. Ordered coffee and sweet rolls to our room. So pleasant with a pretty little girl bringing it to our room. Little Gunnar, Per, Margaretta, and Kristina are such lovely children. Susibeth gets along fine with all of them. The girls have their own room away from the main house. Had a fire in the fireplace all day, wonderful food and two naps!

July 3, 1959. Another restful night with the same pretty girl bringing our coffee to us with the usual "God dag!" I have learned a few words, but very few. We leave this evening at 6:15 by train for Malmö. They say it is a beautiful trip down the west coast, so we are looking forward to it, but we hate to leave our sweet friends here at Frösakull! Walked to the beach and took a few pictures.

July 4, 1959. Had a good trip down last night. Arrived at 9:00 pm and were met by Ingrid, Britta, and Viola. So wonderful to see them all. We came out to Ann-Marie's house in Arlöv where we have the whole big house to ourselves. Barbro is so precious. Cooks such good food. Took a wonderful drive with Britta to some wonderful little towns down at the very end of the country [probably Höllviken and Ystad]. Went to lunch where we could see Denmark on one side and almost Germany on the other.

July 5, 1959. Another marvelous trip to upper Skåne. We saw the King and Queen at an old castle in the country. Also beautiful folk dances and music. This is the prettiest part yet. I really believe though each province has its own particular charm. The girls went swimming [to a beach at Ystad] in the Baltic, but it was too cold to enjoy it. Susibeth saw a little friend from the *Gripsholm*, small world!

July 6, 1959. Stayed in today, as we were pretty tired after two days of driving. Wrote letters and tried to catch up on many things. Ingrid came out tonight and showed us many of her beautiful slides from Bordeaux, Spain, France, and Italy. Barbro is still so precious I don't know what I would do without her. Haven't heard from Tott yet. Said she might come to see me.

July 7, 1959. Wonderful, wonderful Copenhagen! Such a beautiful city. Susie and I just have to come back at least once more. So many wonderful things to buy! Mr. and Mrs. Mattson [friends to Louise Eliasson] were on the boat and just couldn't believe it. They were planning to go to Stockholm the next day but postponed it and invited us out to their home for cookies tomorrow night. I told them they should come to see Louise. [Mother, Ingrid, and Barbro and I took the ferry from Malmö to Copenhagen. We spent a lovely day in the city. Saw *The Little Mermaid* statue, based on the Hans Christian Andersen fairytale.]

July 8, 1959. Malmö. Just had a restful morning. Wonderful fish and tartar sauce for lunch. [We are staying in Ann-Marie's Arlöv villa. Barbro joined us for morning coffee on the patio.] Barbro is terrific. Ingrid called that she had my reservation times for Switzerland for the 15th. I will stay at the Cornavin Hotel for a week. I know it will be wonderful. I will go by train to Geneva and fly back from Zurich on the 22nd. Letters from Jimmy and Betty McMullen. Out to the Mattson's for cookies. Visited Lund [the site of Lund University and the Lund Cathedral, Romanesque architecture and dating from the twelfth century].

July 9, 1959. Malmö. Out to Britta's home where I met her sister's family and her mother. A real big dinner with roast beef, the first since we got here. They showed more wonderful slides. The garden was so lovely. Susibeth, Ingrid and the children were there also.

July 10, 1959. Malmö. Went to the museum in Malmö Castle. Had coffee on the roof with Barbro. Went out to Mrs. Lundquist's [Ingrid and Ann-Marie's mother] this evening for coffee. Another beautiful home with so many art treasures. She gave me a ceramic red rooster for my kitchen. She served strawberry cakes, coffee bread then about an hour later fruit, chocolate and juices. Met Ulla [Larse Lundquist's sister].

July 11, 1959. Malmö. Britta came and took us on another beautiful ride through Lund up the west coast to Helsingborg where we took the ferry to Denmark. Saw the famous Helsingøre [Kronborg] Castle of Hamlet setting and had dinner in a lovely restaurant overlooking the sea. Britta has been so generous with her time and car. Everyone is so lovely to us.

July 12, 1959. Malmö and around. Larse Lundquist's sister Ulla came over for breakfast at 10:00. She took us on

a drive through Malmö Old Town and the museums of Lund
that depict local historic culture. She took us to her castle.
The garden was lovely. She had an apartment in the castle.
We had dinner in Ingrid's apartment.

July 13, 1959. Malmö. Spent the day relaxing,
getting ready for our trips to Switzerland and Stockholm.
Our family will be scattered this week. Dillon is in New
Braunfels [visiting Aunt Lera]. Ingrid came out and had
supper with us, the wonderful crepe suzette as only Barbro
can fix. Then met Britta at the show on the spur of the
moment. Saw Doris Day in "April in Paris."

July 14, 1959. Malmö. Finished packing for
Switzerland and put Susibeth and Barbro on the train for
Halmstad and Frösakull. Went to supper at Viola Fröler's
then to a wonderful Faure concert at the beautiful hall
in Malmö. Britta met us there. Director was Gert-Ove
Andersson and a very lovely young girl, Bertie Malander
played Handel's cello concerto in G Maj. Spent the night
with Ingrid in her old apt, her last night there.

July 15, 1959. Malmö and train. Ingrid and I got up
at 5:00 and I met Anna Ohlsson, my traveling companion
on the ferry. We walked around Copenhagen until 10:00
am then boarded the train finding a darling Danish girl
who was to share our compartment with us. Met others
going to Caux too. Marvelous Danish Smorgasbord in
three hour ferry from Denmark to Germany-Geneva train
ferry. [They are on a boat train.] Germany not nearly so
pretty. Station just being repaired from the war. Beautiful
scenery began at dark.

July 16, 1959. Geneva!! The McMullen's met me at
the train. Bless their precious hearts! Betty and I wept.
They are so wonderful. After some hugging, got set up in
my room at the Cornavin Hotel. Had lunch with them at
their apt. Which is in the same building where the Big Four

Conference is being held. Rested then they took me out to a real swanky outdoor French restaurant for dinner. The twins are 19 year old darlings.

July 17, 1959. Geneva. Susie's birthday and she is celebrating in Frösakull with Barbro. What a lot has happened since 1947! Went with Betty and the twins over into France to buy eggs. Incidentally saw heavenly scenery and had a wonderful experience on a mountain top. Remember the French farmhouse! Had dinner with them and turned in early after showing my and Don's Sweden slides.

In the middle of July 1959, Mother took her trip to Geneva, Switzerland, and I went to Stockholm with Ingrid's sister, Ann-Marie, husband Lars, and son Ockie. They had invited me to take a road trip to Stockholm with them in July. We stayed on the boat hostel *af Chapman*, still moored on the western shore of the islet Skeppsholmen in central Stockholm. It was a great time! We attended a Swedish performance of *My Fair Lady*; I knew the musical well because Mother and Elizabeth Peabody had reviewed it often. The performance in Stockholm lasted thirty minutes longer than the performance I had attended in Dallas because it took that much longer to say it all in Swedish! I understood every word! We also visited the world's oldest open air park, Skansen, and walked the Old Town, Gamla Stan. I remember that Mother had kept my US passport, so Lars and Ann-Marie had an American child in tow with no identification!

On the drive back from Stockholm to Malmö, Lars and Ann-Marie dropped me off at Barbro's in Växjö, where I was collected by Torstein, Ninna's father. We drove west to the summer home just north of Halmstad. I spent my twelfth birthday, July 17, at Frösakull with Kristina's family on the North Sea beach. They gave me a sweet party. I remember there were lots of children around. They spoke very little English and I spoke no Swedish, but we had no trouble communicating. We also visited the town of Halmstad. Ingrid's Minnesota cousin Karen Pederson reminded me, "My grandparents lived in Halmstad; you may recall my mother, at a year old, immigrated with her parents and three-year-old brother, to America from Småland, near Växjö."

⟨⟩ **July 18, 1959.** Geneva. Spent morning making plans for Zermatt trip then drove up the lake with the Clarks and had wonderful American picnic at an English Villa. He is a lawyer with W.H.O. Sailed back with the two Clarks and Betty on a perfectly beautiful moon-lit night. Took 3 ½ hours as there was hardly any wind.

Mother wrote in longhand to Ingrid from Hotel Cornavin in Geneva, Switzerland.

July 18, 1959

⟨⟩ My dear Ingrid,

Please excuse the pencil, but you know how I can misplace things! I am having a wonderful time with my friends. We a going sailing on Lake Geneva this evening after a picnic. Their neighbors have a sailboat.

Yesterday we drove over into France and took a picnic lunch and bought eggs. Very beautiful scenery! [Mother exclaimed often when she told stories of our trip, "Betty drove us to France to buy eggs!" Her enthusiasm and delight about little things like buying eggs in France speaks to her unbounded joy of life and her naivete about the geography of Europe.]

Tomorrow we are going to Mt. Blanc, the highest point in Switzerland. Monday we will go to Montreux and Chillon, then Tuesday Betty, the twins and I will be at the Hotel National for two nights, the 21st and 22nd. They will drop me off at Lausanne on the morning of the 23rd, then I will go by train to Zurich and get the plane at 5:00 pm, arriving at Copenhagen at 7:40 pm. My ticket includes plane to Malmö which will leave Copenhagen at 8:00, arriving Malmö at 8:50, so please don't come to Copenhagen to meet me, as it will be unnecessary trouble for you.

I probably will not write any more, as I am so busy, but remember I love you very much and shall never forget all you have done and are doing for me.

I am feeling pretty good and am resting a lot. Thanks for sending my mail. The big parcel was important papers for me to sign, so I got them right off. Dillon flew to Austin and Lera Bess met him and took him to Aunt Lera's [in New Braunfels], as Jimmy had a stomach virus that week-end. He [Dillon] made all arrangements himself by phone and wouldn't even let J. walk out to the plane with him! Must drop Barbro a line now. Just hold my mail now, please. Love. SUE

P.S. If Barbro comes by, you might let her read this, as my time is running short and I will not have to write about my activities. Found my pen!

The reason I am coming on the 5:00 plane is that they tell me here there is none at 12:50, and anyway that might rush my getting from Zermatt.

Ingrid, I would love to spend one whole day with you alone, if I can, cause I love you so much and I feel I haven't had enough time with you. I would like to wash my hair Friday a.m. either at your house or at Ann-Marie's. If I do it at your apt, and if you go out to Ann-Marie's before I get there will you please bring my hair rollers which are in a plastic bag either on her dresser or in my trunk. I have the bobby pins with me. Betty sends her best regards. SUE

More entries from Mother's travel diary:

C⁄O **July 19, 1959.** Switzerland and France. McMullen's took me to France to see Mont Blanc. Christian Herter [secretary of state from 1959 to 1961, appointed by Dwight David Eisenhower] went up in the Cable Car just 10 minutes before us. Herter has a kind face. Visited Assy, saw the church featured in Life Magazine last year. Had a perfect picnic on a mountain stream looking at the Mont Blanc range.

July 20, 1959. Montreux and Chillon. Betty and the twins and I took the boat trip to Chillon so lovely. Must go home and read "The Prisoner of Chillon" again. Called Anna Ohlsson at Montreux and thanked her again for being so wonderful. Had dinner in a VERY French restaurant with Don and Betty and Don Micks from Gasenville. He is Martha Millican's husband. Invited me to visit the Palais where Don McMullen and Bob Clark work for W.H.O.

July 21, 1959. To Zermatt. [Mother wanted to go to Zermatt to see the Matterhorn because Daddy's father, William Grover Bussard, had made an oil painting of the Matterhorn, probably from a postcard. He shipped it to Daddy, and it hung in our Westlake house living room until Daddy moved from the house. Dillon has it now.] Drove up from Geneva today with Betty and the twins. A beautiful climax. Remember the task ropes? Railroad locks and big doors in the mountain over a bank vault. Staldon to Zermatt, 1 hour 20 min. and like our Hotel National very much. The Walliserhof has a little more glamor, but we are so happy to be here in this quaint beautiful place. The cable car train ride up the mountain to our hotel afforded a fantastic view of the Alps.

July 22, 1959. Zermatt. We went up on the Cog train over 13,000 feet while we got a spectacular view of the Matterhorn and surrounding snow covered peaks and glaciers. Thrilled. Mont Blanc most splendid and bigger. Breathtaking!! Had a wonderful lunch of Fromages down the way apiece [Riffelberg] where there were so many wild flowers. Rested a while then walked down the quaint little main street of Zermatt. Remember the horse bells, the goats and the most interesting cornerstone.

July 23, 1959. From Zermatt to Sweden. Hated to leave Betty and the twins at Zermatt, for they have been so sweet. It is 1:00 and I have already been on 3 trains, but no problems so far. Each a very quick change. These Swiss trains are as accurate as Swiss watches. Two hour wait in Zurich then one hour delay. Met lovely couple named Kuhn from Fresno. Arrived Malmö 10:30. Ingrid and Britta met my plane. The one from Zurich DC6-R Swiss Air. Went to Ingrid's apartment.

I have returned from Stockholm and Frösakull by now. I met Mother at Ann-Marie's house in Arlöv. I remember being thrilled to see her, needing to collect hugs. We shared stories of our respective adventures. We spent a few days on our own in the Arlöv house. Mother sent me into town to find milk and a restaurant. I carried a card with the question "Var är en restaurang?" We did find a café within walking distance for Mother. We sat down and ordered the Wiener schnitzel. Delicious!

    July 24, 1959. Malmö. Ingrid took the day off and we went shopping and had a wonderful lunch at a Swiss restaurant. Also saw a beautiful gladiola flower show from Holland. The Dutch were really in town! Got a charm for Jo's bracelet, watch for Dillon and one for Louise. Never bought 2 watches in one day before. Had a big time in Ebba too. Bought myself some Swedish/Made in Japan beads. [This is the day with Ingrid Mother requested in her letter of July 18, the last time they were alone. I was with Barbro.]

    July 25, 1959. Malmö. Ulla drove us down to Ystad and Falsterbo. Met Toffor, her son, whose confirmation Susibeth went to near Stockholm. Ingrid found a white sofa that she drooled over. Had coffee in Ystad and coffee at Ingrid's later that evening. Went out to Ann-Marie's and Margarita and Irene and Britta came. Saw more children and had a nice time.

    July 26, 1959. Malmö. My Birthday [Mother is forty-six and beautiful. She has ten months to live.] Ingrid brought my breakfast to bed and I was just overcome with

joy to be with her today. She also had pink roses in my
room. Yellow roses in the living room too, made me think so
much of Mother! Tott called to say that she could not come
as she was ill. Britta, Ingrid, and I drove to Hotel Falsterbo
for a smorgasbord lunch.

July 27, 1959. Malmö and Lund. Went to Lund with
Viola and a doctor friend and visited the nurses home
where nearly all our friends lived at some time, then over
to Irene's ward in the hospital and met Margarita who took
us through the children's division. After coffee at Irene's
and coffee at Margarita where Ingrid and Britta met us.
Had a real "grizzly" time. [an expression that means
"joyfully busy" from Mother's childhood] They are so very
much fun. I hope they will visit me sometime.

July 28, 1959. Malmö. Ingrid took us to Copenhagen
today at noon for a last look and a little shopping. Took
Susibeth to Tivoli and she had a big time on two fine
horses. I got the things for Dorothy Brutsché [a friend from
Highland Park Methodist Church] and wished could have
bought more time! The antique shops were wonderful, but I
resisted myself.

Coffee in Britta's Malmö home. Left to right: *Sue, Susibeth, Britta, perhaps her parents, Ingrid*

July 29, 1959. Malmö. This is the day we don't like too much as we must pack everything and get ready to leave. This weekend Carl and Birgitta drove down from Halmstad about 5:30 and we met Ingrid at the hospital where we went through Viola's X-ray department and some wards. It is such a huge place, and so clean! Remember the white linen cloths from Viola. The flax actually grown on her grandmother's farm. She gave Susibeth the darling geese, symbol of Småland.

July 30, 1959. Ebba, Hampus. Well it's good bye today to Malmö and all our wonderful times with Ingrid, Brita, Viola, Ulla, and a host of others. Carl and Birgitta took us to Halmstad and Frösakull where we had a lovely lunch and visit with Ebba and Hampus, Carl's sister and brother-in-law. They put us on the train at 5:00 for Göteborg where Ingrid and Tott met us. Oh it is so good to see these two gals again. Had a wonderful dinner with Ingrid.

July 31, 1959. Göteborg. Susibeth and I went to the beauty parlor this a.m. then we and Ingrid had lunch with Tott at the Botanical Gardens. A beautiful spot, though Heavenly! Because we were with these 2 Swedish angels. Went shopping afterward. How will we ever get Susie's loom home!! Ingrid bought it for her! Went to Tott's parents for supper and had a wonderful time. Remember all the cockney Göteborg English. Mrs. Petterson gave me some old copper molds. [Every time Mother admired a decorative item in the home of someone we visited, the item was often gifted to her! The situation became somewhat embarrassing. She had to stop "admiring" everything! The tabletop loom made it home, but after we returned from Sweden, Mother got sick again, school started, and I didn't have the heart to learn how to use it.]

August 1, 1959. Göteborg and *Kungsholm*. It's goodbye today to wonderful Sweden!! How we hate to leave all these precious friends. Tott came over to the Bishop's

and had breakfast, then we all loaded up and went to the
dock where Ingrid G. took care of all the baggage details.
Bless her! Tott and Ingrid G. got each of us a rose corsage
and they went aboard and stayed until the very last
minute. They are both so very beautiful and Susie and I
watched and cried as long as we could see them. Have B-19
stateroom with two nice ladies from Michigan. Very tired.
[Mother took a photo of Tott and Ingrid G. as they were
standing on the gangplank. The photo is blurry. Either
Mother was shaking while crying OR the gangplank was
being raised while they were standing on it!]

August 2, 1959. *Kungsholm.* This morning around
10:00 a.m. we landed at Bremerhaven, Germany. Took on a
lot of passengers. One could not help noting the difference
in the faces of the people here, so much more serious and
tragic. Only a few tears, too. The ship's band saved the
day however by playing "Roll Out the Barrel." Everybody
was pretty tired today. Got unpacked. [Because of ocean
currents, prevailing winds, and the stop in Bremerhaven,
the crossing from Europe to New York took nine days. The
crossing from New York to Göteborg had taken only eight
days.]

August 3, 1959. *Kungsholm.* Cloudy and rough. This
is the first real rough weather we have experienced.
The ship rocked and pitched until many on board were
seasick. It was really sorta fun for those of us who felt
good. Went to movie at 4:00, "Holiday for Lovers" [1959
romantic comedy starring Jane Wyman, Jill St. John, and
Clifton Webb]. Had a very interesting chat with our room
stewardess who turns out to be a well-educated Swiss girl
of 23. Serving on *Kungsholm* is part of her hospitality
schooling from a school on Lausanne. She is studying hotel
management.

August 4, 1959. *Kungsholm.* There are more white
caps, but more choppy so not so much motion of the ship.

There was a funeral at sea this morning at 5:00 a.m., for an
86 year old ship captain. The ship came to a complete stop,
engines off for a few minutes. Saw the water-tight door
drill for the first time. Played bingo tonight and watched
the dancing. It is so difficult to SIT at a dance! [Having had
the experience on the *Gripsholm*, I knew the drill about
partying into the night. Mother usually turned in early, but
I was allowed to stay up as long as I wanted. There was a
buffet served at 11:00 p.m. every night. The rocking ship is
conducive to sound sleep.]

August 5, 1959. *Kungsholm*. Finally made it into the
shop and spent most of my Swedish money. That wasn't
too difficult! Susibeth is really having a big time on board,
particularly dancing with a 16 year-old boy named Bob.
Went up to the bridge this afternoon—beautiful view of
the sun and water. Dillon would have loved the radar
equipment. Saw travelogue of Kungsholm and recognized
many spots and faces.

August 6, 1959. Clear day on *Kungsholm*. Another
lazy restful day aboard with lots of rest, as I felt a little
like a cold. Susie and I went to ship's doctor about her
tooth. [I don't remember this.] Another travelogue of the
Kungsholm around the world and a real silly English movie
"The Big Money," [1956 comedy, starring Belinda Lee, Ian
Carmichael, and Jill Ireland], then straight to bed without
the 11:00 snack, but Susie stayed up and danced from
10:30–11:00 then woke me to ask if I wanted sandwiches.
Scared me out of my wits!! [Yes, I remember doing that!]

August 7, 1959. Dense fog on *Kungsholm*. Tonight is the
Farewell Dinner, so we will all be getting dressed up. Shall
go to watch the Schottische lesson [I remember learning/
dancing the schottische, a folk dance that originated in
Bohemia] at 11:00 and then beauty parlor. The dinner was
another spectacular affair with paper hats, music and the
beautiful ice display of the Bombe de Kungsholm. Susibeth

had a wonderful time dancing almost every dance. Ended the evening with usual "Varmt Kor" warm sandwiches.

Mother wrote to Ingrid from the MS *Kungsholm*. We had been at sea for a week. She mailed the letter from New York. Although there are no tearstains on the letter, Mother wept over it.

August 7, 1959

〜 My dearest Ingrid.

Just a quick note before everything starts to get busy in preparation for departure from this beautiful ship. It is very foggy today, and the second and third days were very rough, but other than that we have had a very restful time. Tonight is the Farewell dinner.

Ingrid, I can't begin to tell you all my wonderful emotions that I experienced on my visit to Sweden. Bless your angel soul, I was well aware of your capable planning behind every minute of our stay there. I told Susibeth that no one had ever been the recipient of such loving care as she and I had been this summer, and we both thank you from the very depths of our hearts.

I shall try to write real soon to all the rest, but in the meantime tell each of them if you see them or talk to them that we send our love and best wishes.

Sweden was even more beautiful than I had ever dreamed possible, and if I never had another happy day, which of course I shall, I would feel that I had had more than my share of the "goodness of life." In other words, Ingrid, we love you, and thank you again and again. Always your friend. SUE

We are sending a cable to Elisabeth Giertz on Saturday for her birthday. We land Monday.

P.S. August 9, 1959. Ingrid, I met some people who had come over on the Kungsholm in June with the Kipp family. They landed in Göteborg July 3, so I hope you have heard from them by now. August 11, 1959 Tuesday. Mary Frances met us and it was so wonderful. Customs went through everything of everybody on the *Kungsholm*. It helped to get in her car and come up here to her lovely home in the country. She will take us to Idlewild for flight to Washington. Home on Sat.

Ingrid, if you will give me the size of your window and the color and material you want I feel sure I can find something real nice on an August sale. Just let me know what you want and forget the money, as I want to do it for you.

Hastily and with love. SUE

Mother's travel diary entries continue below:

∞ **August 8, 1959.** *Kungsholm*. Foggy and Rough. After breakfast did some packing. Remember the old hot water bottle! Found Susie's dress I had left in the pressing room for two days. Must turn in our custom declarations today. Talent show tonight and lots of fun. Better than the one going over. Remember Susibeth with the little Andersson girls from Dover, Delaware in "Be Kind to Your Parents." Everybody turned in early tonight.

August 9, 1959. *Kungsholm*. Rough but not stormy. Went to devotional service this a.m. at 11:00 conducted by a missionary. A very good talk, but when they sang "Let the Lower Lights Be Burning" there were many moist eyes.

Brightly beams our Father's mercy
From His lighthouse evermore,
But to us He gives the keeping
Of the lights along the shore.

Chorus:
Let the lower lights be burning!
Send a gleam across the wave!
Some poor fainting, struggling seaman
You may rescue, you may save.

Dark the night of sin has settled,
Loud the angry billows roar;
Eager eyes are watching, longing,
For the lights along the shore. (Chorus)

Trim your feeble lamp, my brother:
Some poor sailor, tempest-tossed,
Trying now to make the harbor,
In the darkness may be lost. (Chorus)

I remember hearing Mother [Ruth] sing it so much when I was a child, and it was the first hymn I ever taught myself to play. A rather quiet day, finished packing and saying farewells to friends and B-19.

August 10, 1959. *Kungsholm* and New York. Pulled into N.Y. harbor and docked exactly on schedule at 9:00 a.m.. After about an hour were allowed ashore and was it good to see Mary Frances and Malcolm Williams Jr. there to meet us! After about an hour and a half of finding baggage and going through customs, very friendly but thorough! M.F. took us to her lovely home in Waterford, Conn. Had a marvelous big steak dinner with corn on the cob and all the fixin's!

August 11, 1959. Waterford, Conn. Mary Frances has such a lovely home (Cape Cod style house, no air conditioning!) and family. Enjoyed meeting Malcolm's mother, Tess. They took us around to the United States Coast Guard Academy and the submarine bases and other beautiful spots. Had another marvelous dinner of broiled chicken on their electric grill. Ate out in the back by the apple tree. So lovely. Called Mary Nye and Margaret Hays in NYC about meeting us there. [I was probably with Mother on these excursions, but I also went to the beach with Malcolm Jr. and his sister, Becky.]

August 12, 1959. HOT and HUMID. Waterford and

Washington D.C. Had a nice visit with M.F. this a.m. and
a wonderful noon meal of sword fish steaks, etc. Boy, can
she cook! Her children are so beautiful and so smart. Hate
to leave them so soon, but so thankful for this time with
them. Malcolm and Mary Frances took us to our 8:00 plane
for Washington D.C. stayed to wave goodbye. Epsie Young
met us in Washington and took us to Marg's new home in
Foggy Bottom. Lovely. [Mother's college friend Margaret
Hayes worked at the State Department in D.C. She lived in
an un-air-conditioned townhouse in Foggy Bottom. She was
working at North Texas State University in Denton when
I was an undergraduate, so I got reacquainted with her in
1965 to 1969. I wish I could remember conversations with
her. She attended my first wedding on August 9, 1969.]

August 13, 1959. Washington D.C. HOT and HUMID. But
it is so wonderful to be with Margaret after all these years!
She fixed a good American breakfast and went to her work.
Susie and I went to the Wax Museum and met her for lunch
at the Water Gate Inn, a beautiful spot. Took taxi to Capitol,
Library of Congress, Art Museum and Lincoln Memorial
then home.

Reading her journal, I am again wondering where Mother got the
energy to do all this! I remember this day very well. After the Library
of Congress, we got a taxi. Mother asked the driver where we could
go to cool off and get a snack. We had thought about going to the
Smithsonian. The driver said, "The Smithsonian is not air-conditioned,
but the Modern Art Museum is and you can get a cold drink in the
Museum café." Hence, the choice of the Art Museum! Margaret drove
us through old Georgetown where we had a big Chinese dinner at the
Orient Café. Then she drove by Jefferson and Lincoln Memorials, which
are beautiful at night.

♫ **August 14, 1959.** Still hot in D.C. But we don't mind
with our sweet friends. Charlotte and her daughter Lois

[Lyman] drove over at 10:30 and took us to the White
House. Had a quick lunch after seeing the Washington
Cathedral. Susie and Lois went swimming while Charlotte
drove me by Betty and Don [McMullen's] home and the
Oliver's. Had a big dinner with the Lyman's at a Navy Gun
factory. Never saw so much wonderful food. They visited
with us and Margaret for a while.

    August 15, 1959. Still HOT in D.C. [Mother's last entry
in the travel diary.] Well, our 9:35 flight was cancelled
after getting up at 7:00, so we got out at 7:00 p.m. Bless
Margaret's heart for "sweating it out" with us, but it gave
us a chance to see Lee's old home (overlooking Arlington
National Cemetery) and the Tomb of the Unknown Soldier.
Lost my glasses somewhere out there. Had a grand
flight, arriving in Dallas at 10:05 p.m. It is so good to be
with Daddy and Dillon again. The end of a thrilling and
wonderful summer! But it is good to be home!

HOMECOMING AND MOTHER'S END: AUGUST 1959–MAY 1960

*M*other wrote to Ingrid about one month after our return. I do not remember much about our homecoming, but I know Daddy and Dillon were glad to have us back home. I was preparing to enter the seventh grade at Lakewood Elementary School, Dillon the fifth grade. Mother was still in the zone and on her adrenaline high from the joy of the trip. Life went on. Mother lived to complete projects she had begun before she was stricken with cancer. She lived to see her brother Edgar married. She had already found a replacement organist to perform with Elizabeth. She asked her women friends "to look after my children." She made the trip to Sweden.

In 1958 Mother had begun posing for an oil portrait to be painted by her college friend and professional portrait artist Majorie Phillips. Understanding the state of Sue's health, she painted the portrait as a gift. When we returned from Sweden in August 1959, Marjorie insisted that Mother sit for the completion of her portrait. I accompanied Mother to that final sitting. She wore a favorite blue satin dress and deco-style jewelry. She holds in her left hand a silk fan that Edgar had bought in Paris in 1956. The portrait hung over our piano at Westlake until 1964. It now hangs in my home.

*Portrait of
Sue Dillon
Bussard,
1959, painted
by Marjorie
Phillips*

Mother wrote to Ingrid:

September 14, 1959

୧୬ Dear Ingrid:

It all seems like a dream now that I was ever over to your
wonderful country. I just can't tell you how much it is still
meaning to me, as I feel so much better now. I am so sorry that
I did not feel better while I was there, but I have no doubt in
the world that all the loving care that you and Barbro, Britta,
Viola, and all the rest you gave me has really helped. I am so
much stronger than I was, and I think I told you that Dr. Brown
was more than pleased with the way I looked.

While I was gone, the drug houses came out with another
new pill, which of course he is trying on me as he does all
the new things. This in addition to the two Cytomel (just

thyroid) and the eight Pabalate pills (only an analgesic!)
seem to keep me feeling pretty good. I can turn out a lot more
work now than I have been able to for the past two years and
am having my girl only four days a week. The house hasn't
materialized as yet, but my friend still hasn't sold it. The
realtors are not trying to sell mine anymore, as we felt 90
days was long enough to try, then Jimmy said they had not
tried very hard. Maybe something will work out yet, but I am
very philosophical about such things. Jimmy and I both would
like the convenience of so much storage in the other house,
however.

Did you ever get the slides of Hagavik and Växjö? I do hope
they are not lost, as I think every day of some that were in
that group. My Switzerland ones turned out real well. I am
still showing my pictures but am taking good care of yours and
shall return them before too long. I shall also try to have some
duplicates made of some you might like, or at least send them
to you to look at. I am going to send you some money, Ingrid,
real soon, and if that little chest is still not sold I might have
you fill it with more of the straw mobiles. You will remember
that I bought four—two small and one large plain and one
large with four little dressed dolls on them. We got them at
Illums [a department store in Denmark, still in business]. I
don't remember their exact cost but shall just send you about
twenty-five dollars and have you get as many as you can. I
know I must do it soon in order to get them by Christmas,
which I would want them for.

You didn't answer me about the color of the curtains you
want in your bedroom. If I do not hear I will presume you will
want a pale pink or white—or maybe yellow? Just write me
a card and tell me which, as I want to give you this for your
new apartment. I shall also send you the lipstick mirror, and
whatever else you tell me. Please answer me real soon so that I
can get this done while I have the energy. I never know when I
may run out, you know.

My friend Vivian who had wanted me to meet her in Paris, is very ill, having developed four more tumors, so it won't be much longer. My heart is broken for her, and I don't know what her death is going to do to me. She is so wonderful and so courageous. [Mother is writing about herself also: "I never know when I may run out."]

I dreamed last night I that I was back in Sweden, and it was so wonderful. Believe me, if Jimmy and I can ever do it, I would love to bring him with me. That is the only way I will come again, as I know he would enjoy it so much.

We drove down to San Marcos the week of August 28 or thereabouts. Uncle Jim [Grandmother Ruth's brother] is happily situated, but just sleeps all the time. At least he likes the rest home where he is, and that is something. We spent one night in Austin with Lera Bess and one with Aunt Lera in New Braunfels. It was fun to go with the whole family. [I do remember Uncle Jim, sweet old man. I wish I had been more aware of his life story. Alas, I was but a child. I don't even have a photo of him.]

Elizabeth and I are doing "The Music Man" in Lake Murray, OK on Oct. 8, and I am going to try to get him [Jimmy] to go up with me a day early to rest, as he really needs it. Our business has never been so rushing!

Just keep me informed, Ingrid, about what the expense of sending the slides and cap, etc. are and I will reimburse. Jimmy says he and I will take care of that amount Ed owes you if you will allow us to do it a little at a time, as he was so wonderful to help us work out this trip for me. I'm sure he would feel awful if he knew it, so we will just take care of it as soon as we can. [This money owed to Ingrid by Uncle Ed goes all the way back to when he bought the Mercedes in Sweden in 1956. Ingrid told me that her father had lent Ed the funds to purchase the car.]

I was so distressed to hear of Bo's illness. Lars saw Jimmy and told him. I wrote them immediately, and Birgitta writes today that he is better, though he tires easily. Please tell Britta and Viola that I love them very much and promise to write them real soon. I have not seen any of our Swedish friends since I returned. I just don't know where the time goes, but it does. Susie and Dillon started school last week and are loving it. Dillon is finally getting some front teeth, but the dentist had to lance the gums so that they would come through. I called Sara Everett long distance in Los Angeles Saturday to wish her bon voyage for the Orient and give her your greetings. She flew yesterday and will return about November 21. She was gone when I returned.

Ed and Jo and Mrs. Hunley are getting along about the same. The doctor has told them it will not be over six months probably for Mrs. Hunley. We are so sorry. She is a very sweet little woman. I had the Armstrongs and Hibbards over one night before I even got my Swiss pictures, as they just couldn't wait. Mr. Hibbard just raved over my Sweden pictures taken late at night. Said the horizontal lighting was marvelous, whatever that is! I really was surprised, as I don't know thing one about photography. Of course you took some of them, too, and I told them you did.

I miss you so much, Ingrid, and shall love you forever and ever for the millions of things you have done to make my family happy. Our lives would have never been the same without you!

Bill and Ruth have decided to stay in Dallas, for which we are grateful. They have bought a completely automatic self-service laundry in Ft. Worth. It is about time for fried chicken now, so adjo. I shall never forget your deeeelicious fried chicken. [Willie Mae Johnson, Grandmother's black maid/cook, taught Ingrid how to prepare southern fried chicken in 1949!] Willie Mae has had an operation this summer. Had a breast tumor removed, but it was not malignant.

Be sweet and do drop me a line to let me know we just didn't completely whip you down! Worlds of love. SUE

The friendship between Mother and Ingrid had grown in intensity over the years since 1948. They were closer than sisters. Ingrid had a special empathy for Mother's suffering with cancer, as her medical training informed her understanding of Mother's diagnosis, and the correspondence between them afforded Mother a means to pour out her feelings and frustrations to someone who would not judge her. The relationship seems at times to have been smothering on Mother's part. However, the distance between Texas and Sweden afforded Ingrid breathing room, while allowing Mother to continue her fantasy that Ingrid's friendship held a "healing" power over her, like Mary Poppins, that kept her going.

I remember her being "Mother," but she did not do the things that my friends' mothers did. I do know that she and Elizabeth continued to perform musical reviews for women's groups and Mother often played for style shows. *The Sound of Music* played for a two-week run in the State Fair Music Hall during the State Fair of Texas in October 1959. Mother saw to it that our family attended a performance. She lived every minute of every day.

[This letter is typed on Dillon Scale letterhead and may have been enclosed in a Christmas box Mother had mailed to Ingrid.]

October 5, 1959.

෴ My dearest Ingrid:

Just a hurried note, as I have so many things to do. I am enclosing $10.00. Will you please send by Air mail as many of the little mobiles like I bought at Illums as you can get including postage? I would like the bigger sizes, at least in two of them—one with the dancers and one plain. In other words I would like two of each if the money will go that far. You will be able to get two in one box, as that is the way I did them. You might even get them all in one box which of course would cut down on the weight. I will appreciate your sending as soon as possible, as Jo and I would like to use them for some parties.

I shall wait a few more days for you to answer about the

curtains you want, and if I don't hear, I shall just send what
I think will be pretty! I am so glad that you and Britta and
Ingrid G. were able to go to Italy. I enjoyed your card so much.
I am gradually writing my thank you notes to Sweden, so tell
Britta and Viola not to give up.

I miss all of you so very much. I just wept last night when
Dinah Shore had Ingemar Johansson and sang a couple
of Swedish songs on the program. [He had just won the
heavyweight boxing title over American Floyd Patterson. All
Sweden celebrated.]

I asked for the lipstick mirror, and it seems no one handles
them anymore. There are other types that I might send and
will send something along with the curtains. Be sure to write
me soon if you have a choice or if you have already purchased
something, but I hope you have not.

I am also enclosing the words that you asked about. I took
them off the record some time ago, and you will note there are
a couple of words that even I could not understand. Perhaps
you can make them out yourself from Ann-Marie's records.

Be sweet and give everybody my love. I will hurry to the
post office and mail this. Nothing has happened about the
house yet. She has not sold it, and we just aren't trying too
hard to sell ours. The main reason I want the other house is
that I would have more room to keep my little Swedish friends
when they come! Hope I won't have to wait too long for one of
you! Love you lots. SUE

Saw Jack Everett yesterday and found that Sara was not in
the terrible storms in the Orient. Jimmy had asked Luke last
week if they had heard from her, but he said, "Nope, but we're
not worried. No hurricanes had better ever tangle with our
mother!"

I don't think Mother meant to sound patronizing in her letters, but
she did.

The rest of September and into the middle of October 1959, we just lived. Mother and Elizabeth performed for ladies' organizations, Daddy worked very hard for Dillon Scale & Equipment Co., and Dillon and I studied in fifth and seventh grades at Lakewood Elementary. Uncle Bill and Aunt Ruth, along with cousins Ralph, John, and Ginny, lived nearby in east Dallas. We saw them often. Ralph attended Woodrow Wilson High School as a sophomore, while John and Ginny attended Mount Auburn Elementary School. Ginny started first grade at Mount Auburn. All this time, Mother and Daddy shielded me and Dillon from the severity of her illness, but we already knew it was very serious.

Mother wrote to Ingrid in longhand, which was something very difficult for her. She was probably at the beauty parlor or sitting in a doctor's office.

October 20, 1959

꧁ My dearest Ingrid,

Thank you so very much for your wonderful letter received yesterday! I know how hard it is to write.

I am so pleased that the pictures aren't lost, and am sorry about the black and white, but it can't be helped now. I was just saving space in putting them in our sack. I shall be grateful even for black and white!

Ingrid, I am so very sorry about the curtains. Maybe someone else would like them and I can send you white. Just advise whether or not you are returning them, and I will send white if that is what you want. I am truly sorry, but I just didn't know. I shall send the Lady Esther in my Xmas package.

Tell Ockie that Susibeth would welcome a letter in Swedish from him! She talks about him so much. Both kids got their report cards today—Dillon all 1's, Susibeth one 1 and three 2's which of course is not bad for 7th grade.

Maybe somebody else would like the yellow curtains. Just advise by a sentence or two, Ingrid, and I will act accordingly. I know you want them for the holidays. I have my lace ones up in my bedroom. Remember I bought lace in Växjö? Very pretty. Love to all. SUE

Mother's last two letters to Sweden, written in longhand from Gaston Hospital, are dated November 18 and November 25, 1959. The cancer has progressed with a vengeance. Mother was in terrible pain and losing the battle. At age twelve, I was now allowed to visit her in the hospital. We talked about our magical trip to Sweden, and I told her about school. She wrote to Ingrid:

November 18, 1959

ᑭᑭ My dearest Ingrid,

First thank you so much for the mobiles and the film. There was no mistake, Ingrid. The black and whites were some Susie took with her little brownie box camera.

As you see I am in the hospital again. On Nov. 9 I was playing for Elizabeth at the country club in Ft. Worth when I had an acute attack of bursitis in my left hip. [It was the cancer progressing through her bones, not bursitis.] It was excruciating going from my left foot to the top of my head, but I managed to finish somehow. Then on the way back we stopped suddenly for a light and that finished it. Elizabeth took me to Dr. Brown's office, and he sent me directly here without even going home first. I couldn't even walk and still have a lot of pain. I have an orthopedic doctor too and they are X-raying, etc, so I guess my wings are clipped for a while.

It was such a thrill to see the few slides of Lund, Isterholm, Ulla and you and Barbro—I just can't believe that I ever had such a wonderful summer. You will never know how I love for all the wonderful things you did for us all summer.

I have decided not to play any organ, at least until after the first of the year. [She never played again.] They assure me they see no tumors, but I don't know what kind of therapy they will give me. So far it is mostly bed rest. I am so disgusted right now when I need to do so many things for Christmas. Susie says you sent them the darling Advent calendars too. Thank you so very much, Ingrid, for just loving them. We talk about all of you so much and miss you so very much. Please give them all—family and friends—our love. I will not write too much now as it is very difficult for me.

Be sure to tell me if you still want the white curtains, Ingrid, as I do want you to have what you want! Bye for now. I love you. SUE

Mother's last letter to Sweden was written to the Giertz family in Göteborg. Not only was it a farewell to Sweden, but her farewell to life itself. With Mother in the hospital for Thanksgiving, Daddy, Dillon, and I spent Thanksgiving with Uncle Bill and Aunt Ruth and the cousins. As Mother's letters were circulated among the common friends in Sweden, Ingrid saved it.

November 25, 1959

♋ Dear Family Giertz,

I have wanted to write for some weeks now, but I've had so much bad news and kept hoping things would take a turn for the better before I wrote.

I wrote Ingrid J. that I had entered the hospital on Nov. 9 for a few days and here I still am. Just a week ago tomorrow they [the doctors] informed me that they found "changes" in both hip joints and advised 10 X-ray treatments. Needless to say I was terribly discouraged, as I have seen this pattern by many of my friends and I know this X-ray business can't keep up forever. Ingrid knows how sick they make me and right now I cannot walk. This is due to the treatments they say, and I should be able to walk again, but I have been told so many things that I know only time will tell. I have never suffered such pain as I have these past weeks. I had so hoped to be able to spend Thanksgiving Day tomorrow at home with the family, but that is impossible. They are giving me hypos before the treatments now.

I don't know what I would do without my precious family, friends, and above all God. Also you all will never know what my trip to Sweden did for me, and the blessings I have received from knowing each and every one of you. Please call Tott for me and send this on to Ingrid, as I have such a time writing.

I do hope your trip to Greece did you both a world of good, Bo and Elisabeth. And did Birgitta ever find her trunk? Thank you so much, Ingrid for your cards from your trip too and tell Tott we appreciated hers.

We shall try to keep you posted, but in the meantime it will mean so much to me to know that some Swedish prayers are being said for me! Worlds of Love. SUE

P.S. Jimmy and the kids are fine! Martin, Susie and I enjoy talking of you so much! We have some good pictures of you.

Mother did come home in December, but she was no longer able to write letters, either by hand or on her typewriter. She was able to stand and move with a walker, but she was always in pain. Daddy rented a hospital bed for her, which he put up in their bedroom. One afternoon when I was home from school, I asked her, "Mommy, are you ever going to get well?" She answered, "No, but I will be here as long as I can." Daddy told Dillon and me that this would be Mother's "last Christmas" with us. We walked around with knots in our stomachs and lumps in our throats. The Christmas of 1959 Santa Claus brought new bicycles. We had asked for them in 1958. We did not want them in 1959. We sat down to Christmas dinner at the home of my best friend, Lisa. Her mother had prepared a lovely lunch. There was another guest present to whom Daddy explained that Mother had to lie down because she had cancer. She died five months later on May 23, 1960.

The correspondence that follows shifts from between Mother and Ingrid to between Daddy and Ingrid. Daddy wrote:

February 6, 1960
ᕟᔭ Dear Ingrid,

I'm not sure how long it has been since you last heard from Sue, but I want to bring you up to date regarding her illness.

She was in Gaston Hospital for four weeks prior to the

Christmas holidays. During this period she had ten X-ray treatments in the hip and pelvis area for lesions in the bone. She was home approximately two weeks and instead of getting better, she got worse. About 2:00 a.m. on Sunday morning Jan. 3, she had an excruciatingly painful muscle spasm in her lower back. I called the doctor and an ambulance and we took her to Baylor Hospital that morning, 3:00 a.m.

For a period of 2 weeks I had registered nurses around the clock with her as she was needing hypos and other medication to keep down the pain. Finally she was given a series of 5 intravenous injections of radio-active phosphorus which we hope will control the cancer problem.

On Thursday, Jan. 21, we moved her from Baylor hospital across the street to Gaston hospital where she is at the moment. I've had 2 nurses with her every day (one from 3:00 pm to 11:00 pm, the other from 11:00 pm to 7:00 am) but hope to let both of them go tomorrow, Sunday Feb. 7.

I've had my hands full running the house and looking in on Sue 4 or 5 times a day. We've been very busy at the office also, all of which has kept me pretty busy.

I told Sue yesterday, that if Ingrid were here she would surely be busy. Sue asked me to write to you since she has been so very sick and unable to handle any letter writing since Christmas. We did not send our Christmas cards because of her condition.

I hope we have a remission of her trouble so we can bring her home soon. At the moment I can't bring her home until she can do a little more for herself, but she is beginning to get a little stronger day by day for the past 4 or 5 days.

The kids and I are OK. They are doing a good job in school and growing so fast. Susibeth is a real little lady. I am so grateful that the both of them made the trip to Sweden when they did. You and the others were so good to look after Sue and Susibeth. I wish it were possible for you to see all of her trip pictures.

Please advise Sue's other friends about her. She is a real
sick girl, but is somewhat better, and the day of miracles is not
over. Your presence would be so welcome at this time—it's a
shame you are so far away. Our winter so far has been pretty
mild. We've had some rain, no snow, and a lot of sunshine. I'll
try to keep you posted on Sue's condition. Do drop us a line as
we think of you frequently. Love. Jimmy

Sunday 7 Feb. 1960. The main reason Sue had a set back
after moving over to Gaston Hospital was that she had so many
hypos (morphine) to keep down the pain that it suppressed
her respiration and caused her to have pneumonia. She used
oxygen for 3 or 4 days and is over the pneumonia now. I
finished this letter while sitting with Sue at the hospital. She
sends her love.

On this day, or a day very like it, Mother told Daddy to ask Ingrid to
marry him to help raise Dillon and me. Hence the letters that follow
after Mother's death. Daddy wrote another note to Ingrid while Mother
was still hospitalized.

March 5, 1960
Dear Ingrid:

Edgar wrote Bo a day or two ago advising him of Sue's
present condition. Bo will talk to you, I'm sure. Sue is not
in bad pain nor under heavy sedation at present and we are
letting the night nurse go today, as she gets such good care at
Gaston Hospital. She finishes this series of X-ray treatments
Tuesday Mar. 8th. I know she will be in the hospital thru next
week, then we can possibly bring her home again. She is real
sick and the outlook is not good.

Just before I left for the office yesterday morning, the mail
truck returned the package that Sue had sent to you early in
November. This package included several items, among them
your slides. The package was returned from Malmö because
when Sue printed your name she made the "J" look like an "S"

and they couldn't locate anyone by that name. I'll repack the carton as soon as possible and see that it is addressed properly. We'll keep you posted on Sue's condition. Love. Jimmy

The next eleven weeks of 1960, between Daddy's last letter to Ingrid and Mother's death, are only a foggy memory. Easter fell on April 17, 1960. Daddy took Dillon and me to Easter services at Highland Park Methodist Church. Mother was not able to come home from the hospital. Today, she would have been placed under hospice care.

Early in May 1960, Bishop Bo Giertz came to Dallas to visit Mother and to give her a signed copy of his novel *The Hammer of God.* He was on a book signing tour. I did not see him, but I still have the book, which I read in 2017 before my last trip to Sweden. I visited Bo's daughters Ingrid G. in Stockholm and Birgitta G. in Uppsala on that trip.

Mother succumbed to the ravages of relentless metastatic breast cancer on May 23, 1960. She was forty-six, two months short of her forty-seventh birthday. My last visit to the hospital to see Mother was Saturday, May 14, shortly before she slipped into a coma. I did not see her again. Aunt Lera Dillon Shelander came from New Braunfels to Dallas for the funeral. She stayed with us, slept in my room in the other twin bed, and snored like a banshee all night. She helped me dress for Mother's service. I wore a black-and-white tiny checkered shirtwaist dress with stockings and black patent leather pumps with one-inch heels. Aunt Lera suggested I wear the black belt instead of the red one. She was always close to both Mother and my grandmother Ruth. Her daughter, Lera Bess, was a close first cousin/friend of my mother. I played with her son, Vaner, and daughters, Laura and Susie.

My great-uncle Jim Gilliam died in June 1960, three weeks after Mother died. He left a considerable estate to his niece, my mother, and nephew, Uncle Ed. However, since my mother predeceased Uncle Jim, his entire estate went to Uncle Ed. Daddy tried to get Ed to put Mother's share in a trust for Dillon and me, but he refused to do so.

The service was held at the Ed C. Smith Funeral Home, where Mother had been hired as organist in the 1940s. On the day Mother died, Monday May 23, I remember arriving home from school and seeing lots of cars parked in front of our house. Dillon was already home. Uncle Bob, Daddy's twin; his wife Katheryn; and their daughter, Kathey had driven from Tallahassee, Florida, to be with us and had arrived on Saturday evening, May 21. They stayed for the funeral on May 24, then left for Florida on Wednesday, May 25, the day after the funeral. Daddy insisted that Dillon and I return to school that same day—so very hard. On Friday, May 27, there was a "graduation" assembly at Lakewood Elementary School for the departing seventh graders. I sang in the seventh grade choir. We performed "I Believe." I wept through the whole program.

Daddy notified Ingrid of Mother's passing.

May 28, 1960

꙰ Dearest Ingrid:

Just a year ago Sue was making final plans for visiting you. She and Susibeth left Dallas on June 1st and Dillon and I got along by ourselves for 2 ½ months. The trip to Sweden meant so much to Sue and I appreciated so much all you did for her.

I did everything possible for her to make her illness bearable. During the 6 months she was hospitalized, she had the memories of her trip last summer to think about. I'm sure Bo has told you of his lovely visit with her. She knew, of course, that she couldn't get well, but she did not give up until she went into the coma on Wed. night May 18th.

Sue passed away on Monday noon May 23rd.

The funeral service was Tuesday afternoon conducted by Bill Dickinson, our minister and Sterling Wheeler, our Sunday school teacher—a very lovely service which I would like to tell you about personally.

I have a rather recent picture of Sue at the organ from which the newspaper picture was made [for her obituary]. I'll send you one of these pictures if you'd like to have it.

The kids and I are lined up pretty well at home. Both are

going to camp this summer thanks to Sara Everett as I couldn't possibly send them at this time. I've been in a tailspin for nearly a year and I feel like a terrific weight has been lifted off my shoulders.

I need to take some time off but don't know when or what I will do. Ingrid, I wish you could visit with us a while this summer. So many of Sue's friends know you and have heard her comments on her trip. If you can't visit us this summer, think about a trip over during the Christmas season. It would be so wonderful to have you with us at that time. I've really needed you and have thought so much about you.

You will be seeing Harriet and Jay Armstrong soon— perhaps before you receive this letter. Harriett has been wonderful to us and Dillon thinks Jay is as fine as they come.

Please write me real soon. It is too much to hope for a visit because you are so far away, just 2 days by air, but please know we want you to visit us just as soon as you can.

Kindest regards to Ingrid Giertz. Love. Jimmy

P.S. I haven't sent your Christmas package to you because I haven't had time to repack it and ship it. I'd like to give you some of Sue's things and could do this more intelligently if you were here. I will take care of this in due time.

In 1984, French author Hervé Guibert wrote an autobiographical novel *To the Friend Who Did Not Save My Life*. His portrayal of living with relentless, untreatable AIDS in the 1980s just as surely applies to living with relentless, untreatable metastatic breast cancer in the 1950s. The accepted position of the medical community in the 1950s was that if the patient survived five years after surgery to remove the malignancy, the patient was deemed to be "cancer free" and therefore cured. Although cancer in the 1950s did not conjure the social stigma that AIDS did in the 1980s, those who suffered from such an incurable affliction found themselves separated from the "normal life" of their peers. Mother's gradual realization that she was not going to recover from her cancer put her on a plane different and separate from her friends and family. Hervé Guibert described living with AIDS in the 1980s in terms Mother would have understood while living with cancer in the 1950s.

> I was discovering something sleek and dazzling in its
> hideousness, for though it was certainly an inexorable
> illness, it wasn't immediately catastrophic, it was an illness
> in stages, a very long flight of steps that led assuredly
> to death, but whose every step represented a unique
> apprenticeship. It was a disease that gave death time to
> live and its victims time to die, time to discover time, and
> in the end to discover life.[1]

Although Ingrid's friendship and the trip to Sweden in 1959 could not save her, Mother reached a plane from which she indeed discovered the fullness of time to live to the end of her life.

JIMMY
AND INGRID

*W*hen Mother died on May 23, 1960, Dillon's and my childhood ended, but the woman I was to become would not emerge for many years. I was almost thirteen, entering puberty. All the angst of being a teenager lay before me without my mother. Daddy was, of course, devastated by Mother's death. We all were. He was a clear candidate for a nervous breakdown, but with two children to raise and a business to run, he managed to keep his composure, at least in front of Dillon and me. I believe that the Holy Spirit carried us all through the whole experience. Shortly after the funeral, Bill Dickinson paid a condolence call to Daddy. I was present when Daddy asked Pastor Dickinson how God could have taken her from us. How God could have given her cancer. Bill replied that God did not give Mother cancer. She got sick. When her body was not able to recover, the Lord took her home. I reminded Daddy of this conversation more than once in the years that followed when we were especially missing her.

I know Mother prayed. I know she asked all of her friends "to look after my children." And they did. I was raised by the mothers of my friends: Leona, Luanna, Elizabeth, Harriet, and Sara, to name a few. Perhaps the strongest maternal influence in my life was Aunt Ruth

Bussard, with whom I kept in close touch until her death at age 101 in 2015. And, of course, Ingrid Jaensson, even though she lived in Sweden. Dillon grew closer to Daddy. They became a team.

I became "the lady of the house," but Daddy kept a black housekeeper employed for some years. After all, I was only thirteen. Dillon and I both needed someone to be in the house when we got home from school. That fall, I started eighth grade at J. L. Long Junior High; Dillon was in sixth grade at Lakewood Elementary School. The idyllic childhood Dillon and I had enjoyed on Westlake in the 1950s shattered when Mother died. The 1960 eighth grade class of J. L. Long Junior High School was made up of children from several elementary schools in east Dallas: Lakewood, Stonewall Jackson, Robert E. Lee, O. M. Roberts, and Mt. Auburn. Not all the children I met had been afforded the sheltered upbringing Dillon and I had. For the first time, I encountered boys and girls who smoked in the bathrooms, did not do their homework, talked back to teachers, spoke "dirty talk," and bragged about skipping school. Some of the girls had reputations of being "fast," and some of them just disappeared for six months. Rumors surfaced that they'd gotten pregnant and had to go away.

Daddy continued to correspond regularly with Ingrid from 1960 to 1962. Of course, he wanted her to marry him. His letters indicate that he "carried a torch for her" until June 1962, when we found out that Ingrid had taken a job as administrator of the Swedish Hospital in Seoul, South Korea.

She did not return to Dallas until April 1992. I visited her in Sweden in the summers of 1975, 2000, and 2002, and in October 2004, the year of her ninetieth birthday. She told me then about the love letters, but that she could not marry Daddy—she did not love him that way. She returned to the US one more time in October 2009 to celebrate her ninety-fifth birthday. She visited her cousins in Minnesota, then flew to Austin, Texas, with Håkan Nordmark, her traveling companion and bodyguard. Ingrid had been friends with his grandmother. We all stayed with Dillon in Austin for four days in October 2009, the last time we saw each other. She remained a close friend of mine until her death on March 8, 2012. I returned to Växjö for her funeral service, where I

sang "Amazing Grace" at the service in Växjö Domkyrka. I last visited
Sweden in spring 2017.

Returning to the letters. I have what appears to be pages 3 and 4 of
a letter from Daddy to Ingrid. I imagine he wrote passionate statements
of love and devotion to her and perhaps even mentioned that Sue had
suggested that Ingrid marry him to finish raising Dillon and me. Pages
1 and 2 are missing.

July 10, 1960

⟳ Dear Ingrid,

That's what I wanted to explain.

Susie left last Saturday for a girls camp in the Ozark
mountains near Siloam Springs, Arkansas. She is due back
August 13, 1960.

I will visit Dillon's camp this coming Saturday and bring
him home with me Sunday.

I have this week and next week by myself. I have disposed of
most of Sue's clothes with the exception of some nice dresses
and 2 or 3 suits. Fortunately Louise Eliasson wears the same
shoe size as Sue, so I gave her the complete shoe and slipper
wardrobe (almost 20 pairs I guess). She was very appreciative
and happy to have these.

Do you remember Siv and Lennart Anderson, another
Swedish couple whom you met at our house? Siv had a baby
boy this week and they are so happy. I'm going to visit them
tomorrow afternoon.

Please give my regards to your parents. Isn't it a shame that
we are so far from each other. I would so love to fly with Dillon
to Sweden, but I simply can't figure a trip like that any time
soon. I'll be looking forward to hearing from you.

Love. Jimmy

P.S. Josephine's mother is in the hospital and real bad.
I don't see how she can live much longer—2 or 3 weeks at
the most. I still have this package to send to you (for last
Christmas). I'd like to add some of Sue's things to it but would

like for you to tell what you'd like to have—and I'd like to give it to you in person. See how simple all this would be if you could spend the holidays with us. Love ya.

GYPSY CAMP: A RESPITE FROM GRIEF

In the summer of 1960, I turned thirteen on July 17. My mother had died of cancer on May 23 of that year. Needless to say, I was a teenager at loose ends, in need of friends.

In January or February 1960, Westlake mothers and daughters had gathered at the Westlake home of Luanna Wade to meet "Miss Etta" and to hear the pitch and see a slide presentation on Gypsy Camp for Girls located in the Ozark Mountains just south of Siloam Springs, Arkansas. Among us there were the Wade girls, Wanda and twin sisters Alicia and Alanna, along with Jan King who signed up to attend Gypsy Camp the summer of 1960. It was a four-week session, costing $200—a significant amount in 1960 dollars. Daddy could not afford to send me, but a friend of Mother's, Sara Everett, offered to send both me and brother Dillon to summer camp. So, I went to Gypsy Camp in Arkansas, and Dillon went to Camp Longhorn in the Texas hill country. I loved camp; Dillon hated it.

Early on the morning of Saturday, July 9, 1960, Mrs. Wade loaded Wanda, Jan, and me (the twins did not attend in 1960) into her Buick sedan to begin the long day's drive to Siloam Springs, Arkansas, and Gypsy Camp. I remember that before we got to the highway, Mrs.Wade pulled over, parked the car, and led us girls in prayer for a safe road trip.

We had been instructed to purchase footlockers and were given a detailed list of items to bring to camp. Camp necessities included: personal toiletries, a laundry bag, pillow, sheets, a blanket, ten pairs of shorts and blouses or T-shirts, two bathing suits, four towels, jeans for horseback riding, sun hat, lightweight jacket, skirt or dress to wear into town, white shorts and tops to wear on Sunday, and a gypsy costume (colorful skirt, white ruffled top, costume spangle jewelry). Each camper also brought a tennis racket. Each camper had a $25 cash account at the camp kiosk to cover extra expenses for craft supplies, horseback rides, and an afternoon snack. We shipped the footlockers on the train from Dallas, Texas, to Fayetteville, Arkansas. Bob Coe collected the footlockers from the train station in Fayetteville and brought them to the site in his pickup truck. I can imagine a couple of burly guys carrying the footlockers to the cabins to place at the foot of our bunk beds. I have no idea what it cost to ship the footlockers. The two-story dining hall backed up to the box canyon at the end of the driveway. The cabins, named Angel's Alley, Upper Gypsy, Lower Gypsy, and Romany, were built into the sides of the bluff. I lived in Angel's Alley in 1960 and Romany in 1961. An arts and crafts room perched above the residence that housed Miss Etta and Bob and Daisy Coe (owners and operators). Below Angel's Alley was the latrine: toilets and showers, cold water only. We did most of our "bathing" in the river, including washing hair. Laundry was collected and sent out once a week, probably on Friday, then delivered clean on Monday morning.

Our days at Gypsy Camp began with the ringing of the bell atop the kiosk at 7:00 a.m. We would meet on the grounds in the center of the box canyon at 7:15 for morning calisthenics. One of the camp songs expresses an essence of the atmosphere at Gypsy Camp:

Gypsy Camp, Gypsy Camp
Nestled in the Ozarks blue
Gypsy Camp, Gypsy Camp
Just the place for me and you.
There is so much to be said
For the Orange and the Red
Up at seven and nine in bed,
At Gypsy Camp.

Typical morning activities lasting one hour each included swimming lessons, arts and crafts (I tooled a leather pouch and made a copper wall hanging of a sailing ship), tennis, and boating (flat-bottom wooden boats with paddles). We could sign up for a horseback ride once a week during one of the class times if we chose to do so. Classes began at 8:00 a.m. after breakfast and concluded at noon, when lunch was served in the common dining hall. Cabins took turns offering grace at meals.

The food was mediocre at best but filling.

Early in the camp session, before the first Wednesday campfire, new campers drew lots to determine which clan they would join. Each clan/team was led by a queen and intermediate and junior princesses and overseen by two of the cabin counselors. I served as Orange Queen in 1961 at age fourteen. The returning campers were already "members" of either the Orange or the Red clan. The Wednesday evening campfires for which we donned our gypsy costumes were themed, scripted events that focused on "clan" assignments and the history of Gypsy Camp, the values of caring for nature, stories about the Ozarks, and cultivating friendship.

On Tuesday evenings, we put on dresses and rode in the back of the Coe pickup truck to Fayetteville to attend the movies. This was the era of teen romantic beach movies with Annette Funicello and Frankie Avalon. On Sundays, campers put on "dress whites," and the staff and counselors held a nondenominational worship service. Catholic campers were taken to mass in Siloam Springs.

Quiet time/siesta was from 1:00 to 3:00. We earned points for napping and writing a letter home. At 3:00, the kiosk opened. We purchased soft drinks and candy bars. There was open swim until about 4:30. We earned five clan points for swimming fifteen laps from the dock to the buoy in the middle of the river. Each cabin got to take the boats on the river to cook a sunrise breakfast on a sandbar/island just around the bend from camp. Two or three adult (college students/former campers) counselors accompanied us. On another day the boats and campers were trucked upstream so we could take a float trip down the river back to camp. The Illinois winds through the beautiful canyons of the Ozarks—gentle current and ripples one can hardly call rapids. We loved it!

That second summer, 1961, Jan, Wanda, her twin sisters, and I took the train from Dallas to Fayetteville. Our footlockers traveled in the baggage car. We were met by Bob Coe with his pickup truck. We sat on our footlockers in the bed of the pickup as we rode the thirty miles from the Fayetteville depot to Gypsy Camp.

Throughout the camp sessions, every event of the day completed by every camper earned points for the team. The last week of camp was highlighted by a tennis tournament, rowing races, and swim tournament—with individual and team awards. The end-of-term banquet attended by family members and campers, wearing gypsy costumes, featured a talent show. Wanda, Jan, and I were the "Bandana Trio." We strummed ukuleles and sang a folk song. Part of the scripted ritual was the reciting of the poem "Goodbye, Little Cabin." Jan was chosen to deliver it from memory at the banquet in 1961. She auditioned for the honor. Awards for swimming, tennis, and boating were handed out. The high-point camper was named, and the clan that earned the most total points was awarded the "cup." I was awarded a blue ribbon for having the best form for swimming the breaststroke (Ingrid had taught me in 1957). Some campers I particularly remember are Wanda, Alicia, and Alanna (members of Red clan) and Jan (Orange). In 1961, Gloria was Orange senior princess and high point camper, but the Reds won the cup. Another camper I remember is Dana (Jackson, Mississippi) and counselors Memory and Norma.

I did not return to Gypsy Camp after 1961. Jan and Wanda and the twins returned in 1962 with another neighborhood girl, Nancy. As for me, preparing for high school was more important. There have been Gypsy Camp reunions over the years, but I have not attended one. I know all of us were enriched by the camp experience; for me it was therapeutic.

Gypsy Camp was abandoned in 1978, but my husband, Ron, and I found the site as we drove south out of Siloam Springs on July 16, 2018, on our way to visit my cousin Kathey and her husband, Ed, in Little Rock, Arkansas. The lady at the visitor center in Fayetteville remarked that she had heard of Gypsy Camp, but she did not know exactly where it was. "Just drive south toward the Illinois River and look for a turn-off." We did drive south toward the Illinois River and spotted the drive, marked by a sign that read "Gypsy Camp & Canoe." A young couple had bought the property only three weeks before. They offer float trips down the Illinois River in rafts and canoes. As we drove onto the property, I immediately recognized the bluff on one side and the river on the other. The new owners let me walk into the property to view the remains of the cabins and dining hall. The camp site looked much smaller than I remembered. I learned from the new owners that Bob Coe had died in 2017. They had purchased the property from his estate. I wished them success in their business venture, and Ron and I continued our journey to Little Rock.

Daddy wrote his next letter to Ingrid during my time at Gypsy Camp. He was lonely, missing Mother and needing Ingrid.

August 7, 1960
 Dearest Ingrid:

I took off last week for some much needed rest and relaxation. Spent Monday and Tuesday at home. Then on Wednesday I went down to Austin where I spent three days at a very nice motel with a lovely swimming pool. My brother Bill and his family live in Austin now, so I enjoyed visiting with them.

On Saturday I picked Dillon up at his camp not far from Bandera and we went back to Austin that afternoon. Got in a good swim Saturday afternoon and Sunday morning, then came home Sunday evening.

It is awfully hard for me not to think seriously about us (you and me). The children truly love you and you know my feeling for you. When we analyze our situations we have much in common and I feel we should get together as soon as conveniently possible to talk things over. I am extremely proud of you and of your accomplishments and would like to think seriously of a future together.

My personal affairs are beginning to shape up and look better. As time goes along I can see a real need for a "mommy" who can help us and love us and to whom in turn we can give happiness and love. We are not the least bit interested in anyone else but you. If you think our getting together is utterly impossible or if you do not share this feeling, please tell me. I want to correspond with you and will refrain from writing love letters if you want me to.

I know I can make you happy (I am even a good cook) and wish I could send you the money today to visit us. So much for the love angle. It's in your hands. I've had several interesting letters from Susie. She is enjoying her camp experience and tells me she wants to go back next year.

Dillon does not want to go back to camp next year, but instead prefers a trip with his daddy. Am I completely out of my mind to contemplate a honeymoon vacation? Susie is due back a week from today after having been gone a month. I'll be glad to see her and was glad to see Dillon; however, I enjoyed the two weeks rest, relaxation and contemplation while both children were gone.

Ed and I hope to get our business in such a shape that each of us can take 2 weeks off twice a year or 4 weeks at a time. Our business is doing well but it requires hard work on the part of both of us.

Uncle Jim Gilliam in San Marcos passed away three weeks ago. Edgar was the executor of his estate and we buried him here at Dallas with his mother and father.

Josephine's mother is still lingering in the hospital and can pass away just any time. I feel sorry for Josephine for she is experiencing the same situation that I experienced with Sue and it is awfully hard on her.

I don't recall when I last wrote you, and it is possible that this letter will cross in the mail with a letter from you. At any rate, please write me after you have had a chance to really think about this. I'm quite serious but don't want to act foolish or put you on the spot. It is not our fault that we live in different lands. Perhaps there is a plan and a reason that we were thrown together 11 years ago. Love. Jimmy

Yes, Daddy was "out of his mind." He did not save Ingrid's reply, but I imagine she let him down as gently as possible, as they remained friends until he died in 1993. Living some three thousand miles apart was a blessing for them both.

Uncle Edgar had been married since the winter of 1960 to Josephine, nee Hunley. Dillon and I were instructed to call her "Aunt Jo." My uncle's emotional health improved with a wife to look after him, but his physical health was always problematic. He was president of Dillon Scale by right of inheritance and drew a salary, but he never worked to earn it. Daddy covered for Edgar, just as Ruth and Sue had always done.

The letters Ingrid wrote to Daddy have not survived. However, I can imagine how uneasy she must have felt about his romantic overtures. She told me in 2004 that she did not love him in that way. She had turned down several marriage proposals over the years—two men in Sweden, Uncle Ed and Jack Everett in Dallas, and now Daddy. I am aware that Ingrid's family would have been delighted to see her marry, but she was an independent, ambitious woman with a career.

Daddy's next letter, written a month later, gives voice to his loneliness and need to just talk to someone. It must have been therapeutic for him to share his thoughts with Ingrid, just as it had been for Mother. Actually, there is no one else who knows the background to whom he can write. Mother has been gone not yet four months.

Sunday, September 11, 1960

〰 Dearest Ingrid—

I finally opened the box which Sue sent to you last fall and which was subsequently returned because the name was not legible. In this carton were new curtains, some of your slides, 2 boxes of cake mix, some recipe magazines, a book of yours titled "Gösta Berlings Saga," and an overdue birthday greeting with a letter from Sue to you which you will treasure as a hallowed memory. [This may be referencing Mother's letter to Ingrid of Oct. 5, 1959. Ingrid's birthday was Oct. 4.]

All of this has to be repacked which I will try to do this week and I'll try to get it into the mail to you by Saturday Sept. 17th.

The children have started back to school. Dillon is in the 6th grade at Lakewood Elementary School and Susibeth is in the 8th grade at J. L. Long Junior High School.

Edgar is in the hospital in Colorado Springs where he

will undergo lung surgery in about a month. He will be away from the office at least 8 to 12 weeks, confidentially, it can be indefinite, depending on the results of the operation. I think he has written Bo some of the details. If not, I will tell you more about him later. Accordingly, I am running the business and really have my hands full.

This is all the more reason that I need a homemaker so very much and I cannot put you out of my mind. If you could give me some idea as to when you might visit us, I could then get my thinking settled and do some planning. Ingrid, I have a lot to offer you and we could be very happy together if you would consider it. There are so many things to discuss and this is a situation vital to both of us, unless of course there is someone else.

Please write to me soon and give me your honest opinion particularly of when you might come back to us. I'll agree we do need to talk for there are so many things we can't discuss by correspondence. I would send you the money for a round trip if I had it, but it will be a year or more before I recover from the expense of Sue's illness. I have paid for Sue's and Susibeth's trip to Sweden and I'm so glad they took the trip. It meant a lot to both of them and gave Sue some wonderful memories to think about during her last illness.

I want so much to visit Sweden, but I need to see you before that time, as it would be 3 or 4 years longer before I could get away from Dallas. If you could possibly work out a 2 or 3 months leave of absence from your position, we could then get some things worked out and you could give your family some specific information and assurance that they wouldn't be losing you entirely.

I am reading this letter over, it sounds like I am assuming a lot. That is not the case. The point is that I love you and need you. If the feeling is mutual, we can work something out. It may take a little time, but let's give it a chance.

Your last letter was dated Aug. 17th. I hope a letter is on the way from you. I'd like to write you at least twice a month and would so like to hear from you more frequently.

Love. Jimmy

P.S. Incidentally, if I am not addressing my letters to you correctly, please PRINT your address the way you want me to write it.

The letter of August 17 is missing. Ingrid did not respond to Daddy's latest overture in a timely manner. She was not in love with him, and she was grateful for the distance between them. Daddy received the disappointing news that Ingrid would not be traveling to the US anytime soon in a letter dated November 2,1960. He was still emotionally raw, as it had not been a year since Mother's death. Ingrid knew how vulnerable Daddy was and that she must not encourage him in any way. Ingrid had dropped into our lives in 1948, almost like Mary Poppins. True to her nature, Ingrid "took care" of people. She took special care of Mother. She gave more of herself to my family than anyone could expect from a devoted friend and kindred spirit, but Mary Poppins would never marry.

November 20, 1960

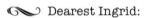 Dearest Ingrid:

I was so glad to receive your letter of 11-2-60 and I'm sorry I haven't written you sooner. I know how busy you must be—I'm so busy also but let us not wait too long to write each other. I understand and am truly sorry that it is not possible for you to plan a trip over here in the near future. It is really rough running a home and a business single handed, but it can be done if necessary. We can at least be good friends and if we can get together in the not too distant future, we can then talk things over and maybe work something out.

I'm distressed to learn that Ingrid Giertz has been ill, and I hope she is much better by now. Edgar came home from the hospital a week ago yesterday. He is recuperating very well but will not be back to the office until after the 1st of the year. His surgery included the removal of 4 ribs. All tests now have been TB negative and he is gaining weight, so he is definitely on the mend. We are spending Thanksgiving next Thursday with Harriet and Jay. I've seen their Swedish pictures a couple of times, however Jay messed up the last roll of film and missed the best pictures of their Swedish trip and of you. Please write to me soon.

Love. Jimmy

Daddy is still carrying the torch of love for Ingrid even though he is beginning to accept the fact that all she can promise him is platonic friendship. The Armstrongs lived in Grapevine, Texas. I remember the drive to their place in the country. It was a sunny, mild November day. I remember that Thanksgiving very well. As part of the dinner, Harriet served steamed cauliflower topped with drizzled browned butter. I have prepared it often. We got through our first holiday season without Mother, but I remember being on the verge of tears most of the time—knot in the stomach, lump in the throat.

Daddy's next letter is dated January 4, 1961.

Dearest Ingrid:

Thank you so much for your letter of Dec. 18th, your Christmas greetings and Christmas packages. The book "The Warship Vasa" arrived yesterday and it is truly a most interesting and fascinating book. I do appreciate your sending it to me.

We made it through Christmas and New Year's pretty well. It was just a year ago Jan. 2, 1960 that Sue had to go into Baylor Hospital. She was real bad and I didn't believe she would live through the month. She has been on my mind so much during this holiday season.

Edgar looks not good at all and may be improving only very slowly. He came by the office yesterday for a little while—the first time in about 5 months.

My responsibilities are quite heavy but I'm getting along OK. Running the business and my home keeps me busy—but I do

get lonesome at times. I hope to have my business in shape so I
can go to Florida in June and spend a couple of weeks with Bob.
I wish it were possible for you to visit us this summer—you
have many friends here who would be delighted to see you.

The kids and I had Xmas dinner with Jo and Ed. Then we
went out to the Armstrongs' for the rest of the day and the
evening. I've seen their Swedish pictures a couple of times but
not enough shots of you. Jay ruined his best roll of pictures
taken in Sweden.

Several weeks ago Don and Betty McMullen from Geneva,
Switzerland [the friends Mother visited in 1959], flew thru
Dallas. Harriet, Jay, and I met them between flights. It was
good to see them as it had been 10 or 12 years since I have
previously visited with them.

I am the only single person in our Mr. and Mrs. Sunday
School class, but I feel very much at home with this group
of very wonderful people. I lead the singing every Thursday
night. I'm on the Board of Stewards of Highland Park
Methodist Church this year and will be doing some extra-
curricular church work. I think I must be just about as busy
as you are. [By now Ingrid was an administrator in Malmö
Hospital.]

Susibeth and Dillon were at Sara Everett's for a New Year's
Eve party. Sarah had 24 children from 8 p.m. Saturday night
to 9:30 a.m. Sunday. The kids stayed up until 3 a.m.—but they
were really tired when they got home.

Please give my regards to Ingrid G., Bo, Barbro, etc. I sure
do have a lot of Swedish friends. Love. Jimmy

Daddy's "Mr. and Mrs. Class" met on Thursday evening. There was a
chaperone on duty during class. Dillon and I would go with Daddy. The
church fed us hot dogs for dinner. Sometimes we did homework; most
of the time we played games. For a short time, I stayed with Elizabeth
Peabody when I became friends with her son David.

Sara hosted a New Year's Eve party for her grandchildren and their friends. This particular year she invited Dillon and me. There I met a boy who would become one of my best friends all through junior high and high school. We are still friends today, some sixty-plus years later. Sara was one of Mother's friends whom she asked to "look after my children." Her husband and Daddy were business associates.

The correspondence between Daddy and Ingrid took a long pause after January 1961.

In Tallahassee, Florida, when we visited Uncle Bob and family in June 1961, Daddy met a woman named Margaret M. She was a divorcée with a son, Alan, two years younger than Dillon. Daddy was extremely vulnerable. Ingrid had turned down his proposal of marriage and broken his heart. Daddy was a widower with a steady job and two adolescent children. Daddy fell in love. She played him. He brought Margaret and Alan to Dallas, where they were married in Cox Chapel of Highland Park Methodist Church by Rev. Bill Dickinson after a four-week courtship.

Shortly after the wedding, our new family returned to Tallahassee, where Uncle Bob and Aunt Katheryn hosted a cocktail party for them to introduce her and Daddy to their Tallahassee friends. I remember Katheryn saying, "We can't find anyone who knows her!" Margaret and Alan moved into our house on Westlake. Dillon had to share a room with Alan; Margaret became the "wife/mother of the house"; and Daddy spent several hundred dollars on new furniture for the master bedroom. I do remember that she was sweet to me, and I was more than ready for a mother.

That fall, I was in ninth grade at J. L. Long Junior High, Dillon was in seventh grade, and Alan was enrolled in fifth grade, both at Lakewood Elementary School. On the surface, everything seemed okay. In September, after school had started, Margaret flew back to Tallahassee "to take care of some legal paperwork and to visit a sick friend." Daddy asked her if the sick friend was a man. She answered, "Yes." We children stayed home in Dallas with Daddy. When she returned to Dallas, Uncle Bob informed Daddy that he had had Margaret investigated and found out that she was having an affair with her hairdresser. She had married Daddy to make her lover in Florida jealous. The six-week-old marriage was annulled. Margaret and Alan returned to Tallahassee, never to be

seen or heard from again. Daddy had his heart broken a second time
and was burned financially. I was disappointed; Dillon was relieved.
Daddy kept his sanity, and we three moved on as a family.

There is no mention of the events of the summer/fall of 1961 in any
letters between Daddy and Ingrid from January 1961 until June 6, 1962.
What would he have told her? She probably learned of it from Harriet
and Sara. Daddy retreated into himself, worked for Dillon Scale, and
raised his children. Then came significant news from Sweden.

June 6, 1962

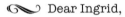 Dear Ingrid,

The children are out of school to their summer vacation and
we are making plans to leave Friday June 15th for two weeks
in Florida. We'll spend our vacation with Bob [Daddy's twin]
and his family on the Gulf of Mexico on the beach due south
of Tallahassee, Florida. We were over there in 1957 and last
summer.

Bob has a new 17 foot boat with a 75 horse power motor and
we can get out in the Gulf 10 or 15 miles. I plan to simply relax
for two weeks and get in some good fishing.

Now I find that you may go to Korea in the fall. The children
said, "Daddy, why can't Ingrid go to Korea by way of the
United States?" That question is foremost in my mind. Isn't
there some possible way for you to route your trip this way
and spend a few days with us? When I look at the globe, the
shortest route by air is over the pole: Sweden to Alaska to
Korea. If you are going to be away for some time, I do so want
to see you and hope there is some way for you to visit us
enroute.

We plan on arriving home from Florida no later than Sunday
July 1st as I must return to the office on Monday July 2nd. We
are all well and very busy. Susie goes into senior high school in
the fall and Dillon enters junior high. They are wonderful kids
and so smart. Love. Jimmy

I have no idea how Daddy found out that Ingrid had been posted by the Swedish government to work on the founding of the Swedish Hospital in Seoul, South Korea. She did not come to Dallas on the way, as we had hoped. I don't think she wrote to him, but someone from Sweden must have, or Daddy might have found out from Sara Everett or Harriet Armstrong. Then there is another long hiatus in their correspondence between June 1962 and his next letter to her, dated December 20, 1967.

Daddy had met Mary Kay in an adult Sunday school class at Highland Park Methodist Church in the fall 1962. She had been recently widowed with a five-year-old daughter and a nineteen-year-old son. Daddy found her attractive. During their two-year courtship, he made a beaten path between her house in Highland Park and our house in Lakewood. He even received a speeding ticket or two.

They married in September 1964, the fall of my senior year. I was seventeen. By that time, Mary Kay had made it clear that she would not move into our house, as she wanted to keep Kay in Highland Park schools. She also made it clear that she did not want to live with Daddy's children, but she was perfectly willing to let my father raise her five-year-old daughter. Daddy's solution was to sell the Westlake house and move Dillon and me into an apartment—*by ourselves*. A regime change had taken place. Queen Mary prevailed.

I was a senior at Woodrow; Dillon was a sophomore. To his credit, Daddy did come to the apartment every morning to make sure we were up for school. He made us breakfast and saw to it that we had lunch money and basic food in the fridge for supper. He even bought us a car to drive to school: a 1963 Corvair, the one tagged by Ralph Nader as "unsafe at any speed."

During that year, Dillon and I were on our own from 7:30 a.m., when we drove ourselves to school, until the next morning, when Daddy would come. After school, we did our homework. Sometimes I fixed supper, but usually we ate at the local Wyatt's Cafeteria. We attended all the Woodrow football games. Dillon spent time with guy friends; I spent time with my girlfriends, and I had a boyfriend. I truly believe that it was the power of the Holy Spirit that protected us both during that year. When Dillon came down with the flu, I took care of him and sat with him when he woke up with a 102-degree fever and delirium. As the time for me to graduate from high school approached, I had to insist that Daddy bring Dillon into the house with him and Mary Kay. No one in their right mind would allow a sixteen-year-old boy to live in an apartment alone! Daddy took heat and criticism from the parents of our friends—especially from the parents of my high school boyfriend and our pastor!

Daddy and Mary Kay did move to a house in Highland Park where there was room for Dillon to live and for me to stay when I came home from college for holidays and the summer. While I pursued an English major at North Texas State University in Denton, Texas, Dillon had been uprooted from Woodrow, where he was "somebody," only to enroll as a junior in Highland Park High School, where he was "nobody." He was miserable. However, to Dillon's credit, he knew how to stay out of trouble. He wanted to be a commercial airline pilot—something you can't become with even a juvenile arrest record. Dillon grew closer to Daddy during those years. I withdrew from him.

I was hurt and angry with Daddy and Mary Kay for over twenty years. That anger came to a head in 1979, shortly after Jim Baldwin and I married. Daddy called to ask if I wanted to have Mother's piano, which he and Mary Kay had in the house they shared. I told him I did not have room for it. This was the piano that had been in our house all through my childhood. Mother had taught me to play on that piano. Several months later, I happened to drive by their house. They were having a garage sale. On the sale tables were several items that had come from Sweden and had belonged to Mother, among them a Kosta Boda handblown glass vase with a $.50 tag on it. I immediately claimed it, along with several other items, and told Daddy that this vase was valuable, both monetarily and sentimentally. When Mother died, Daddy had sold several pieces of antique furniture she had acquired. As a child of twelve, I had no authority or even interest in most of those things, but the piano had stayed, and I still played it from time to time. That same day, Daddy told me he had sold Mother's piano for $400! When I registered vehement objection, he remarked that I had said I didn't want it. I countered that I never said I didn't want it; I just didn't have room for it! I have never been so angry with Daddy before or since. I wept bitter tears from years of pent-up anger and the rawness of a wounded heart. With the help of my dear husband, Jim, I was eventually able to let go of the anger and forgive Daddy.

Sometime after Daddy and Mary Kay married, the correspondence between Ingrid and Daddy resumed. Uncle Ed died in November 1967 from pneumonia and complications of the tuberculosis that he had been dealing with since 1938. Ironically, he was the sickliest of all his immediate family, but he outlived them all. His father, Marvin Dillon, died of a heart attack in 1943; his mother, Ruth Dillon, died of heart failure in 1958; and his sister Sue, my mother, died from metastatic breast cancer in May 1960. I remember coming home from North Texas to attend Uncle Ed's funeral. Daddy wrote to Ingrid to let her know. I had not yet corresponded with Ingrid as an adult. I asked Daddy for her address.

My father, James Layton Bussard, having recovered his dignity and no longer carrying a torch for Ingrid, wrote to her in December 1967 to notify her of Edgar's death.

       ❧ Dear Ingrid:

If you have not already been informed, you will be saddened to know that Edgar died on November 30. His health has been deteriorating over the past several years and he has been in and out of the Hospital 2 or 3 times a year. He went into the hospital on Monday noon with a cold, came down with pneumonia and died early Wednesday morning about 3:00 a.m. Josephine buried him on the lot with her grandparents at Lancaster, Texas, south part of Dallas County. He is the last of the Dillon family and it is sad to think of it.

Our own family is precious and I will send you a picture of us very soon. Dillon is taller than I and Susie is cute and petite—looks a lot like Sue. Dillon is a high school senior and will go to college next year. Susie is a 2nd year college student at North Texas State University where Sue and I graduated in 1935. Edgar had moved up to chairman of the board and I was made President of the company in July. I now have a real good general manager and find my situation getting easier and better, thank goodness.

Josephine said she would write Bishop Bo Giertz. I hope she did as he thought highly of the Dillon family.

It would be nice to hear from you—what you are doing and something about your travels. The kids—particularly Susie would love to hear about Okie and Susanne. I'm very happy with my family and appreciate getting a second chance for a good life. Sincerely, Jimmy

A year later, Daddy wrote in response to Ingrid's Christmas letter. He and Mary Kay were living in Dallas. Dillon had graduated from Highland Park High School, and I was a junior at North Texas State University. Daddy wrote a "catch-up" letter to update Ingrid about his situation with Dillon Scale and about me and Dillon as young college students. Mary Kay and Ingrid knew about each other, but they had not yet met.

December 20, 1968

꩜ Dear Ingrid:

We appreciated your Christmas note so much. This has been quite an interesting year in the activities of our family. Susie is a junior in college (3rd year) and will be home for the XMAS holidays tomorrow. She is in North Texas State University at Denton, Texas where Sue and I took our degrees in 1935. Dillon is in his first year to University of Texas, Arlington near Dallas and got home for the holidays yesterday. He is working for me at the office until he goes back to school Jan. 3rd.

Dillon visited Bob and his family in Florida for a week or two this summer. Susie visited Bill and his family in New Orleans. Kathey, Bob's daughter Susie's age is in Paris in school. She arrived in Paris in September and we found out today that she married in November. Bob is in Paris now and will spend the XMAS holidays with Kathey and her new husband.

In order to save my job and the company, I bot out the stock
I didn't own and assumed full control and am endeavoring to
reorganize the company into a profitable business.

Johnnie Johnson [Ingrid's cousin she visited in 1948]
comes by occasionally. He is fine, retired, and not getting any
younger. Harold Beadles and Jess Wortham are still with me—
Jess is 71 and going strong. Because of business pressure I did
not take a vacation this year. The past 3 years Mary Kay and
I have been going to Colorado to visit her sister-in-law. This
year in July we bought a 25' cabin cruiser (a lovely boat) we
have it moored in Garza Little Elm Lake near Dallas. All of the
children water ski and we enjoy it so much especially on the
weekends.

It's interesting to learn that Lars Giertz is in Houston. I
have little occasion to go down to Houston but will certainly
look him up if I do go there.

I haven't seen or talked to Sara Everett for some time. Saw
something in the paper recently about her activity with the
American Pen Women. I'll try to call her one day soon.

Also, I'll suggest that Susie write to you during the holidays.
So glad you wrote to us. Love. Jimmy

I remember talks around the family dinner table when I was a child.
The conversation about college was not about when I would go to
college, but when I would go to North Texas. My family's legacy with
NTSU goes back three generations: Grandmother Ruth had earned
a teaching degree in 1909 from North Texas State Normal College;
Mother and Daddy had earned their teaching degrees from North Texas
State Teachers College in 1935; I earned my bachelor's and master's
degrees in English from North Texas State University in 1969 and 1973.
Needless to say, teaching is in my family's DNA.

About Daddy's buying Dillon Scale, actually, Mary Kay's mother lent
Daddy the money to buy out Josephine, Uncle Ed's widow, as she owned
majority shares from inheritance. She would have sold the company
that Uncle Ed had driven to near bankruptcy and put Daddy out of a

job. I did not find this out until many years later. He repaid it.

I did write to Ingrid in 1967 and stayed in touch with her from time to time. I graduated from NTSU in May 1969. I skipped graduation to punish Daddy. In retrospect, I wish I hadn't, but I was still upset with Daddy because of the decisions he had made in 1964 where Dillon and I were concerned.

I met a graduate student, Robert, over Christmas 1968. He was a friend of Dillon's. We started dating my senior year, fell in love, and married the following August (1969). I took a teaching job with Mesquite Independent School District. Robert became a social worker in Dallas for Texas Department of Human Services. We were married five years, long enough to put each other through graduate school. I earned a master's degree in English from NTSU, and Robert earned a master's in social work from SMU. We divorced in 1975.

Shortly after Robert and I separated, I met James Byron Baldwin Jr. We were both in the middle of getting a divorce from our spouses at the time, so we took things slow. The summer of 1975, after Jim and I got together, I decided to go to Europe and visit Sweden. I was teaching English at Mesquite High School and living as a single, independent woman. My friend at Saint Mark Presbyterian Church, Anne W., had also gone through a divorce in 1975. I told her I was going to Sweden that summer and asked if she would like to be my traveling companion. She accepted, and we began to plan the trip. We were able to book teacher discount flights to London, where we spent a week; then we took the DFDS boat train from Harwich on the east coast of England to Copenhagen, Denmark; then the hydrofoil to Malmö, and the train to Växjö! We spent a week at Hagavik, followed by a weekend on Öland, where we visited Bishop Bo Giertz in his summerhouse and the town of Borgholm, all places Mother and I had visited in 1959. As we were walking down the main street of the town of Borgholm, I swear I saw, walking ahead of me, a vision of two women and a little girl. I felt a rush of recognition. I saw myself in 1959 at age eleven with Ingrid and Mother. I was overcome with emotion of the memory. Anne and I also visited Stockholm and the park Skansen.

The last letter I have from Daddy to Ingrid is a short note contained

in a Christmas card. Dillon had married Karen S. in 1974. Daughter
Amanda was born in 1977.

> December 22, 1977
>
> ⟨∾⟩ Dear Ingrid:
>
> Happy holidays to you and yours—we had a delightful
> dinner with Susie on Tuesday, p.m. She is doing really well.
> Dillon and Karen have had a baby girl about 3 months old
> (Amanda Sue, born Sept. 22, 1977) real cute. Our Kay worked
> in Lahaina—Maui—Hawaii this summer. Mary Kay and I spent
> a week there in August, a lovely vacation. My twin Bob and
> brother Bill were with us for a weekend 1st of November. The
> first time in 15 years we 3 boys had been together at the same
> time. [Daddy is sixty-four at the time of this letter.]
>
> We sold our house on Colgate and bot a condominium
> in May, we really like it. Instead of yard work I enjoy the
> swimming pool. We are all well and busy. Our very best to you
> and yours this holiday season. Love. Jimmy

Jim Baldwin and I continued to date and grow close in our
relationship. He was a social worker who found foster and adoptive
homes for hard-to-place children for the Texas Department of Human
Services. I was an English teacher at Mesquite High School. We married
in October 1978 and lived happily until his death from HIV/AIDS in
February 1993. A hemophiliac, he had received contaminated blood
product in 1984. The Jim Baldwin Family Room located in the regional
DHS office building in Arlington, Texas, was dedicated in his memory
in 1995.

Daddy died of prostate cancer in March 1993. Needless to say, the
decades of the 1980s and the early 1990s were a difficult time.

SIGNIFICANT EVENT IN 1981

A flyer posted in the Lakewood Bank and a letter my longtime friend
Lisa wrote to our retiring postman, Bill Ledbetter, in January 1981
increases the reach of this story. I was married to Jim Baldwin at the

time and teaching at Mesquite High School. Life was good. As I was
no longer a client of Lakewood Bank, I was unaware of the retirement
party for our postman in 1981. He would have started delivering the
US mail in 1944!

Community Room of the Lakewood Bank

A Reception honoring

WILLIE (Bill) LEDBETTER

Who has faithfully served our Lakewood Community

for 37 years

Sunday, January 18th 2 to 4pm.

Contributions accepted at door mailbox

Here is the text of Lisa's letter to Bill:

January 15, 1981

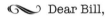 Dear Bill,

You and I sure go way back! I can remember following you
around the neighborhood before I started to elementary school.
You would lift me up on your shoulders to cross the vacant
lots because I was bare footed and there were stickers. The
vacant lots are gone now—the stickers miraculously replaced
by manicured lawns.

For some years, there were those of us—you, me, and that
big German shepherd—wasn't her name Queenie? That was
before the days of the leash law.

Since then I can say that almost 95% of the letters I have
received from my mother end with "Here comes Bill, I better
close" or "Bill's waiting for me to finish this—got to go". I don't
know how they will end now—but I know we'll both miss that
familiar closing. It never failed to bring a smile to my face.

On the days I couldn't walk with you, I often put out a glass
of ice water. Oh, we were pals!

Then, when I grew up and moved away from home, an

interesting thing began to happen. On the outside of the envelopes that contained letters to my folks, I'd write a tiny message to you—"Hi Bill!" and after a while, you began writing "Hi Lisa" on the letter picked up then at the house that was being mailed to me. And always a part of coming home to visit was meeting you at the door with a big hug, smelling again the leather of your mail pouch and remembering when I was a little girl trying once again to carry it. It came down past my knees and was very heavy.

In these present days of so much change, I feel pretty lucky. I still have two wonderful parents, that still live in the same wonderful home where I grew up and for more years than I am old, we've had the same wonderful mail man! You've certainly deserved your retirement. Congratulations. I hope you enjoy it to the fullest. I have tears in my eyes as I change my little message from "Hi Bill" to "Goodbye Bill." I love you. Lisa

PS. Whenever I'm in town, and you'd like to take a walk, come by!

I do remember our mailman, Bill. And like Lisa, we often gave him ice water on a hot day or a cup of coffee or hot chocolate in the winter.

INGRID VISITS THE USA IN THE 1980s, 1990s, AND 2000s

*W*ith my visit to Sweden in 1975, Ingrid and I became friends on our own terms. We corresponded regularly. She saved letters from me dated April 10, 1985 until my last letter to her, dated December 11, 2011. I saved letters from Ingrid dated December 5, 2002, until January 18, 2012, her last letter to me. Ingrid suffered a series of strokes in late January 2012, then again in February and March 2012. She died on March 8, 2012. She was ninety-seven.

One afternoon in the spring of 1985, I received a phone call from Ingrid. She and her sister, Ann-Marie, were in Minnesota to attend the wedding of a cousin and son of Dennis and Karen Pederson. They are part of the same extended family she had visited in 1948. I was so glad to hear from her, and I invited her and Ann-Marie to Dallas, but alas, it was not possible. She asked me, "Is Sara Everett still in life?" Ingrid was only seventy-one at the time and still had twenty-six more years of life ahead of her. She had telephoned Sara but had not been able to get in touch with her. Sara and Mother had been close friends. They had met through Daddy's business association with Monkey Grip Rubber Company, founded by Sara's husband. Sara was older than Mother, but probably by not more than ten years. I asked Daddy to look into it, and

he sent me the notice of Sara's death. I wrote to Ingrid and enclosed
the obituary from the *Dallas Morning News.*

April 10, 1985
ᏻ Dear Ingrid,
  You probably have guessed what this letter is about before
you opened it. Sara Everett died the first week of this month.
I don't know the exact date. The enclosed obituary was in the
newspaper for Sat. April 6. You may recall that Sara was a
Christian Scientist. She did not believe in mourning the dead.
When Mother died in 1960, Sara did not attend the funeral
but remained at our house on Westlake to receive calls and
keep watch. I know that she loved Mother, but I did not see
her shed a tear or look sad. I remember her as always smiling
and optimistic. I think it took so long for her to die because she
did not want to let go of life. I'm sure you have mixed feelings
now—sadness at the death of a longtime friend but also relief
that her struggle is over.
  1985 has been a busy year for us. Daddy was diagnosed
with prostate cancer. In February, he had radical surgery. The
cancer had not progressed beyond the gland, so the doctor
is confident that he removed it all successfully. Daddy has
returned to work for half-days, and he says he feels fine. He
plans to retire in June 1986 at age 75.
  My school year will be finished in six weeks, then I have
most of the summer off. I think my Jim will have his right
knee joint replaced this summer to complete the corrective
surgery on his legs. [The ravages of hemophilia had made him
a cripple.] We will know for sure in May. Love. Susibeth

  I did not include in the letter to Ingrid that Daddy had contracted
hepatitis from a blood transfusion he received at the time of the prostate
surgery. It took a year for him to recover. The radical nature of the
surgery left him impotent and incontinent. The cancer metastasized the
next year. Daddy had radiation treatments, which cooked his intestinal

tract. He never fully recovered and died in March 1993. Prostate cancer today is treated with much gentler and less invasive procedures. Actually, my Jim had both knees replaced in February 1987, after having had his left hip replaced in 1984. He was able to stand and walk straight until his death in 1993.

Ingrid and I continued to exchange letters two or three times a year between 1975 and 2012. I wish I had saved more of them. I am eternally grateful to her for saving Mother and Daddy's letters from the 1950s and 1960s and several of mine from the years that followed.

I do not have the letter Ingrid wrote telling me that she and Britta were coming to the US in the spring of 1992. They planned a stop in Dallas over the Easter weekend in April 1992. Jim and I were living in our Ashbrook house—2,400 square feet, corner lot with a swimming pool, bought in 1985. We loved it. Ingrid and Britta stayed in Argyle, Texas, with Harriet Armstrong, who was widowed by then.

As it worked out, I met Ingrid and Britta at the Dallas Art Museum after school on Wednesday, April 15. I collected them at 4:00 p.m. Ingrid wanted to drive through the old neighborhood, which we did. So many memories, not enough time. Jim and I took them to dinner, then choir practice at St. Mark Presbyterian Church on Wednesday night before Easter Sunday. Then we drove them back to Argyle. On Easter Sunday, April 19, 1992 Harriet hosted a lunch for friends of Ingrid. It was at this gathering that Ingrid and Mary Kay laid eyes on each other for the first and only time. In attendance were Daddy and Mary Kay, Jim and me, Dillon and his son, Casey. It was a lovely time, just not long enough to tell all the stories and no private time with Ingrid. Ingrid invited us all to Sweden. Dillon and his family made the trip the following summer.

During the summer of 1992, Dillon, Karen, Amanda, Corey, and Casey attended a Jehovah's Witnesses International Convocation in Berlin, Germany. Dillon rented a van and courageously drove the family across Germany from Berlin to Bremerhaven, Port of Rostock, where they boarded a car ferry to Sweden. They crossed the Baltic Sea to the Swedish Port of Trelleborg, then drove 130 miles north through Sweden to Växjö, then on to Hagavik, Ingrid's summer home, built by her father in 1935. Ingrid, with her customary hospitality and grace, hosted the whole family: parents Dillon and Karen and children, Amanda (age fifteen) and twins Corey and Casey (age thirteen). By now, Mary Kay and I had a civil relationship. We were both taking care of husbands with complex health issues, so we needed to be able to talk with each other. Jim Bussard, Mary Kay's husband and my father, died on March 4, 1993, only one month after my husband. The letters I composed to Ingrid notifying her of their deaths were the most difficult I have ever written.

I did not visit Sweden again until the summer of 2002, after I was widowed and had retired from Mesquite ISD and moved to Manitou Springs, Colorado. I wrote to Ingrid on March 9, 2002: "I would like to come visit you this summer. The time I can come is in the first two weeks in July. I have not booked a flight yet. I will wait to hear from you before I do that." Ingrid had access to email by now, but she never owned a computer. I would email her friend Alf Sandell or her nephew Thomas Lundqvist if I needed to get word to her quickly. I did visit her in July, stayed nine days at Hagavik, celebrated my fifty-fifth birthday with a party to which she invited Britta, Barbro, Birgitta G., Martin G. I also got to see Ninna and Vijay, Barbro's niece and her husband. Ninna and I had not seen each other since 1975. We are friends to this day.

My next visit to Sweden came in October 2004 for Ingrid's ninetieth birthday. I arrived in Malmö the week after her party when she was free to spend private time with me. I stayed with her in her apartment. It was during this visit that she gave me the first batch of letters that Mother had written to her and a photo album from her time in the US 1948–1950. It was also during this visit that she told me Daddy had proposed marriage to her. Ann-Marie hosted me for dinner with the family. I played bridge with Britta, Alf, and Ingrid. By now Britta was an invalid, and died the next year. When I returned home to Colorado after visiting Ingrid, I was being courted by Ronald K. Ruiz. We fell in love and married the following fall, on September 23, 2005, in the ballroom of the Cliff House in Manitou Springs, Colorado. He died on February 4, 2020.

Five years later, in July 2009, I received a telephone call from Ingrid.

"Susibeth, this is Ingrid. I am coming to US in October to celebrate my ninety-fifth birthday. Håkan will come with me. I will start in Minnesota; then I will come to Denver to see you." I replied to Ingrid, "I do not live in Denver, and anyway, Ron and I will be in Austin visiting Dillon. Book a flight from Minneapolis to Austin, Texas. Let me know the dates. We can all stay at Dillon's house. He has room for all four of us."

I arranged all this before consulting my brother. I called him with the news. "Hi, Dillon. Guess what? Ingrid and Håkan are coming to the US this fall to celebrate her ninety-fifth birthday! She and Håkan will arrive in Austin on October 7. Ron and I will arrive on October 6. We will all stay in the upstairs bedrooms. Ron and I will look after Ingrid and Håkan. They leave early on October 10; then Ron and I will leave that afternoon. Don't worry about a thing." There was an uncomfortable, long silence on the other end of the phone line. "Dillon, I had to make an executive decision here." His concern was "What will we do with them for four days?" I assured him there would be no problem. We, of course, had a wonderful time. Ingrid was amazing! She wanted to see the local IKEA store in Round Rock. At age ninety-five, she walked through the whole store pushing a cart. We did stop at the cafeteria for coffee. Ingrid remarked to me, "Something is the matter with Karen. She is not the same woman who came to Sweden fifteen years ago." Ingrid was right. Karen was very ill.

Not surprisingly, October 2009 was our last visit with Ingrid. During that visit, Ingrid remarked, "I have lived a wonderful life." We continued to correspond. I wrote to her about Karen's illness and subsequent death. In April 2011, Karen passed away. When Karen entered her final illness, Ron and I drove to Austin to stay with Dillon. When Karen passed, we were there to lend emotional support to our grieving family. Ingrid wrote to me from Hagavik:

June 2011

⧼ My dearest Susibeth,

Finally, I got to answer your long wonderful letter around Karen. She was a very fine woman but sick for a big part of her

life. I know you did so much for her and Dillon. I wish I could
have helped you. You are my dearest child and I could give all
my considerateness for you and Dillon. I gave my heart to you
both when Sue must leave you to a new mother who would
not love you but I could not marry her husband Jim. We have
talked about it. [Ingrid often told both Dillon and me that we
were "very clever." The story comes full circle.]

Today we have sunshine, but a lots of rain since I settled
down at Hagavik. A cousin of mine has been here from
Montana. She is Lutheran minister. Right now the lake is
like a mirror. You are welcome to all your friends in Sweden.
A-M and Lars keep together in Arlöv under Midsummer time.
Barbro with her sister Karin's family. Håkan with mother on
Gotland. Lisbeth with family and Eva, a fine midsummer with
her grandchildren and dance around the pool [she means "the
pole"].

I have had a little heart attack. I got a car belt so tight that
the heart almost stopped. My garden has got too much rain.
Friday Eva and Thomas are coming. They are so very nice to
me. Talked to Martin G. yesterday. He has many grandchildren
and a lovely home with Sara, and so has Ingrid and Jån
M. Håkan is coming home today. When you get old you feel
lonesome. For you and Dillon I will always go out from my
heart. Your old friend. Ninnie

After receiving this letter, I telephoned Ingrid at Hagavik. It was about
10:00 p.m. in Sweden, so I think I woke her up. She sounded horrible
and admitted that she was there by herself and was suffering from a
cold. I called a week later in the afternoon to apologize for disturbing
her. By then she had recovered from the cold and sounded like herself.
That was the last time we talked.

I visited with Ingrid's family in April 2012 when I attended her
memorial service. They told me about her last year. Basically, she
declined—both physically and mentally. Her last summer at Hagavik

was 2011. Thomas and Eva told me that ever an adventuress, Ingrid was planning a trip to Australia in 2012, but she no longer had the energy or stamina to undertake such a trip.

As life comes full circle, Ingrid and I corresponded frequently in her last years, often our letters crossing in the mail. Her 2011 Christmas letter came early in 2012. Already, her English syntax and handwriting were not so clear, but I knew her voice well enough to make sense of the text. The energy required to write in another language is evident with every word.

January 2012

❧ Dearest Susibeth,

Thank you for your nice birthday letter. I have been very busy since I came back from Hagavik. You are the first one I thank for all flower bouquets I got. It was a big day so now I am 97 years. I am grateful that I can go by myself without help. Now I have a rollator [shopping cart on wheels] when I buy my food and wines.

We had a pretty cool summer but still fine time with neighbours you know. So next summer I hope will be warm. You know you are very welcome. I have thought very how Dillon is going. I understand that the nice children take care of him. Maybe he meet a new friend from another church.

The photos in the letter I will that you take about them. I took them 1949 when you was a little sweet girl. We was happy people. I remember my first Christmas when we had a pink Christmas tree. I made a lots of cookies. Do you remember Lucia? When the candles in my head were dripping on my blonde hair. I had big work to get it off. I do not have any photos left. I know that we took with a little camera. Do you remember that the furniture was blue and yellow? Swedish colors. I felt at home. Mrs. Dillon and Ed came very often. It was a happy time. We picked pecan nuts. It was Oktober.

The next time I visited Dallas [1957] you had moved to

a new place [the house on Westlake]. The next time I came
[1992] 3 of my dear friends had passed away [Sue, Sara, and
Ed]. Such is life. Ann Marie and I have each other with one
Swedish mile between. She is doing pretty well after heart
dilation. Lars little absent minded. They have a good life
together in their nice home.

Ockie has a fine position at Stockholm's county council as
director, 3 fine boys, the oldest one study at the University.
Now they are thinking of a finding a possibility for the middle
to study in USA for two weeks not far from NY on a course.
With very good reports the little one is very clever Ockie says.
Susanne works in a hospital for old people. Her oldest son is
married and has 1 daughters and is expecting a girl in March.

Just now Lisbeth from Hagavik called me and said they had
snow, as it was now so Christmas like. She is retired and so is
her husband. She was fine.

I have talked with Barbro. It is full speed on her. She
associates very much with her sis Karin's girls and boys.
They have big families all of them. One of them which you
know wanted to keep in touch with you. May[be] it was for
Christmas.

You understand that we love you and you know that you and
your husband always are welcome the next summer. Håkan is
very busy with the museum and historical speeches. He was
2 weeks ago and he fixed a very good Italian dinner. He had
insisted I talk with Martin Giertz and some historical persons.
He was full of experiences.

To my wonderful Susibeth which I love I give a warm
Christmas hug and affection to Ron. Come to see us next year.
I do hope to be here some years more. Your dearest friend
in Sweden. To Dillon give him my best thoughts to his fine
children. [Not signed, but of course it is from Ingrid.]

Ingrid's handwriting was always a challenge to read. As she got older,
the challenge increased. I appreciate the love energy she put into the

letters she wrote to my family and me.

My last letter to Ingrid was written December 16, 2011:

 ⟨∿ My dear friend Ingrid—

As often happens our Christmas letters crossed in the mail. Today I received cards and letters from you and Ann-Marie. So glad to have the anniversary photo of her and Lars. I hope you enjoy the CD of the Christmas Concert I sent. It is compiled from several performances. My voice is on it in some of the selections.

Thank you so much for the photos from the days of my childhood. I recognize all but two of them taken in the early 1950s before Mother became ill. One of the photos is of Eloise Pavey with four little girls at a birthday party. I am not in that one and I don't recognize any of the children. The other photo I don't recognize has the writing on the back about a 25th wedding anniversary party. It wasn't for Mother and Daddy because she died shortly before their 25th anniversary in 1960. I will show them to Dillon when I see him. He will probably come to Colorado this winter for a visit. He is enjoying being single—the freedom to come and go as he pleases and not having to look after anyone but himself. He is doing very well.

I am so very glad that you are still able to live in your apartment [a three-story walk-up] and look after yourself. Thank you for the standing invitation to Sweden. We would love to come. If it is possible for us to come in 2012, I will let you know. Who knows what the future holds. Ron and I enjoy our life in Colorado mountains. We will ski throughout the winter as time permits. This week there is not yet enough snow at the resort where we ski, so we probably won't ski until after the new year.

This winter I enjoy cooking for friends and family. I mostly cook Italian when we have friends over. Everyone seems to like it. I remember Lucia Day very well. I remember peppar kakar and saffron bread. I buy peppar kakar at the IKEA store, as

well as Kungsoren brand Swedish Coffee Roll Mix. I make it
for New Years. I will write to you again as new events develop.
Much love to you, dear Ingrid. Susibeth

Ingrid's last letter to me, dated 18 January 2012, is indeed a treasure.

    Dearest Susibeth—

I still keep your name you got one time long time ago.
Thanks for your wonderful Christmas songs. Lovely, you
are fine choir. I am sorry because I can't sing, but I love to
listen. [I had sent a CD of the First Presbyterian Church choir
"Christmas Joy" concert selections recorded in the Pikes Peak
Center for the Performing Arts.]

All fine Christmas holidays are behind us. We had a quiet
time I spent with A-M and Thomas family. The climax was A-M
and Lars' 65 yrs wedding anniversary. Eva made a delicious
champagne dinner, and we took photos that we will send you
later on. They are doing pretty well. Eva helps me once in a
while.

Eva and Thomas are taking a tour of Germany over the
weekend and Eva's mom is dead. Eva is retired from this
year and Alf is not so good. He feels tired and is not able to
concentrate on driving the car. We talk over telephone mostly.
I talk to Barbro very often. She is busy with her sister's
children, they are grown up so she has "grand grand boys and
girls." Kristina talks about you. If you have planned to see us
one day you are welcome from all of us.

Tell me which president do you wish the next. I follow in
our newspapers. We have not had any snow this winter. I am
longing for spring and make my garden in Hagavik. Håkan will
be here in the end of Feb and help me with a fine dinner for 2
old friends from his musical team. They are both doctors and
work over the whole world. Their brother was my best friend
during the pupil time in Lund and at the school of medicine. Alf
just called. He want to have your mail address. Right now he

feels lonely, but he has 2 sons with families.

Lots of greetings to Ron. You are both welcome to Sweden anytime. I hope we get a fine summer. Lots of love from Yours Ninnie Ingrid

Alf was Ingrid's friend who managed her email. He also drove us around Malmö and Lund when I visited her in 2004. He did not attend her funeral in 2012.

After entering Ingrid's last letter, my eyes grew moist and my heart ached. I would like to say I answered this one immediately, but I regret that I set it aside to answer later. After all, Ingrid was going to live to be a hundred and there would be time for more letter exchanges, phone calls, and, yes, even another trip to Sweden. I believe she had her first stroke in January 2012. She was hospitalized in Malmö, where she seemed to recover. She was even ready to go home when she had her final stroke in early March 2012 before she could leave the hospital. She died peacefully on March 8, 2012, with her family at her bedside. I was notified by email from Ingrid Giertz-Mårtenson a few days later. Ingrid's funeral service was set for April 27, 2012, in the domkyrka in Växjö. It was easy to decide that I must attend her service, since I was sure that most of the people I had met through Ingrid would be there.

It might be the last time I would see many of them. During the decision process, I was in email communication with Eva and Thomas. They assured me that I was welcome, but that they could not "take care" of me. I explained to them that I was fully capable of traveling alone, finding a hotel, and managing my own transportation needs as appropriate. I booked the ticket. Then the family asked me to sing "Amazing Grace" at Ingrid's service. I flew into Copenhagen on April 23, then took the train to Växjö, where I checked in to the local Best Western for four nights. At the BW hotel, I also met Ingrid's cousins from Minnesota, Dennis and Kären Pederson. Ingrid had told us about each other over the years. I also met Kären's cousin Ingela from Halmstad. What a privilege to meet them! We are now friends

I had reconnected with Kristina "Ninna" on my visit to Sweden in 2002, and we had stayed in touch, but we did not meet in 2004. Ninna collected me from the Växjö BW hotel that afternoon and drove us to her sister Teta's home for a lovely dinner with Barbro, now ninety-two and widowed. What a wonderful reunion! I had not seen these dear ladies since 2002! I spent the next day with Ninna, visiting the town of Växjö, which by then was familiar to me. We ate lunch at Barbro's apartment—the same three-story walk-up where Mother and I had laid our heads in 1959! She had prepared chicken marsala, accompanied by a lovely crisp bread.

Barbro me from the BW Hotel and drove us to the domkyrka in Växjö the day of Ingrid's service, April 27, 2012. She sat with me as I waited to sing "Amazing Grace." I went through warm-up vocals at the hotel and prayed that morning for emotional strength and a good voice, which the Lord granted me. I sang "Amazing Grace" with passion and conviction, accompanied by a talented young organist who transposed my score of the hymn down a step for my aging sixty-four year old voice.

The weather was cold and damp. After the service, the family and congregation of mourners walked to the Tegnér Cemetery burial plot where Ingrid would be laid to rest with her parents and brother. We were given white flowers to toss onto the casket as each of us said a final goodbye. After the burial, the congregation of about sixty friends and family adjourned for lunch at Evedals Värdshus on the shore of Helgasjön, where we dined on salmon, new potatoes, asparagus, and a crisp white wine. We could see Hagavik cottage across the lake. During lunch, a spring thunderstorm blew over. After lunch, I gathered with members of Ingrid's family for photos. As I was looking around, Barbro was nowhere to be seen. I left the luncheon with Kären and Denis Pederson. I do not even remember if I said a proper goodbye to Barbro. She died two years later and is buried in the Tegnér Cemetery, near Ingrid. Time moves so fast!

Thomas Lundqvist, son of Ann-Marie and Ingrid's nephew, and his wife, Eva, inherited Hagavik from Ingrid in 2012. Thomas has told me that he first came to Hagavik, Ingrid's family summer home built by her father Carl Jaensson in 1935 on the shore of Helgasjön near Växjö, when he was in utero. The site Hagar (which means "pasture") was first mapped in 1793. From "Hagar" came the name "Hagavik." A railroad was built between Växjö and the village of Evedals in 1895. Only the depot remains. Thomas and Eva have completely remodeled the house and live there now in retirement. They hosted me, Håkan, and Dennis and Kären for lunch at Hagavik the day after Ingrid's service. On display in the window sills was an array of Ingrid's keepsakes. She loved all things blue. Each of us was invited us to choose a remembrance. I brought home a glass blue bird that now perches on my curio shelf. Ingrid left me a Kjell Engman vase in her will, which I also carried home. I gaze on these treasures every day. I lingered at Hagavik as long as I dared, then took the 6:00 p.m. train from Växjö to Copenhagen, where I spent the night in the Clarion Hotel at Kastrup Airport, then flew home the next day. Later in July 2012, Ninna and Vijay journeyed from Sweden to Colorado Springs and spent four days with Ron and me in Manitou Springs, visiting the Rocky Mountains.

I have maintained connections with dear friends in Sweden. Susanne Sköld, Ingrid's niece, told me that on her death bed Ingrid made her promise to stay connected with family and friends in the US. We are all thankful for email and Facebook, and for Susanne's faithfulness to that promise. She and I email regularly, and she keeps me informed about her family and grandchildren. In 2016, Ron and I traveled to Minnesota and spent four wonderful days with the Pedersons. They showed us all the places Ingrid had visited, including the family plot in the local cemetery, the American Swedish Institute, and beautiful Minneapolis. We continue to stay in touch with each other.

Between April 26 and May 9, 2017, in response to a palpable tug on my heart, I visited Sweden again, this time accompanied by my friend Judy from First Presbyterian Church in Colorado Springs. Judy was a wonderful traveling companion, and I am grateful that my friends in Sweden welcomed us both with open arms. We were met at Copenhagen Kastrup Airport by Susanne and her daughter, Kristina, who showed us Malmö and Lund. Susanne asked. "What do you want to see in southern Sweden?" I answered, "I want to see the Sweden you know, the places that mean something to you and your family." We visited the Burlöv old church and cemetery where her family had married, baptized children, and celebrated lives of the departed. Susanne's father, Lars Lundqvist, had died in early April. His memorial was celebrated the day after Judy and I departed for Denver, CO, US.

Judy and I spent four days in Växjö. I purchased flowers from a street vendor and walked through Tegnér Cemetery to visit Ingrid's and Barbro's graves. It was a poignant moment when I laid the flowers on their graves. We attended the Sunday service in the Domkyrka. Judy and I toured Växjö and the area around Hagavik with Thomas and Eva. Then we dined on salmon, new potatoes, and asparagus prepared by Eva at Hagavik with Håkan. Lisbeth and Janus (neighbors next door to Hagavik) hosted us for supper that evening, then took us into Växjö for a May Day parade, choral festival, and fireworks.

The next day, Ninna and Vijay collected Judy and me from Hotel Esplanad in Växjö. They took us to glassworks. We stopped four days in Lammhult with Ninna and Vijay, where we stayed at their restored eighteenth-century cottage home in the country. We stopped for lunch at "Suzie's Café," a charming 1950's retro venue that served authentic American style hamburgers with french fries and bottled Coca-Cola! There was a pink vintage Cadillac parked out front! They drove us on a tour of the Småland countryside, stopping at old churches, local shops and a monthly folk club gathering of their friends in Växjö. Ninna served Swedish meatballs, mashed potatoes, and salad for dinner.

After four wonderful days with Ninna and Vijay, we boarded the train to Uppsala to visit Birgitta G. We stayed with her daughter, Magdelena. In Uppsala, we visited the Domkyrka where Bo Giertz had been installed as Bishop in 1950. We also met Ingrid Giertz-Mårtenson and husband Jån, and Ockie and his family in Stockholm. After two days, we boarded the train from Uppsala to Malmö, where we visited Ann-Marie in her nursing home residence. We had tea and a delightful visit. After bidding *adjö* to Ann-Marie, Susanne and Kristina, Judy and I made our last train ride to Copenhagen Kastrup. The next day we boarded a flight home to Denver, Colorado. Susanne's father, Lars Lundqvist, had died in early April 2017. His memorial was celebrated the day after Judy and I departed for Denver, Colorado, US. Ann-Marie died in 2019 at age ninety-nine.

WHY I WROTE
THIS BOOK

*T*his memoir began with tracing the Dillon and Gilliam families
from the early 1800s. The story developed with the romance
between my maternal grandparents Marvin Dillon and Ruth Gilliam in
1910, their marriage in 1912, and the births of their children, Sue in
1913 and Edgar in 1915. When Sue and Edgar became adults with
professional and personal lives of their own, fate decreed that Ingrid
Jaensson from Växjö, Sweden, born in 1914, would come to the US and
Dallas, Texas, in 1948. Immediately, she became friends with the Dillon/
Bussard family: my grandmother Ruth Dillon and her children Edgar,
Sue Dillon with her husband Jim Bussard (married in 1936) and their
children, Susan Beth, born in 1947, and James Dillon, born in 1949.

Ingrid returned to Sweden in November 1950. In the decade that
followed, Ingrid's extraordinary enthusiasm for America and the
opportunities it afforded emigrés motivated her to encourage her own
friends in Sweden who wanted to come to America to choose Dallas,
Texas, as a place to land where they would find a social network, Southern
hospitality and friends, as well as jobs and educational opportunities.
My father, Jim Bussard, and my uncle Edgar Dillon sponsored many
of Ingrid's friends who came to Dallas to work or go to school. In that

capacity, Mother met and became friends with Viola Fröler in 1952 (no children), Barbro Weber in 1953, and members of the Giertz family from 1952 to 1958.

In 1959, Mother and I made the "dream trip" to Sweden. Because of Ingrid's connection to them all, we were blessed to have established endearing friendships with three extended families there. The children with whom I became friends in 1959 are now senior citizens, as am I. All of us are in our seventies and dealing with health challenges. Ingrid Jaensson's family included her sister, Ann-Marie, and Ann-Marie's husband, Lars Lundqvist; their children, Ockie, Susanne, and Thomas; and their descendants. Barbro Weber's family included her parents; her sister, Karin's, children, Kristina, Margaretta, Per, and Gunnar; and their descendants. The Giertz family included Bishop Bo Giertz; his children, Lars, Birgitta, Ingrid, Martin; and their descendants. These three families cut across the social strata of Swedish culture. The families met each other casually through Ingrid, and some of them attended her funeral in 2012. However, each family comes from a different part of the country, and their professional and social lives do not intersect. The relationships I have as Sue's daughter with each of these families is a unique entity unto itself.

Friendships forged by a shared movement of spirit between individuals create a relationship entity independent of the individuals within the relationship itself. This memoir records the development of such entities. Inevitably, the bond forged by Ruth and Sue with Ingrid that I have maintained with Susanne, Ninna, and Ingrid G-M in Sweden weakens with the passing of each generation. If the story is not handed down to those family members who have not lived it, the entity will die. Therefore, I leave this memoir of "charismatic goodness" to the families and cultural descendants of Ruth, Sue, and Ingrid.

All of the people mentioned in this memoir are real. The events described herein have been reconstructed from letters, Sue's diaries, and family stories that are believed to be true. We are grateful for the lives well lived by those who have gone before us. It is incumbent on those of us still living our own stories to pass family lore to children and descendants yet to be born. May all their lives be enriched by this memoir.

ACKNOWLEDGMENTS

To my family and friends with whom I share this labor of love: I hope you enjoy it and gain some insight into how we are all connected. There are many people I must thank for helping me put this history together. Thank you to my stepson, Danny Ruiz, for suggesting the GoFundMe page and to those who supported the publication of this memoir by contributing to it.

Thank you to the editorial and production staff of BookVillages, LLC. A special thanks goes to my copy editor, Tia Stauffer and my publisher, Karen Pickering. Thanks also to my designer, Scot McDonald, who produced the layout and created the cover design.

Thank you to Sam Zettersten for translating Ingrid's Swedish letters into English. Thank you to Susanne Sköld for transcribing passages that reference my family from Ingrid's letters that she wrote home in 1948 to 1950. Thank you to Kären and Dennis Pederson for sharing the story of their Swedish ancestors who emigrated in the early twentieth century to the US. Thank you to Ingrid Giertz-Mårtenson, Birgitta Giertz, Ninna Manna, and all my friends in Sweden who shared photos and stories about Ingrid and my mother, Sue.

Thank you to my brother, Dillon, and childhood friends Lisa, Wanda, Alanna, Alicia, Jan, and Livonia, who contributed to the stories I have included. I owe a special thanks to my Gilliam family cousins, Patsy Ruth Smith and Betty Wortham Rush, who knew and loved the Gilliam and Dillon families, and who contributed memories of Marvin, Ruth, Edgar, and my mother, Sue, to this story. Thank you to my Dillon family cousin Annie Bess Anderson for reading the manuscript, for contributing photos, and for sharing her ancestry research which, produced significant details and insights into the Dillon side of the story. Thank you to the Bussard cousins —Ralph, John, Ginny, Karol Kay, and Kathey—for growing up with me in childhood. Thank you to my friend Jan Doades, who not only read the manuscript but who also offered financial support, constructive criticism and editorial suggestions.

Thank you to Julian Fellowes, who created *Downton Abbey* and who wrote the screenplay for *The Chaperone* by Laura Moriarty, a story about independent women who took charge of their own lives. In his interview following the PBS showing of *The Chaperone*, he mentions that the lead actress, Elizabeth McGovern, has the gift to portray "charismatic goodness." I unabashedly attribute that borrowed phrase to Ruth, Sue, and Ingrid. He then goes on to encourage the viewers to step out and take a chance on fulfilling a dream, "to learn Japanese or write that book!" I chose to write the book.

The last thank-you is for Lawrence Wright, Pulitzer Prize–winning author and my classmate from Woodrow Wilson High School, class of 1965. He wrote a memoir in 1983 titled *In the New World: Growing Up with America from the Sixties to the Eighties*. At our fiftieth class reunion in 2015, Lawrence encouraged me to pursue the writing of my own memoir.

NOTES

The Friendship and Courtship: 1910–1911

1. William R. Hunt, "Jean, TX," *Handbook of Texas Online,* accessed March 17, 2021, https://www.tshaonline.org/handbook/entries/jean-tx. Published by the Texas State Historical Association.

2. "Texas Education Timeline," accessed March 17, 2021, https://gato-docs.its.txstate.edu/jcr:27972b92-caac-48c5-9a04-baec65647f43/Texas%20 Education%20Timeline.pdf.

3. Kathryn Phend Watlington, "Changing the School Year: The Texas Experience in Moving to a Twelve-Grade Academic Program" [doctoral dissertation, Texas A&M University, 2014], 2–3, http://oaktrust. library.tamu.edu/bitstream/handle/1969.1/153420/WATLINGTON-DISSERTATION-2014.pdf?sequence=1.

4. Nancy Pope, "Daily Deliveries Down to One—1950," Smithsonian National Postal Museum blog, April 17, 2016, https://postalmuseum.si.edu/ node/2123.

The Engagement and Wedding: 1912

1. Wikipedia, s.v. "Wills Point, Texas," accessed March 17, 2021, https:// en.wikipedia.org/wiki/Wills_Point,_Texas.

2. "About Us," Dillon Equipment Company website, accessed March 18, 2021, https://dillonequipment.com/about-us/.

3. Dillon paperwork; "About Us."

Homecoming and Mother's End: August 1959–May 1960

1. Hervé Guibert, *To the Friend Who Did Not Save My Life* (1990; n.p.: MIT Press, 2020), 262.

ABOUT THE AUTHOR

Susan Beth "Susibeth" Bussard grew up in Dallas, Texas. She attended public school, graduating from Woodrow Wilson High School in 1965. She was raised in the Methodist and Presbyterian churches, and pursued higher education at North Texas State University, earning a bachelor's and a master's degree in English. She taught English and Latin for twenty-nine years for Mesquite Independent School District before retiring in 1999 to Colorado Springs, Colorado, where she taught Latin at The Classical Academy from 1999 to 2005.